HOW TO
COACH

BOB THOMSON

2ND EDITION

HOW TO COACH

First Steps and Beyond

Los Angeles | London | New Delhi
Singapore | Washington DC | Melbourne

Los Angeles | London | New Delhi
Singapore | Washington DC | Melbourne

SAGE Publications Ltd
1 Oliver's Yard
55 City Road
London EC1Y 1SP

SAGE Publications Inc.
2455 Teller Road
Thousand Oaks, California 91320

SAGE Publications India Pvt Ltd
B 1/I 1 Mohan Cooperative Industrial Area
Mathura Road
New Delhi 110 044

SAGE Publications Asia-Pacific Pte Ltd
3 Church Street
#10-04 Samsung Hub
Singapore 049483

Editor: Susannah Trefgarne
Assistant editor: Ruth Lilly
Assistant editor, digital: Sunita Patel
Production editor: Katherine Haw
Copyeditor: Jane Fricker
Proofreader: Christine Bitten
Indexer: Bob Thomson
Marketing manager: Dilhara Attygalle
Cover design: Naomi Robinson
Typeset by: C&M Digitals (P) Ltd, Chennai, India
Printed in the UK

© Bob Thomson 2020

First published 2014

This edition first published 2020

Library of Congress Control Number: 2019944361

British Library Cataloguing in Publication data

A catalogue record for this book is available from the British Library

ISBN 978-1-5264-8479-6
ISBN 978-1-5264-8478-9 (pbk)

At SAGE we take sustainability seriously. Most of our products are printed in the UK using responsibly sourced papers and boards. When we print overseas we ensure sustainable papers are used as measured by the PREPS grading system. We undertake an annual audit to monitor our sustainability.

CONTENTS

LIST OF FIGURES, TABLES AND TEMPLATES

ABOUT THE AUTHOR

Bob Thomson is a Professor at Warwick Business School. He is an experienced coach and supervisor of coaching, and established the University of Warwick's Certificate and Diploma in Coaching. He also acts as an internal mediator, helping members of staff in conflict with one another to find a way forward. He is accredited as both a coach and supervisor by the European Mentoring and Coaching Council. He is also a Senior Fellow of the Higher Education Academy.

He has written a number of books on coaching, and learning and development:

- *Growing People: Learning and Developing from Day to Day Experience*
- *Don't Just Do Something, Sit There: An Introduction to Non-directive Coaching*
- *The Coaching Dance: A Tale of Coaching and Management*
- *Non-directive Coaching: Attitudes, Approaches and Applications*
- *First Steps in Coaching*
- *Understanding Yourself and Others: Practical Tools from the World of Coaching*

Don't Just Do Something, Sit There was published in Chinese under the title, which reflects the notion of Socratic questioning, *Modern Midwifery: The Art of Coaching.*

He may be contacted by email at bob.thomson@wbs.ac.uk

AUTHOR'S NOTE

The text of this book is based on that of my previous book, *First Steps in Coaching*, which was published by Sage in 2014. The word count of the new text is one third longer than the previous book. There are a number of additions to many of the chapters, but the main changes are:

- Two new chapters on coaching across cultures and on supervision
- A rewrite of the final chapter, with a focus on accreditation
- New material on acceptance and commitment coaching, and on presence as a coach

The new book also has an online resource site with a number of video clips to illustrate key ideas.

PREFACE

One of the joys of learning to coach is that it's a wonderful journey that doesn't end. I've written this book to accompany you on the next steps of your coaching journey, whether you're starting out on a new adventure or whether you're already an experienced traveller seeking to explore some new territory. I hope that the text contains useful ideas for people learning how to coach and for experienced coaches who wish to develop their practice further. The ideas are relevant for external coaches, for internal coaches working within an organisation, and for line managers seeking to use a coaching approach as part of how they manage people.

Coaching is a privilege. As you listen to a client, helping them explore their hopes and concerns, you are invited to glimpse inside their world, sometimes hearing thoughts that they've never shared with anyone before. There can be a deep sense of satisfaction when you enable a client to see things afresh or commit to actions to achieve their goals. Engaging in meaningful and productive conversations that make a difference is a great way to spend your time.

Coaching is a practical skill. As such, it's something that you can only learn through experience. Throughout the book I'll invite you to try out ideas and see how they work in practice. I shall also encourage you to reflect on and make sense of your experiences and your conversations with other people. And I'll offer you a range of ideas and models for you to consider and decide how useful they will be to you as a coach.

Coaching is an art. As you coach you are continually making judgements about what to do next in a conversation. You build a coaching relationship over time, in part through your skills but also through your presence. You bring your self to your clients, in encounters that can be more or less authentic.

The book falls into three parts. The first part – Learning the Basics – offers an introduction to coaching and the basic skills needed to coach well. Chapter 1 offers a definition of a primarily non-directive approach to coaching that we'll use throughout the book, sets out the GROW model which is widely used to structure coaching conversations, and suggests that raising awareness and encouraging responsibility are at the heart of effective coaching. In Chapter 2 we look at various behaviours that lie along the spectrum from directive to non-directive coaching, and consider the difference between coaching and mentoring. Chapters 3, 4 and 5 discuss in some detail the three fundamental skills needed to conduct a coaching conversation – listening to understand the client, asking open questions to encourage them to think, and playing back what they have communicated to you. Chapter 6 considers the importance of learning from experience and includes a couple of practical activities that you might engage in to develop your coaching skills.

In Part Two – Developing your Practice – we move beyond the basics of coaching to explore a number of issues that will help you to develop further as a coach. Chapter 7 considers the practical matters that need to be agreed when you contract directly with a new client, such as the time, place, frequency, length and cost of coaching sessions, and looks at three-way contracting which involves an organisational sponsor as well as the individual client. Chapter 8 explores a number of other practical aspects you need to consider, including making notes, keeping records, evaluating the impact of your coaching, and ending a coaching assignment. Chapter 9 then looks at important ethical issues, including confidentiality, boundaries, supervision and questions of diversity.

In Chapter 10 we examine a number of tools that you might introduce in a session to help a client think through their situation – scaling, drawing rich pictures, exploring metaphors, reflective writing and the empty chair exercise. Chapter 11 looks at how you might give feedback to a client, help them to generate feedback for themself, and gather feedback on your own performance. It also looks at 360 degree feedback and the use of psychometric instruments.

Throughout the book we emphasise the importance of the relationship between the coach and client. We look at this in detail in Chapter 12, exploring the views of Erik de Haan and Carl Rogers, and discussing how an Adult–Adult relationship between coach and client differs from one which is Parent–Child. Chapter 13 explores various aspects of how the coach can use their self in coaching, including how they might utilise what they notice within themself as the conversation unfolds. It also looks at the ideas of Maria Iliffe-Wood on how a coach can operate in four modes of presence to share themself in different ways in the service of their clients. In Chapter 14 we consider the inner game that is going on within the mind of the coach as they converse with a client, and consider the interferences that might get in the way of coaching well.

The final part – Extending your Approach – explores a number of advanced topics that can help you to coach gracefully and fluently. In Chapter 15 we look at how you might introduce a conceptual model or framework to help a client make sense of their situation, and consider some of the key ideas in a cognitive behavioural approach to coaching, and in acceptance and commitment coaching. Chapter 16 describes three widely used approaches – Solution-focused coaching, Neuro-linguistic programming and Gestalt – and invites you to consider how you might use some of these ideas in your practice. In Chapter 17 we address the difficult challenge of helping a client who lacks confidence or has low self-esteem. We look at the idea that each of us is a community of selves, and at the use of Motivational Interviewing to help someone who is ambivalent about change.

Chapter 18 explores how you might use a coaching approach as a line manager, and describes a coaching dance where the manager moves between telling people what to do and asking them for their ideas. In Chapter 19 we look at coaching a team of people and how you can use the GROW model and the basic idea of raising awareness and encouraging responsibility when working collectively with a team rather than an individual.

The type of coaching that we are exploring in this book is a Western, even British, notion. In Chapter 20 we consider how coaching has been adapted for use in China and in Islamic society. Chapter 21 explores the key topic of supervision of coaching, and discusses a primarily non-directive approach to supervision which parallels our definition of coaching. The final chapter considers how you can continue your journey of development as a coach, and discusses coaching accreditation.

I have the good fortune to work as a coach, to write about coaching and to help others learn how to coach. Each of these activities informs and enhances the other two. I would like to thank all of my coaching and supervision clients for letting me listen as they explored the challenges facing them.

The book is supported by an online resource site featuring a number of video clips to illustrate some key ideas. Many of these are taken from a coaching session I did with Lina to be used by Christian van Nieuwerburgh and David Love in their book, *Advanced Coaching Practice*. Other clips are from Lina's reflections with Christian immediately after our conversation, or from my own debrief with Christian. The final set of clips were made by Will Percy on his experiences of bringing coaching to a Chinese context. Many thanks to Lina, Christian and Will for their contributions.

Finally, thanks to everyone at SAGE Publishing, especially Susannah Trefgarne, Talulah Hall, Katherine Haw and Jane Fricker, for their encouragement and practical help in the writing of the book.

ONLINE RESOURCES

Visit **https://study.sagepub.com/thomson2e** to watch the following videos:

PART ONE:
LEARNING THE BASICS

1

WHAT IS COACHING?

Introduction

In this chapter we shall consider a number of definitions of coaching, beginning with my own definition that is the basis of my practice and which we'll be using throughout the book. We also consider an equation that sits at the heart of coaching:

Awareness + Responsibility = Performance

My definition of coaching

There is no agreed definition of coaching. If you were to ask the ordinary person in the street what comes to mind when they think of a coach, many people will reply with some notion of a sports coach. Over the years, I have had tennis and golf lessons in which someone who understood textbook technique used a mix of instruction, feedback and encouragement to help me improve my game. I found this useful, and the lessons helped me to enjoy both games more fully.

However, that's not the view of coaching that we shall be exploring together. Here is my own definition that is the basis of my practice and which we'll refer to throughout the book. It regards coaching as primarily non-directive. I've refined this definition over the years as I've reflected upon my own practice as a coach, and each phrase in the definition has been carefully chosen.

Coaching is a relationship of rapport and trust in which the coach uses their ability to listen, to ask questions and to play back what the client has communicated in order to help the client to clarify what matters to them and to work out what to do to achieve their aspirations.

There are a number of points I'd like to highlight in this definition.

First and foremost, coaching is a relationship between two people. The definition offers a couple of pointers to the nature of an effective coaching relationship – one based on rapport and trust. The fact that the coach is operating non-directively will create a different relationship than if the coach were directive. We shall explore in some depth the nature of a coaching relationship in Chapter 12. (Strictly speaking, coaching is a process rather than a relationship. However, to emphasise the importance of the relationship, I begin my definition with the words '*Coaching is a relationship* …'.)

Second, the definition states that the role of the coach is to help the client to articulate their goals and how they will set about achieving them. The words which follow '*in order to* …' are those which make the definition non-directive. Non-directive coaching is about facilitating, not instructing, advising or guiding. It is working with someone, not doing something to them. In the next chapter we shall look in more detail at directive and non-directive approaches.

Third, the definition introduces three basic conversational skills in coaching that will be explored a little later in the book – listening, questioning and playing back. However, while these skills are important, the more fundamental ability that the coach needs is to establish rapport and trust in the relationship.

Coaching is an art not a science. The coach is continually drawing on their experience and their intuition to shape what they do next.

If you are already an experienced coach, you will probably be familiar with much of the material in this chapter and indeed in Part One of the book. Nevertheless, I hope you find some of the ideas a stimulating reminder of the basics of coaching and that some of the material in Parts Two and Three offers you some new perspectives. If you are on the early stages of your journey as a coach, then I hope that the ideas in Part One offer you a sound foundation for your future practice, and that you can go on to use the content of Parts Two and Three to make further progress on your journey. I also hope that the ideas throughout the book will encourage any line manager who is keen to support the performance and development of their staff in a way that goes beyond a traditional command and control approach. Finally, I invite anyone in a teaching or development role to use freely any of the material that you think will facilitate the learning of your students or participants.

The Association for Coaching's definition

There are a number of professional bodies in the coaching world, and we'll draw on some material from their websites later in the book of the Association for Coaching. In answer to the prompt *What is Coaching?* the website of the Association for Coaching offers the following definition and comments on coaching:

> Coaching is a facilitated, dialogic and reflective learning process that aims to grow the individual's (or team's) awareness, responsibility and choice (thinking and behavioural). The advancing popularity of the profession reflects a need arising in business and society for people to find solutions to the complexities they face in their life, career and profession.

> When individuals, teams and business leaders first come to coaching it is often because their recent experiences have driven them to seek coaching support to aid them in finding enhanced ways of being and working. Something needs to change, improve or be enhanced. It might be that they have a hunch, a feeling or an intuition that something is troubling them and is causing them some form of disorientation.

> The issues an individual may be experiencing could be feelings of being 'stuck', feelings of lack of progress, frustration, or feelings of going back and forth with no apparent resolution. When they come to coaching they are at a point of transition and by engaging a coach they work together to uncover and de-layer in order to identify the essence of the problem and implement change.

> www.associationforcoaching.com/page/WhyCoaching

The opening words of the AC definition are important: *Coaching is a facilitated, dialogic and reflective learning process … .* The role of the coach is to facilitate a conversation and to encourage the client to reflect and learn. The aims are to grow the client's awareness, responsibility and choice.

These comments from the AC website seem somewhat negative. While some people do come to coaching because they are stuck or troubled, others come to enhance performance that is already very good, or to take a further step on a successful career.

Coaching in context

The term *coach* in the sense that we are using it was first used around 1830 as a slang term at the University of Oxford for a tutor who could carry a student through an exam. Around 1860 it began to be used in a sporting context, and coaching is now well established in the sports world. Indeed if you ask the ordinary person about a coach they are likely to think first of a sports coach. In 1975 Tim Gallwey, who was both an educationalist and a tennis coach, wrote a very influential book called *The Inner Game of Tennis* which is fundamental to the type of coaching we are exploring in this book. His ideas were taken up by people such as Graham Alexander, John Whitmore (a champion motor racing driver) and Myles Downey. They found that the business world was more receptive than the sports world to Gallwey's ideas. The development of coaching also owes much to a wide range of fields, such as ideas in humanistic psychology from people such as Carl Rogers and Abraham Maslow; the human potential movement with activities such as est training and encounter groups; a wide variety of ideas and approaches from the worlds of counselling and therapy; and perspectives from fields such as management and leadership, organisation studies and personal development.

Views of some other writers on coaching

Julie Starr offers this view:

> Put simply, coaching is a conversation, or series of conversations, that one person has with another. The person who is the coach intends to produce a conversation that will benefit the other person (the coachee) in a way that relates to the coachee's learning and progress. (Starr, 2011)

Jenny Rogers proposes this definition of coaching, which she says is 'a simple one that conceals complexity':

> The coach works with clients to achieve speedy, increased and sustainable effectiveness in their lives and careers through focused learning. The coach's sole aim is to work with the client to achieve all of the client's potential – as defined by the client. (Rogers, 2008)

She goes on to list six principles that distinguish coaching from other disciplines:

1. The client is resourceful
2. The coach's role is to develop the client's resourcefulness through skilful questioning, challenge and support
3. Coaching addresses the whole person – past, present and future
4. The client sets the agenda
5. The coach and the client are equals
6. Coaching is about change and action

Maria Iliffe-Wood (2014) offers a number of guiding beliefs that underpin her approach to coaching and which fit well with a primarily non-directive stance. These include:

1. I am not here to supply answers
2. It's ok for me not to know
3. Clients learn best when they work things out for themselves
4. It is a collaborative experience

Geoff Pelham draws on the metaphor of coaching as a journey in setting out his view:

> It is about assisting someone to gain a sense of direction and purpose, which is often lost in the absorption with everyday life, and then set out on their self-chosen path. Coaching is about enabling someone to find their own next step, and to take this step in a skilful and effective way. (Pelham, 2016)

He goes on to emphasise the fundamental principle of coaching that is the bedrock of his approach: 'people have the capability to take responsibility for, and make decisions about, their own lives, rather than someone else doing this for them'.

Personal reflection

I myself began to learn how to coach by taking a programme at the School of Coaching in London. When I applied to the programme I already had some experience working as a voluntary counsellor. We'll see later in the book that the ideas of Carl Rogers and his person-centred approach provide a foundation for my own views on coaching and facilitation. At the selection interview, Myles Downey – someone else whose ideas we shall visit throughout the book – asked me what I thought the difference was between coaching and counselling.

(Continued)

The answer I gave at the time – and it strikes me years later as quite a good answer given on the spur of the moment – was that coaching is counselling with a purpose. I don't mean to suggest that counselling doesn't have a purpose – it certainly does. What I meant was that coaching uses many of the skills of counselling but with a focus on performance. Its focus is results rather than problems.

Another way of thinking about the difference between counselling and coaching is that counselling explores the present and the past, and may at times consider the future. Coaching is focused on the present and the future, though it may at times look at the past.

You might like to spend a few minutes noting what you yourself see as the differences between coaching and counselling.

In the next chapter we'll discuss the difference between coaching and mentoring.

Incidentally, Myles Downey's definition of coaching is:

Coaching is the art of facilitating the performance, learning and development of another. (Downey, 2003)

Awareness and responsibility

John Whitmore's book *Coaching for Performance*, first published in 1992, was very influential in shaping the approach to coaching which we are exploring. When I worked in the early 2000s in management development for the gas pipeline company Transco, I had the privilege of working alongside John and his colleagues as together we ran workshops to help Transco managers develop their coaching skills.

In his book (Whitmore, 2002) he writes that, 'Building AWARENESS and RESPONSIBILITY is the essence of good coaching'. You can translate this into the following equation:

Awareness + Responsibility = Performance

Whitmore notes that:

The first key element of coaching is AWARENESS. ... It is the gathering and the clear perception of the relevant facts and information, and the ability to determine what is relevant. ... Awareness also encompasses self-awareness, in particular recognizing when and how emotions or desires distort one's own perception.

He suggests that:

- Awareness is knowing what is happening around you.
- Self-awareness is knowing what you are experiencing.

He goes on to say that:

> RESPONSIBILITY is the other key concept or goal of coaching. ... When we truly accept, choose or take responsibility for our thoughts and our actions, our commitment to them rises and so does our performance. (Whitmore, 2002)

As a coach, your questions are designed either to raise your client's awareness – of their hopes and fears, of how they feel about their current situation, of what they might do to change things, and so on – or to encourage them to take responsibility – what are they going to do, and by when, for instance. The premise is that someone who is aware of what they need to do and how to do it, and who also takes responsibility for acting, will perform. What performance means depends on their situation – it might be hitting a golf ball well, managing a team, completing an essay, or playing the flute.

You will see as you read through the book that we continually refer back to the importance in coaching conversations and relationships of raising your client's awareness and encouraging them to take responsibility for action.

I remember John Whitmore saying during some of the workshops that we ran together that *Awareness without Responsibility is just Whingeing*.

EXERCISE 1.1

WHAT IS YOUR DEFINITION OF COACHING?

You might be content to work with one of the definitions offered above. However, you may wish to browse through some books or search the internet for definitions used by other writers.

- Crystallise your thoughts by writing your own definition of coaching that you will use in your own practice.

It will be interesting to see if your definition evolves as you work through this book or in the light of your experience of practising coaching.

(Continued)

Here is another definition of coaching that is somewhat different from mine. Peter Hawkins and Nick Smith offer this definition as their 'working hypothesis':

> Coaching is the focused application of skills that deliver performance improvement to the individual's work in their organization, through robust support and challenge. The coaching process should yield learning and personal development for the executive, and help them contribute more of their potential. This collaborative relationship will be short-term and practically focused, and will be marked by clear, strong feedback. (Hawkins and Smith, 2006)

In this definition Hawkins and Smith have in mind executive coaching, but their definition could be modified to include, for instance, coaching someone who isn't currently working.

You might like to summarise what you see as the different emphases in my definition and Hawkins and Smith's definition, and consider which feels most appropriate to you at this point in your development as a coach.

2

DIRECTIVE AND NON-DIRECTIVE COACHING

Introduction

In this chapter we shall look at the directive to non-directive spectrum of coaching behaviours, and consider different things you might do in a coaching conversation along this spectrum. We then describe a simple framework for moving to the directive end of the spectrum. We next distinguish between being directive about the structure of a coaching conversation and being directive about the content. We introduce the GROW model, a widely used framework to structure coaching conversations, and illustrate this with an exercise called silent coaching which demonstrates the power of a non-directive approach to a coaching conversation. We end by comparing coaching and mentoring, suggesting that mentoring is positioned more towards the directive end of the spectrum.

The directive to non-directive spectrum

Some years ago I received a wonderful piece of feedback from one of the participants on the Certificate in Coaching that I used to run at the University of Warwick. She said that I was very directive about being non-directive. With this in mind, I want to emphasise that, while my own preference is to be primarily non-directive, this doesn't mean that you should coach in this way. One of the things I hope you will take from reading this book is clarity about how directive or non-directive you yourself wish to be in your own practice. I think it's invaluable to be clear in your own mind about your stance on this, both in your overall approach and in the moment as you choose what to say or do next within a conversation.

Another student on the Certificate in Coaching came to a clear conclusion that he needed to be directive in his role. He worked with unemployed young people in a large city. As well as being unemployed, many of his clients had other problems such as drug misuse or homelessness. He had 30-minute appointments with each client, and he had tough targets about finding jobs or placements for them. Given all of this, he concluded that he needed to be highly directive in telling his clients what they needed to do. From a distance, this struck me as entirely sensible.

While it is possible to take an extreme position, and indeed some counsellors would seek to operate exclusively at the non-directive end, in practice many coaches will operate at different points on the spectrum in different situations.

When you are coaching you are continually faced with choices about what to do next and how to respond. What question should I ask now? How do I deal with this silence? The session seems to be going nowhere, so what should I do? And so on. There are a host of possible responses, and choosing which response is an art rather than a science. A vital notion to bear in mind when you say or do anything is your intention. When you ask a question, give advice or offer a summary, what is your intention at that point?

I suggest that as you develop your practice as a coach it is very important to clarify in your own mind your position about being directive or non-directive. Being clear about your approach will help you continually in choosing what to do next in a coaching session or in managing a coaching relationship over time. Moreover, being non-directive creates a very different relationship with the client than being directive.

I would also add that I believe it is impossible to be totally non-directive as a coach. As the client speaks, your face or your body language can reveal your reaction, either conscious or unconscious. When you ask a question or play back to the client what you understand of their world, you are inevitably selective in choosing your words, even if your words are originally their words. And when you decide not to respond, you are nonetheless making a choice. However, it is undoubtedly possible to be more or less non-directive as a coach.

Directive and non-directive behaviours

Here is an exercise to consider this question of where you operate as a coach on the directive to non-directive spectrum. Below is a list of 10 behaviours, listed alphabetically, that you might engage in as a coach. Take a few minutes to rearrange the behaviours along a spectrum from the most directive behaviours at one end to the most non-directive behaviours at the other.

- Asking open questions that raise awareness
- Giving advice
- Giving feedback
- Instructing
- Listening to understand
- Making suggestions
- Offering guidance
- Paraphrasing by rephrasing the client's words
- Reflecting back using the client's own words
- Summarising an extended piece of conversation

I use the exercise, which I first encountered at the School of Coaching, to highlight that as a coach there are a number of behaviours you might engage in, and to introduce this fundamental question of how directive or non-directive you wish to be.

Figure 2.1 offers one answer to the task of arranging the behaviours along the directive to non-directive spectrum.

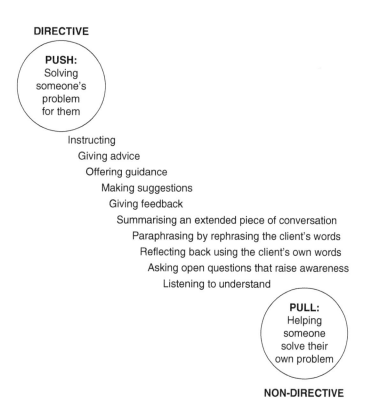

Figure 2.1   Directive and non-directive coaching behaviours

Thus behaviours such as instructing, giving advice and offering guidance are at the directive end, while listening, questioning and reflecting back are at the non-directive end.

The diagram also suggests that when you are coaching in a more directive style you are more likely to be looking to solve someone's problem for them or to **push** them towards a solution that you have in mind. On the other hand, when coaching non-directively your role is to help the other person to find their own solutions or to **pull** the ideas from them.

If you do wish to vary your approach in different situations, it helps to do this with a conscious awareness of what you're doing and why you're doing it.

EXERCISE 2.1

WHERE DO YOU OPERATE ON THE DIRECTIVE TO NON-DIRECTIVE SPECTRUM?

Your position on how directive or non-directive you are in your practice may evolve as you gain and reflect on experience. However, here are some questions to take stock of how you currently operate. You might reflect not only on coaching conversations but in other situations that you find yourself in as a manager, consultant, colleague, teacher, parent, friend, or whatever.

You may find it useful to repeat the exercise in the future and see how your practice shifts over time.

1. In what situations do you tend to operate from the directive end of the spectrum?
2. In what situations do you tend to operate from the non-directive end of the spectrum?
3. What factors influence your choice on where to operate along the spectrum?

Moving to the directive end of the spectrum

Myles Downey points that:

> There is an in-built limitation in the directive approach, which is that the coach has to know the answer already, or be able to work it out. (Downey, 2003)

However, he also emphasises that:

> It is important to understand that the directive end of the spectrum is also available to you as a coach. ... There will be times when ... to withhold an answer, feedback or advice would not be helpful. However, the magic inhabits the non-directive end of the spectrum. (Downey, 2003)

He proposes these guidelines on how a coach might give advice, make a suggestion or offer feedback to a client:

- First, ask the client if they would like your advice, suggestion or feedback at the moment.
- Second, if the client agrees, then say what you wish to say, which is moving to the directive end of the spectrum.
- Third, move immediately back to the non-directive end, resume coaching, and let the client choose how to respond in the light of your advice, suggestion or feedback.

You may find that when you offer a suggestion you are tempted to develop or justify it. Expanding on a suggestion you have just made may be appropriate but it does mean that you are remaining towards the directive end of the spectrum, perhaps pushing the merits of your idea. To move to the non-directive end, simply let the client respond, possibly by asking an open question such as *What do you see as the pros and cons of this idea?* Note that a question such as *What are the benefits of this idea?* may still be directing the client, unless it is followed by an equivalent question such as *What are the costs of this idea?*

Directive about structure and directive about content

I'd like to make a distinction between the structure and content of a coaching conversation. I believe that one of the key roles a coach plays is to manage the conversation in the service of the client. In my own practice I am very directive in structuring the session. I will, for example, manage the time, move the conversation on, propose an exercise, let a silence run on or break a silence, invite the client to summarise, and so on. And I am continually choosing which question to ask next. I'm clear that this is focusing the client's attention, hopefully in areas that are important to them, not me.

I will when appropriate check with the client that they are willing to, for instance, draw a picture or do an exercise, and will drop the idea if the client really doesn't want to do it. And I might play back to the client that they've mentioned two important topics and invite them to choose which we explore. I still regard this as managing the structure of the conversation.

However, I am at the same time very non-directive about the content of the conversation. For example, if I ask a client to draw a picture about how they'd like things to be in five years' time, I don't offer any suggestions about what that picture might or should contain. And when I ask a question, I don't ask a leading question that suggests a desirable answer. An example of a leading question might be: *Would it be a good idea to look for a new job?* This could in effect be giving advice that the client ought to look for a new job.

I find that people who are learning to coach and who wish to operate mainly non-directively often become muddled about this distinction. In trying to be non-directive about the content of the client's thinking they may fail to structure the conversation purposefully. To sum up my own approach, I'm directive about the structure of the conversation and non-directive about the content of how the client chooses to think or act.

The GROW model

Coaching generally takes place through conversation. Here is a simple framework that you can use to structure a coaching conversation. The GROW model is a very practical framework to enable another person to think through their situation and come up with a plan of action. The four aspects which give the model its name are:

<u>G</u>oal   What are you trying to achieve?

<u>R</u>eality   What is currently going on?

<u>O</u>ptions   What might you do?

<u>W</u>ill   What will you do?

The GROW model was developed originally by Graham Alexander in the 1980s in his work with senior executives. It was brought to a wider audience by John Whitmore in his book *Coaching for Performance*, first published in 1992. Whitmore explains why he considers it more useful to explore the client's goals before looking at the current reality. He writes:

> Goals formed by ascertaining the ideal long-term solution, and then determining realistic steps toward that ideal, are generally far more inspiring, creative and motivating. (Whitmore, 2002)

EXERCISE 2.2

SILENT COACHING AND THE GROW MODEL

Here is an exercise to experience working through the stages of the GROW model. To do the exercise you need to have in mind an issue that you'd like to spend 20 minutes thinking about. The issue needs to be a real current issue involving yourself where you're not sure how to proceed.

Begin by writing down in a sentence the issue that you want to think about.

Here are a number of questions to structure your thinking about the issue. Simply write down your answer to each question as you work through them.

Goal

1. What are you trying to achieve?
2. Imagine that you have successfully addressed your issue. What does success look like?
3. And what does success feel like?
4. In regard to this issue, what do you really, really want?

Reality

5. What is happening that makes this an issue for you?
6. What are the key features of the situation?
7. Who is involved?
8. What assumptions are you making?
9. What – if anything – have you already done to address the situation?
10. And what has been the effect of what you have done so far?

Options

11. What options do you have?
12. What else might you do?
13. If you had absolutely no constraints – of time or money or power or health – what would you do?
14. If you had a really wise friend, what would they do in your shoes?

(Continued)

Will

15. Your answers to the last four questions have generated a set of options. Which options will you actually pursue?
16. For each chosen option, what specifically will you do?
17. What help or support do you need?
18. What deadlines will you set for yourself?
19. What is the first step that you will take?

Here is a final question, which is about the process you've just been through rather than the content of what you've written:

20. What was the effect of these questions?

I often use the exercise in the early stages of a programme to help people learn how to coach. It's called silent coaching because the people answering the questions are silent. I let people know before they start writing that I won't ask them to share any of their reflections with anyone, so their exploration can be as deep or personal as they wish it to be.

I do ask them, if they wish to, to share their answer to the final question. This is a question about the process, not the content. I ask them not to say anything about the issue itself, just the effect of the questions. It is generally the case that many, though not necessarily all, have made some real progress in exploring their issue.

The exercise demonstrates a number of things. First, it introduces and highlights the usefulness of the GROW model. Second, it shows the power of asking short, open questions in a structured way. And, third, it illustrates the power of a non-directive approach. When I use the exercise in workshops, many participants make progress in exploring their issue even though I have no idea whatsoever what their topic is!

If you are working with colleagues in a coaching pair or trio, you'll find it useful to have the GROW framework in mind to help you manage the conversation. Note, however, that not all conversations lend themselves to the GROW framework. For example, if a client wants to think through whether to accept the offer of a new job or stay in their current role, a conversation structured to help them think through the pros and cons of the two options might be more helpful.

As you become more familiar and comfortable with the GROW framework you'll also find that you need to use it flexibly. Sometimes the client's goal will be very clear, and you don't need to spend a lot of time in this stage. On other occasions, you may have to take considerable time to help the client clarify their goal and then, once the goal is clear, the action steps are obvious. At other times, you may discover that exploration of reality or options leads to the insight that the goal as originally formulated isn't achievable and so you need to track back to help the client to revise – or perhaps abandon – their goal. You might also feel that it's easier to start with R and the exploration of reality, so that the model becomes RGOW – which isn't as neat a mnemonic!

Over time too you'll develop your own set of questions. There is nothing magical about the precise questions set out in the GROW exercise. Indeed, as we will consider in the chapter on questioning, the most useful questions are those that emerge from listening to understand the client. Note, however, that all of the questions in the exercise are open rather than closed questions, often beginning with the word *What ...?*

In my own coaching practice I have the GROW model at the back of my mind as I converse with a client. I sometimes explicitly work through the stages of the model to structure a coaching conversation, and on other occasions I use it more implicitly to mentally check where we're up to and if, for example, it seems time to move on to explore Options. I also find that in many coaching conversations it does seem more natural and useful to help the client explore their Reality before asking about their Goal.

Mentoring

A question often asked is: *What is the difference between coaching and mentoring?* These are two related activities, and it is helpful to be clear which activity you are engaged in. To describe the difference we need to define our terms.

Just as there isn't an agreed definition of coaching, similarly there isn't a recognised definition of mentoring. Here is my own working definition of mentoring that parallels my definition of coaching:

> Mentoring is a relationship in which the mentor draws on their experience, expertise and knowledge to support and guide a less experienced person in order to enhance their performance or encourage their development.

I see mentoring as likely to be in a situation where a more experienced person helps another to work out their way forward, in part by sharing their experience, offering suggestions and giving advice. These are behaviours at the more directive end of the spectrum, and they may be entirely appropriate depending on the context and the agreed objectives of the mentoring arrangement. In contrast, I view coaching as being primarily at the non-directive end of the spectrum.

To illustrate the difference, I once heard someone say *I could coach Barack Obama but I couldn't mentor him*. In other words, he could use his listening and questioning skills to help Barack Obama think things through (if he was willing to do so!) but he couldn't offer advice to him based on prior experience of being an international statesman.

I would add that I think you're more likely to be able to charge for your services if you style yourself as a coach, whereas as a mentor you may be expected to be offering your help for free.

In her book *The Mentoring Manual* Julie Starr offers this definition:

> A mentor is someone who takes on the role of a trusted adviser, supporter, teacher and wise counsel to another person. A mentor adopts a primarily selfless role in supporting the learning, development and ultimate success of another person. (Starr, 2014)

She goes on to add some key aspects of the respective roles:

- The mentee has something that they desire or want to achieve.
- The mentee has respect for the mentor.
- The mentor has knowledge, experience and perhaps opinion or insight in areas of value to the mentee.
- The mentor has a level of maturity around a topic that enables them to offer views and opinions based on understanding.
- The mentor has some level of benevolence towards the mentee – they offer compassion, care and generosity.
- Responsibility for learning, progress and results ultimately rests with the mentee. (Starr, 2014)

Origin of the words *coaching* and *mentoring*

In the sense that we're using the term, the word *coach* first appears in English literature in the nineteenth century, meaning someone who tutored a student to carry him through the Oxford University entrance exams. The word derives from the name of a small Hungarian town, Kocs, where a popular type of horse-drawn carriage was built.

Mentoring has been around since the time of the ancient Greeks – and doubtless before that. According to Greek mythology, when Odysseus set out for Troy he left the education of his son Telemachus to his friend Mentor – from whom we get the word *mentor*.

In one of the No. 1 Ladies' Detective Agency books, *The Full Cupboard of Life*, Mama Ramotswe reflects

> on the truth that when people ask for advice they very rarely want your advice and will go ahead and do what they want to do anyway, no matter what you say.

That applied in every sort of case; it was a human truth of universal application, but one which most people knew little or nothing about. (McCall Smith, 2003)

I think that a good mentor is aware of dangers like this in giving advice, and so will offer their advice or guidance judiciously and selectively. Moreover when they choose to offer advice, they do this with clear awareness that this is what they're doing. They can share their own experiences in a way that leaves the client free to take what they want to use and leave what they don't want. And they are also able to operate at the non-directive end of the spectrum, listening to understand and asking open questions.

I suspect that some mentors who have been very successful in their professional field are only able to offer advice based on what worked for them, without realising that other behaviours are possible. A senior manager with a command and control style of operating will struggle to be a rounded mentor.

Myles Downey illustrates how a mentor will be more valuable when they can operate from both ends of the spectrum. He writes:

A mentor who is reliant on, say, an avuncular style and dependent on having had significant experience of the organisation, business and life may well provide great benefit and be a wonderful person to be with. However, at the very least such a mentor would need to be able to listen effectively in order to ensure that the pearls of wisdom were indeed pearls in the eyes of the recipient. On a more positive note a mentor who has vast experience, and can use it to good effect, and who can also employ a non-directive approach when appropriate will have much greater impact. (Downey, 2003)

Peter Hawkins and Nick Smith suggest that mentoring is often about helping a mentee to make a transition from one stage of their career to the next. An untrained mentor who draws heavily on their own experiences may offer advice, some of which might be useful. However, it will be of limited value, they suggest, because:

- The situation and psychology of the mentee will almost certainly be different from that of the mentor.
- Advice-giving is nearly always less effective than skilfully facilitated exploration.
- Successful transitions nearly always involve unlearning previous ways of behaving and thinking, as well as acquiring new ones.
- Successful people in one phase of development are often unable to stand far enough back to help those trying to emulate their success.
- It is important to see the current transition in the context of the individual's long-term journey. (Hawkins and Smith, 2006)

Coaching and mentoring – a view from the CIPD

The website of the Chartered Institute of Personnel and Development contains the following views on coaching and mentoring in the workplace:

> Coaching and mentoring are development approaches based on the use of one-to-one conversations to enhance an individual's skills, knowledge or work performance.

> Coaching aims to produce optimal performance and improvement at work. It focuses on specific skills and goals, although it may also have an impact on an individual's personal attributes such as social interaction or confidence. The process typically lasts for a defined period of time or forms the basis of an on-going management style.

Although there's a lack of agreement among coaching professionals about precise definitions, there are some generally agreed characteristics of coaching in organisations:

- It's essentially a non-directive form of development.
- It focuses on improving performance and developing an individual.
- Personal factors may be included but the emphasis is on performance at work.
- Coaching activities have both organisational and individual goals.
- It provides people with the opportunity to better assess their strengths as well as their development areas.
- It's a skilled activity, which should be delivered by people who are trained to do so. This can be line managers and others trained in coaching skills.

Mentoring in the workplace tends to describe a relationship in which a more experienced colleague shares their greater knowledge to support the development of an inexperienced member of staff. It calls on the skills of questioning, listening, clarifying and reframing that are also associated with coaching.

One key distinction is that mentoring relationships tend to be longer term than coaching arrangements. In a succession planning scenario, for example, a regional finance director might be mentored by a group level counterpart over a lengthy period to develop a sound approach to dealing with the board, presenting to analysts and challenging departmental budgets.

Mentoring relationships work best when they move beyond the directive approach of a senior colleague 'telling it how it is', to one where they both learn from each other. An effective mentoring relationship is a learning opportunity for both parties, encouraging sharing and learning across generations and/or between roles.

www.cipd.co.uk/knowledge/fundamentals/people/development/coaching-mentoring-factsheet

Warwick Business School Mentoring Programme

One of the activities I do at Warwick Business School is to provide initial training and continuing professional development activities for the mentors who are involved in the WBS Mentoring Programme.

Open exclusively to students and alumni of Warwick Business School, the programme offers mentees the opportunity to have a mentor who is a volunteer from the WBS alumni community. There are currently approximately 250 active mentors, and each year the scheme takes on between 100 and 120 new mentees. It is a global scheme, with a hub in Singapore and a developing one in India. It has been particularly helpful for WBS graduates taking the next step in their career. Mentors help to provide the motivation, confidence and support to help mentees make their own decisions about their future steps.

Mentees are carefully matched with an appropriate mentor for a two-year mentoring relationship. The mentor acts as an unbiased, confidential support and sounding board. Many of the mentoring relationships take place remotely, using technology such as Skype. Wherever possible, however, mentor and mentee have an initial face-to-face meeting.

There is also a selection process for mentors – not everyone who applies is matched with a mentee. One of my colleagues rejected one applicant, a successful executive, who said that his motivation in volunteering to mentor business students was that he enjoyed telling people what to do!

In the initial training, which is offered either as a face-to-face workshop or a series of online webinars, I use the exercise on the directive to non-directive spectrum and the silent coaching exercise that we looked at earlier in the chapter. I emphasise the importance of each mentor being aware of their choices in operating directively or non-directively.

One of the challenges faced by many of the mentors is how to balance offering advice or guidance – which indeed is frequently asked for by mentees – and facilitating the mentee's self-exploration.

EXERCISE 2.3

YOUR EXPERIENCES OF MENTORING

Think back over your life and career. Identify one or two people who acted as some form of mentor to you. This may not have been a formal arrangement.

1. What did they do that was particularly helpful to you?
2. What might they have done differently to be of even more help to you?

Now think of some times when you acted as a mentor – formally or informally – to someone else.

1. What did you do that seemed to be helpful?
2. What would you do differently if you were mentoring that person again?

3

LISTENING TO UNDERSTAND

Introduction

Recall from Chapter 1 the definition of coaching that this book is based on:

> Coaching is a relationship of rapport and trust in which the coach uses their ability to listen, to ask questions and to play back what the client has communicated in order to help the client to clarify what matters to them and to work out what to do to achieve their aspirations.

In the next three chapters we shall explore the three key conversational skills needed to coach well – listening, questioning and playing back. We begin with listening, which is the fundamental skill you need to coach well. The importance of listening is captured by Alison Hardingham, who says that active listening:

> is the single most important skill for a coach. It is what enables the coach to understand the coachee and her world. Every other intervention the coach makes has to be based on that understanding, and the more complete that understanding is, the more effectively the coach will intervene. (Hardingham, 2004)

In this chapter we'll first consider different levels of listening, identifying the type of listening that is needed to coach well. We go on to discuss the importance of listening beyond the words spoken by the client, and consider non-verbal aspects of communication. We then look at listening to the client's story, and the place of silence and of interrupting the client within coaching conversations. We end by discussing active, attentive listening, and how this kind of listening is fundamental in creating a good coaching relationship.

Levels of listening

There are different ways of listening to someone, most of which are unsuitable for coaching.

First, and it is not an uncommon experience, is *not listening at all*. I know one woman who describes the quality of her husband's listening at times as *Listening while watching Sky Sports*.

A second and pretty common way of listening – particularly in social situations – is *listening, waiting to speak*. This is when I want to talk and will wait for as short a time as possible before starting to speak. Sometimes I might wait for you to pause, but equally I might interrupt you in mid-sentence. Nancy Kline (1999) writes, 'We think we listen, but we don't. We finish each other's sentences, we interrupt each other, we moan. … We give advice, give advice, give advice.'

A third way of listening – and it is typical of the kind of listening that goes on in many meetings – is *listening to disagree*. I want my point of view to prevail or to get my way. I'm listening for the weak points in what you say, and when I spot one I pounce. This is a selective form of listening. In some situations – in a court of law or in much academic discourse – this is the normal form of conversation, and it may be entirely appropriate. However, it is essentially adversarial – it is about winning and losing.

A fourth type of listening – and this way of listening is vital if you want to coach well – is *listening to understand*. In listening to understand, I am trying to see the world as it appears through your eyes. I am trying to appreciate what you're thinking and how you're feeling. I want to understand your dreams and your hopes, your fears and your doubts. The word that is often used here is *empathy*.

Note that it's important not only to understand your client and their world, it's also essential to communicate your understanding to the client. Your non-verbal acknowledgements, the questions you ask that build upon and extend their thinking, and your playing back of what you've understood of their world are all ways of indicating to the client that you have listened and understood.

Beyond listening to understand there is a further form of listening that is helpful in coaching – *listening to help the client to understand*. As long as your client understands, you don't have to know what they are thinking. In any case, you won't fully understand their reality in all its complexity and subtlety anyway.

I once coached someone from Beijing whose accent meant that it was difficult for me to grasp all that he was saying. He in turn found it difficult to understand me when I was speaking. But by continuing to show him respect and to pay close attention to him, I believe that I was able to help him think through his situation in ways that were meaningful to him. It didn't matter that I didn't fully understand.

Figure 3.1 summarises these five different levels of listening.

Listening to help the client
to understand

Listening to understand

Listening to disagree

Listening, waiting to speak

Not listening

Figure 3.1   Levels of listening

There is another distinction I'd like to make, which is between *listening to understand* and *listening to respond*. As you begin to learn to coach, you are likely to find that you spend quite a bit of time thinking about what question you're going to ask next. This brings the risk that, in being more concerned about how you're going to respond, you stop listening to understand the client.

If you catch yourself doing this, just be aware that this is what's going on for you and bring your attention fully back to the client. Simply focusing on what they are saying will help you listen to understand. I also sometimes find it helpful, when my client has said something that I'd like to explore further but don't want to interrupt their train of thought, to make a very brief note on my notepad – a word or perhaps a phrase they've used – to remind me to come back to this.

EXERCISE 3.1

LISTENING TO LISTENING

As an exercise, observe and characterise the kind of listening that is going on in some of the meetings or conversations that you are involved in.

- Who isn't listening?
- Who is listening, waiting to speak?
- Who is listening to disagree?
- Who is listening to understand?

Another thing you might monitor is the quality of your own listening. Notice how it varies in different situations or when you are with different people.

- When do you not listen?
- When do you listen, waiting to speak?
- When do you listen to disagree?
- When do you listen to understand?

Listening to what isn't being said

When someone speaks they communicate both verbally and non-verbally. If I say 'On Tuesday I caught the 8.30 train to Bath', it is fairly easy to capture and play back what I've said as it's entirely factual. I haven't revealed anything about how I felt about my trip to Bath.

In a coaching conversation, as your client is exploring issues which are very important to them and possibly uncovering things they hadn't fully realised before, there is likely to be a strong emotional element in what they're experiencing. Sometimes the client might verbalise this by saying, for instance, that they're feeling angry or confused. However, they may not verbalise this but reveal it in their facial expression or tone of voice or body language. To coach well, to understand empathically your client, you need to tune into the non-verbal aspects of their communication as well as hearing the words that they speak.

I'm not impressed by simplistic notions of body language which claim, for example, that someone who crosses their arms is defensive. They might simply be cold. Similarly, someone tapping their foot may indeed wish to get away from something, but other explanations are possible. Nevertheless, it's useful simply to notice how your client is sitting or when their posture changes, tentatively bearing this in mind as you listen to them.

Likewise, it's worth being aware of times when your client's words say one thing and their tone of voice or the look on their face seems to convey another message. If I say in a dejected tone that things are great, it's probably my non-verbal communication which more accurately indicates how I'm feeling. In Chapter 15 we'll look at some ideas from an approach called Transactional Analysis. One of the basic rules of communication in TA is that when a message is mixed – that is, the verbal content does not reflect the non-verbal or psychological communication – then it is the non-verbal message which has the most impact on the other person.

As we shall consider in more detail in Chapter 5, if you play back to your client what you have picked up non-verbally you need to do this carefully. In my earlier example, you can confidently and accurately repeat back to me that I went to Bath by train on Tuesday, because I told you this in words. However, if you are picking things up based on your client's non-verbal communications, you may need to be more tentative when you play back to the client. One way of doing this is to begin your statements with an expression such as *I'm wondering if you're feeling ...* or *I'm getting the impression that you're ...* .

There is one other point I'd like to make about non-verbal communication in coaching. As the coach, your own body language, facial expression and tone of voice are communicating to your client. If you're looking bored, failing to make eye contact or stumbling over your words, you're sending messages which the client is likely to pick up at a more or less conscious level.

EXERCISE 3.2

LISTENING TO NON-VERBAL COMMUNICATIONS

Here is a simple exercise you might like to try which illustrates the importance of body language and facial expressions – though not tone of voice – in communication. Choose a meeting – or a part of a meeting – that is not especially important for you. Imagine that you've switched off the sound and are simply observing the body language of the other participants without attending to the words they are saying. What do the various non-verbal communications tell you about the positions of the various participants?

You can, as it were, then switch the sound back on and check how congruent the words being spoken are with the non-verbals you've observed.

Listening to the client's story

Alison Hardingham says that listening to the client's story is her favourite technique for helping a client become more self-aware. She invites clients to tell their story by simply saying something like *Tell me your story – where you began, how you came to be here, what your journey was.*

When a client hears themself telling their story, they have an increased sense of themself and their distinctiveness. They are also likely to be more acceptant of themself because they've been heard without criticism or judging. They are also giving themself feedback at a really useful level – feedback that answers the question *Why?* When the client understands how they came to behave in certain ways, this can help them decide whether it feels right and safe to change. As the client shares their story, they may have insights that they hadn't realised before or make connections between past experiences and present ones.

Once the client has shared their story with the coach, it remains as a resource that either of them can draw on whenever they meet.

She writes:

> Because our values, beliefs and sense of who we are in the world have their roots in our early experiences, listening to a coachee's story in the sense I have just described it provides a huge amount of information about those most important aspects of her. The coach can help this information emerge, by listening for and reflecting back things the coachee says about what was important in her family of origin, what she was known for even as a child, what her hopes and dreams were, and so on. (Hardingham, 2004)

She notes that it's not always appropriate to ask the client to share their story in this way. For example, the coaching might have a very specific agenda. Some clients do not want to share or explore at this level of depth. Moreover, it's important to be clear that coaching isn't therapy, and the role of the coach isn't to heal emotional wounds or mend family relationships. If the client wants to work on these issues, then they need to do so with a qualified therapist or counsellor.

One way in which I sometimes ask a client to share their story is to invite them to draw a line which represents their life to date, and to mark on this significant events or decision points. This can be useful in an opening session to get a sense of the client and what matters to them. We'll look at this in Chapter 10 on tools you might use in a coaching session.

Silence

An important aspect of some coaching conversations is silence. In *Dialogue and the Art of Thinking Together* (1999), Bill Isaacs writes of four types of silence that may be experienced in a group:

- *Awkward* silences, where people feel uncomfortable
- *Tense* silences, where there is disagreement and conflict
- *Thoughtful* silences, where people are reflecting and looking inwards
- *Sacred* silences, where wisdom has replaced chatter

A key challenge to a coach is to be comfortable with silence. Nancy Kline (1999) speaks of the times when the client might go quiet as they think deeply about something: 'Listening to their quiet, you will not know *what* they are thinking. But you will know *that* they are thinking ... ideas are forming, insights are melding, most of which you will never hear about.'

Being clear about your intention is important before you break a silence. If the silence in a coaching conversation is awkward or tense, you need to consider whether and how to break the silence. If, however, your client is busy thinking then it's essential that you don't interrupt the silence. Breaking a silence simply because you feel uncomfortable isn't appropriate. Breaking a silence because your client seems to be feeling uncomfortable may or may not be appropriate.

Susan Scott writes of her work as an executive coach that:

> During my conversations with the people most important to me, silence has become my favourite sound, because that is when the work is being done. Of all the tools I use during conversations and all the principles I keep in mind, silence is the most powerful of all. (Scott, 2002)

She draws a lovely comparison with classical music and the pauses between the notes. She says:

> Anyone can play the notes. The magic is in the intervals, in the phrasing. That's where silence comes in. When we are completely engaged in talking, all of the possibilities for the conversation grow smaller. (Scott, 2002)

Faced with a silence where your client is busy thinking, simply give them your attention and wait till they're ready to speak. Sometimes you will be surprised by what they say next. And, even if they say nothing, they may still have reached an important insight or made a significant decision. As long as your client understands, you don't have to.

Interrupting

This chapter is all about the importance of listening to understand the client, and we've just argued that it's vital not to interrupt the client when they are busy thinking. There are occasions, however, when – in the interests of the client – you help more by interrupting them than by letting them talk on.

It may be, for example, that the client is explaining their situation in great detail, giving information that they already know and which you don't need to know to coach them effectively. This isn't a good use of either of your time, and interrupting them – politely but clearly – is likely to be helpful. Or, it may be that you're nearing the end of the scheduled time and you judge that it will be more useful for the client to focus on deciding what actions they're going to take after the session.

It could be that the client is talking as a way of avoiding what they really need to be focusing on. This may be a conscious manoeuvre on their part, or they may be doing it unconsciously. You might in this situation say something such as *I'd like to take us back to …* in order to refocus the conversation. Alternatively, you might wish simply to say *I'm wondering what this has to do with the issue you wanted to explore today.* It may turn out to be important for the client to unburden themself by sharing all the detail with you.

If your relationship with the client is strong enough, you might consider naming what you see happening in the conversation – for instance, saying *I'm wondering if you're describing things in such detail as a way of avoiding something important.* Prefacing your comment with *I'm wondering if …* makes it open to consideration rather than a dogmatic statement.

I believe that a vital part of your role as a coach is to manage the conversation in the interests of the client. As I mentioned in the previous chapter, I am directive about the process but not about the content of the conversation. Hence, I may sometimes interrupt the client to manage the process.

Jenny Rogers offers some useful pointers on how to interrupt:

- Negotiate the expectation that you will interrupt in your first session with the client.
- Trust your intuition that it is time to do it.
- Set aside your worries about whether the client will dislike you for doing it.
- Ask permission.
- Use body language to help.
- Ask the client if you really need to know all the detail. (Rogers, 2008)

Christian van Nieuwerburgh distinguishes two types of interruption that a coach might use in the interests of the client. **Procedural interruption** is to help manage the conversation – for instance, to remind a client who has started to revisit earlier material that there are only 10 minutes left in today's session. **Emphatic interruption** is when the coach wishes to emphasise something that the client has just said which seems important but is being overlooked or underplayed – for instance, when a client is understating a strength or an achievement. He says that, 'All interruptions should begin with an apology and an explanation of why the intervention is being made' (van Nieuwerburgh, 2017).

Active, attentive listening

Listening to understand your client is an active process. It requires concentration, and can be tiring. Alison Hardingham suggests three reasons for describing listening as active:

- First, it is active because the listener is doing things.
- Second, it is active because while it is going on, changes are happening.
- Third, it is 'active' because it takes effort and application to do well. (Hardingham, 2004)

She also writes that, 'Sometimes active listening achieves the goal of coaching all by itself.' There are times when just saying things out loud is enough for the client to resolve what's troubling them.

Michael Mitton also notes that attentive listening is an active process. He writes:

Attentive listening is creating space – it is constructive. It is not sitting passively in front of a verbal water jet. It is actively applying often intense concentration to facilitate the person we are listening to, to help them move on in their journey. (Mitton, 2004)

Nancy Kline talks about how important it is to give great attention to your client. She describes attention as listening with palpable respect and fascination. She says that:

When you are listening to someone, much of the quality of what you are hearing is *your effect on them*. Giving good attention to people makes them more intelligent. Poor attention makes them stumble over their words and seem stupid. Your attention, your listening is that important. (Kline, 1999 – italics in original)

Julie Starr describes a level of listening that she terms *deep listening*, an elusive form of listening where the awareness of the coach is entirely focused on the client. She writes of deep listening that:

For the person being listened to, as they are speaking they will undoubtedly feel understood and they might also experience a deeper form of relatedness to the listener. (Starr, 2011)

She offers some ground rules for listening in the form of five things that you should not do when your focus is on listening deeply to understand the client. Do not, she writes:

- Attempt to give the speaker ideas, solutions or suggestions relating to the situations they are discussing
- Refer to or discuss any of your own similar circumstances, experiences or feelings
- Attempt to control the direction or content of the conversation
- Seek to look good or impress the other person in any way, e.g. by asking 'clever' questions, by offering impressive facts or information, etc.
- Try to coach them …

Listening to understand is active, attentive listening. However, sometimes when you are coaching your attention may wander and your mind drift off into your own thoughts. If this happens, first notice it and then gently bring your attention back to the client.

Listening creates relationship

Listening to understand is the most important skill you need to coach well. The other two conversational skills needed in coaching, questioning and playing back your understanding, are both based on first listening attentively to your client.

This might seem a good enough reason to claim that listening is vital to good coaching. However, there is a second and more fundamental reason why attentive listening is vital. Meg Wheatley writes:

> Why is being heard so healing? I don't know the full answer to that question, but I do know that it has something to do with the fact that listening creates relationship. (Wheatley, 2002)

Coaching is first and foremost a relationship, a relationship of rapport and trust. You build this relationship by listening with respect and empathy to your client. Myles Downey (2003) argues that, 'Without a relationship there is no coaching. In fact the only real mistake that a coach can make is to damage the relationship irreparably.'

I am sometimes asked if I get bored listening to people day after day in coaching. I don't, and I think the key is to be genuinely interested in the other person and their unique story. It's really helpful simply to be curious about each and every one of your clients. In conversation the opposite of curiosity is certainty. When you think you know what the other person is going to say, you stop listening.

Nancy Kline emphasises the importance of attentive listening. She says that:

> Real help, personally or professionally, consists of listening to people, of paying respectful attention to people so that they can *access their own ideas first*. Usually the brain that contains the problem also contains the solution – often the best one. When you

keep that in mind, you become more effective with people. And people around you end up with better ideas. (Kline, 1999 – italics in original)

So, while listening is important in all forms of coaching, listening with respect and attention is especially and fundamentally important in non-directive coaching.

EXERCISE 3.3

SOME QUOTES ON LISTENING

Here are some of my favourite quotes on listening from different authors. As an exercise, read through the quotes and pick out one or two phrases that particularly resonate for you.

Anyone who cannot listen long and patiently will presently be talking beside the point and be never really speaking to others. There is a kind of listening with half an ear that presumes already to know what the other person has to say. It is an impatient, inattentive listening, that despises the other and is only waiting for a chance to speak and thus get rid of the other person.

Dietrich Bonhoeffer, *Life Together* (1954)

Attentive listening is creating space – it is constructive. It is not sitting passively in front of a verbal water jet. It is actively applying often intense concentration to facilitate the person we are listening to, to help them move on in their journey.

Michael Mitton, *A Heart to Listen* (2004)

Why is being heard so healing? I don't know the full answer to that question, but I do know that it has something to do with the fact that listening creates relationship.

Meg Wheatley, *Turning to One Another* (2002)

During my conversations with the people most important to me, silence has become my favourite sound, because that is when the work is being done. Of all the tools I use during conversations and all the principles I keep in mind, silence is the most powerful of all.

Susan Scott, *Fierce Conversations* (2002)

(Continued)

To relate effectively with a wife, a husband, children, friends, or working associates, we must learn to listen. And this requires emotional strength. Listening involves patience, openness, and the desire to understand – highly developed qualities of character. It's so much easier to operate from a low emotional level and to give high-level advice.

Stephen Covey, *The 7 Habits of Highly Effective People* (1989)

When you are listening to someone, much of the quality of what you are hearing is *your effect on them*. Giving good attention to people makes them more intelligent. Poor attention makes them stumble over their words and seem stupid. Your attention, your listening is that important.

Nancy Kline, *Time to Think* (1999)

4

QUESTIONING

Introduction

In the previous chapter we explored attentive listening, which is the fundamental skill you need to coach well. Questioning is the second most important conversational skill in coaching. Asking questions is one of the main ways in which you manage and structure a coaching conversation, helping the client to focus on what is most useful for them.

Alison Hardingham (2004) writes that 'Questioning … together with active listening probably achieves 80% of the positive outcome of coaching.' Moreover, listening and questioning go hand in hand – good coaching questions emerge from listening with empathy and curiosity to the client.

In this chapter we begin by exploring what makes a good coaching question, and then compare open and closed questions. We go on to look at how you ask a question, and suggest that it's helpful to ask crisp questions – that is, open questions simply expressed. We then describe different types of question you might ask in a coaching session, and caution against asking leading questions which already contain the answer. We end by suggesting a modification to the GROW model.

What makes a good coaching question?

Recall the equation that we looked at in Chapter 1 which sums up what you're trying to do as a coach:

Awareness + Responsibility = Performance

Most of the questions you ask in coaching should either be to raise the client's awareness or to encourage them to take responsibility – or possibly both.

Julie Starr writes:

> The ability to ask great questions is one of the most important skills a coach develops. Great questions are simple to answer, give direction to the conversation and gently influence someone else's thinking. A simply worded question, delivered at the appropriate moment, can shift or shape someone's thinking dramatically. (Starr, 2011)

Since my preference as a coach is to be mainly non-directive, I'm somewhat uncomfortable with Julie Starr's phrase '*gently influence someone else's thinking*'. My view is that a useful question in non-directive coaching focuses – rather than influences – the client's thinking.

You will sometimes ask questions to gather information from the client so that you can appreciate their world. However, asking questions that the client already knows the answer to doesn't actually help them. For instance, let's suppose that your client is exploring how to manage their team of six people. It might help you to know a little about these six people in order to ask useful questions. But you don't need detailed descriptions of their roles and career histories. And, if you catch yourself gathering lots of factual information, mentally ask yourself what your intention is. You may be avoiding helping the client to focus on the real issues that they need to address – and possibly colluding with them in this.

As you develop your coaching skills you may realise that you don't actually need that much information. As long as the client understands you don't need to understand.

Alison Hardingham (2004) says that, 'Good questions come, just like active listening, from a deep interest on the part of the coach in the coachee's experience of the world.'

Jenny Rogers (2008) writes that, 'one of the secrets of good coaching is to know how to ask questions that ... liberate the client by broadening the search for answers, take the client into new pathways, and challenge the client's thinking'. She sets out this useful checklist of characteristics of effective questions:

- They raise the client's self-awareness by provoking thinking and challenge.
- They demand truthful answers by cutting through obfuscation and waffle.
- They are short.
- They go beyond asking for information by asking for discovery.
- They encourage the client to take responsibility for themselves.
- They stick closely to the client's agenda.
- They lead to learning for the client.
- They are more than likely to begin with the words 'what' or 'how'. (Rogers, 2008)

Open and closed questions

In thinking about the kinds of question you might ask as a coach, it is very useful to distinguish between open and closed questions.

An open question is one which begins with a word like *What … ?* or *How … ?* or *Why … ?* It is more likely to prompt thinking in the client and a detailed response. Hence it is more likely to raise the client's awareness or encourage responsibility.

A closed question often begins with a verb, such as *Have you … ?* or *Could you … ?* or *Do you think that … ?* It can usually be answered *Yes* or *No* or with a one-word reply, often with little thought required.

Open questions are normally more useful than closed ones in coaching. Moreover, a closed question can generally be easily turned into an equivalent but more thought provoking open question. As an illustration, compare these two questions:

- Do you like your job?
- What do you like about your job?

The second question will generally encourage more thought and a fuller explanation.

You may be lucky and find that the client interprets a closed question as an open one, and gives an expansive answer, but it is safer to ask the open question in the first place.

I regard some questions as semi-open. Consider, for example, the question *Is there anything else about X?* Grammatically, this is a closed question, but often the client hears it and responds as though it were an open question.

I also often ask a simple open question beginning with *What else … ?* to encourage the client to think further. I also use phrases such as *Say a bit more about Y* or *Tell me more about Z*. I see these as very open statements inviting the client to explore further, and regard them as equivalent to open questions.

One danger in asking closed questions is that, because they don't generate much thinking or yield much information, you end up asking a whole series of questions and the conversation begins to feel like an interrogation. If you find yourself caught up in such an exchange, one option is to take a pause and ask the client a simple, open question, such as:

- What's on your mind?
- Where are we up to now?
- What do you want to look at next?

Occasionally, a closed question is just what is called for, particularly if you don't want a detailed response. For instance, you may want to check out your understanding by saying something like *Have I understood you correctly?* Or, you may want to move the conversation on by asking, for example, *Are you ready to look at options?* Or, you may wish to establish if your client really is committed to an action by asking a question such as: *So, will you speak to your boss today?*

EXERCISE 4.1

CONVERTING CLOSED TO OPEN QUESTIONS

It is easy to convert a closed question into a more useful, thought provoking question. As an exercise, translate these questions into short, open questions.

1. Did you like the film?
2. Is Chris the best performer in the team?
3. Do you want pizza for dinner tonight?
4. Shall we go to Spain on holiday next summer?
5. Do you understand the financial case?
6. Have you thought of resigning?

How do you ask the question?

Julie Starr highlights that how you ask a question is important:

> Any question is given further meaning by the quality of your voice when you ask it. Questions may be made clearer, colder, more supportive or more aggressive simply by the tone, warmth and speed of your voice. (Starr, 2011)

One form of open question that you need to be careful in asking is a question beginning with *Why?* This can often come across as unduly challenging and might provoke defensiveness in the client. For example, imagine different ways in which you might ask *Why did you do that?* and how they might be heard by a client.

A helpful idea if you want to challenge your client but are concerned that you may come across as overly critical or judgemental is the notion of *softening* the question. You might, for instance, ask a *Why?* type of question in one of the following ways:

1. I was wondering what led you to do that.
2. I'm interested in your reasons for saying that.
3. What do you think that will achieve?
4. What is it that makes this important for you?

Note too that these examples not only soften the question but may also give it a more specific focus than a more general *Why?* question. The first formulation is backward looking, for instance, and the third is forward looking.

Crisp questions

A common mistake made by learner coaches is asking questions that are too long. They also frequently ask a number of questions together. For example, they might say:

> What type of career are you looking for? Where would you like to be in five years time? I mean, do you want to stay as an accountant or move into management? Which will give you most job satisfaction, do you think? Or do you want to leave the organisation and move elsewhere?

There are five questions here, and they are likely to leave the client feeling confused about what is being asked. Often, if the learner coach simply left it at the first question, it would be a good question. In this case, simply asking *What type of career are you looking for?* and waiting for the answer might be really helpful.

Jenny Rogers says that:

> As a coach, when you ask long questions you are at risk of turning the spotlight of the coaching onto yourself. Long questions normally come out of uncertainty. … As a coach, you cannot afford the luxury of doing your thinking out loud. It will only confuse your client if your questions have long preambles followed by many dependent clauses, garlanded with phrases intended to give yourself time to think: *sort of, you know* and *I mean.* (Rogers, 2008)

The word I like to use to describe the right question is *crisp*. A crisp question – simply expressed – helps to focus the client on the most useful issue for them at that moment in time. Note that this is more art than science. You couldn't prove that another question or another phrasing of a question would not have been better still. But sometimes you know – or occasionally the client will tell you – that you've asked a really useful question.

In the next chapter we look at playing back to the client your understanding of what they've been saying. A useful combination is first to summarise – hopefully accurately – what they've said and then ask a crisp question to move the conversation on. This is more much effective than asking the question and then offering your summary as a way of explaining or perhaps justifying your question. If you follow your question with a long explanation of why you've asked it, there is a risk that the client – and perhaps you yourself – may have forgotten what the question was when you stop speaking.

EXERCISE 4.2

YOUR OWN QUESTIONS

Over the next week or so, pay attention to the questions that you yourself ask in meetings or one-to-one conversations. Simply notice:

- How many words does it take you to ask a question?
- How often do you ask multiple questions together?
- How often do you ask a question followed by an explanation or justification of the question?

Other types of question

Here are some different types of question that you might use at an appropriate time in a coaching conversation.

- A **clarifying** question can help a client refine their thinking when it's vague or fuzzy. For instance, *What exactly do you find difficult when writing a report?*
- A **probing** question invites a client to think more deeply or be more precise or face up to a possible contradiction in what they've been saying. For example, *What is the real issue here?* or *How does your plan to do X fit with your issue Y?*
- A **differentiating** question asks the client to compare and contrast different aspects of their situation, encouraging them to think more deeply. Examples include *What is the most difficult part of your role?* or *What is the most important of your reasons for doing Z?*

- A **hypothetical** question invites the client to explore possibilities and may free up their thinking. For instance, *If you had more confidence in your assistant, what would you delegate to them?*
- A **reframing** question aims to help the client see their situation in a new way. As an illustration: *So far we've been discussing the difficulties involved in this change. What possibilities does it open up?*
- A **scaling** question asks the client to rate some aspect of their situation on a scale of 1 to 10. For example: *On a scale of 1 to 10, how committed are you to carrying out this action?* We'll look in more detail at scaling questions in Chapter 10.

Leading questions

There is one type of question that I'd urge you to avoid in coaching. A **leading** question is one which already contains the answer or at least a suggested answer. A leading question is often advice disguised as a question. Examples of leading questions are:

1. Do you think it would be a good idea to do X?
2. Have you tried doing Y?
3. Would you agree that Z would be more useful?

I think there are a number of possible reasons why a coach, particularly an inexperienced one, might ask a leading question. First, they may see a way forward and offer this in the form of a leading question in a genuine attempt to help. Second, they may feel uncomfortable listening to someone talk about an unresolved issue or problem – offering a solution seems a way of making things better for the client and removing the discomfort that both may be feeling. Third, a learner coach may not yet be confident or capable enough to ask good questions or tolerate a silence.

As we considered in Chapter 2, there is a place for suggestions in coaching. When you have a suggestion to make then it's more honest and helpful to offer it clearly as a suggestion. For example, you could rephrase the above leading questions as these suggestions:

1. I think it would be a good idea to do X. What do you think?
2. If you want my opinion, it would be helpful to do Y. What is your view?
3. In my view, it would be more useful to do Z. What do you see as the pros and cons of Z?

In these rewordings, the coach moves clearly down to the directive end of the spectrum, offers their idea, and then asks a balanced and open question which invites the client to consider this.

You may find that you sometimes ask a question expecting the client to give a particular answer, and you might even experience a feeling of disappointment if the answer is not as you expected. Although you may not be leading the client, notice that you have some attachment to the answer. A really useful notion when coaching is to *ask the question with no attachment to the answer.* In other words, be completely open minded about how the client might respond, and work with whatever they reply.

What do you do when you don't know what question to ask?

David Whitaker, coach of the UK team that won the men's hockey gold medal at the 1988 Olympics, offers the following guideline to help you when you're not sure what to say next in a coaching conversation. He says: *If in doubt, build the relationship.* In his view, anything that develops the relationship between yourself and your client can only help. For example, playing back an empathic understanding of the client and their world is likely to build the relationship.

Myles Downey (2003) echoes this when he writes that, 'There is only one mistake that you can make in coaching and that is to irreparably damage the relationship.'

Another approach when you're not sure what to say next – which is likely to be more suitable when your client understands the coaching process – is simply to ask them *What is the most helpful question I could ask you now?* And you might preface this by acknowledging that you are not sure what to do next.

One thing that I sometimes do when I'm not sure what to do next is to offer a summary of where I think we're up to in the conversation, or perhaps ask the client to summarise where we're up to. One benefit of a summary is simply that it gives you time to think. We'll look at this in the next chapter at playing back to the client what they've said.

You might combine these ideas by summarising, indicating some possible ways of taking the conversation forward, and inviting the client to choose what they'd like to do next in the session. For example, you might respond to a client along the lines:

There seem to be three aspects of the situation that are important to you: X, Y and Z. We probably have time to look at just one of these today. Which one would you like to explore?

Socratic questioning

My book *Don't Just Do Something, Sit There* was translated into Chinese with a title that translates back as *Modern Midwifery: The Art of Coaching*.

The Chinese title reflects the notion of Socratic questioning. Socrates taught his pupils by asking questions and drawing the answers from them. My translator picked up on the importance of a non-directive approach using open questions. Plato, one of his students who wrote up much of what we know about Socrates, described him as a midwife, helping others to give birth to their ideas through his questions.

In his dialogue *Theaetetus*, Plato writes of Socrates:

> I have this in common with the midwives: I am sterile in point of wisdom, and the reproach which has often been brought against me, that I question others but make no reply myself about anything, because I have no wisdom in me, is a true reproach; and the reason of it is this: the god compels me to act as midwife, but has never allowed me to bring forth. I am, then, not at all a wise person myself ...

> www.gradesaver.com/theaetetus/study-guide/quotes

We might regard Socrates as the first non-directive coach!

In an article entitled 'Using Socratic questioning in coaching', Michael Neenan writes:

> A Socratic stance in coaching ... focuses on asking a person a series of open-ended questions to help promote reflection; this, in turn, is likely to produce knowledge which is currently outside of her awareness and thereby enable her to develop more helpful perspectives and actions in tackling her difficulties. Through this method, people are able to reach their own conclusions rather than being told what these should be by the questioner. (Neenan, 2009)

Modifying the GROW model

I often find it helpful to ask two distinct questions near the start of a coaching session. The first is something along the lines of *What do you want to talk about today?* This invites the client to introduce the **Topic** for the session.

The second is *What would be a useful outcome for you from our conversation today?* I sometimes ask this in a form such as: *If today's session is really useful for you, what will you be taking away from it?* Either of these establishes a more focused **Objective** for the conversation. I also may use this type of question if we've reached a point in the session when I want to check what the client thinks will be the best use of the time left that day.

Having established an objective for the session, you might then go on to work through the various stages of the GROW framework. Hence, we could modify the GROW model to become the TO GROW model:

Topic   What do you want to talk about today?

Objective   What would be a useful outcome from this conversation?

Goal   What are you trying to achieve?

Reality   What is currently going on?

Options   What could you do?

Will   What will you do?

The TO of TO GROW

In 2017 I was filmed having a 35-minute coaching conversation with Lina. This was one of a number of sessions by different coaches being recorded for use by Christian van Nieuwerburgh and David Love in their book, *Advanced Coaching Practice* (2019). After the conversation, Christian interviewed Lina on her experience of the session, and then interviewed me on my own reflections. At various points in the book, we shall invite you to view a number of clips from these recordings to illustrate some ideas.

Link to Video 4.1
Establishing a topic and an objective

Please watch this clip of the opening four minutes of my coaching conversation with Lina. In this, I establish the Topic that Lina wants to explore, discuss some of the Reality of her situation, and then establish Lina's Objective for the session.

EXERCISE 4.3

SOME QUOTES ON QUESTIONING

Here are a number of quotes on questioning from different authors. As an exercise, read through the quotes and pick out one or two phrases that you think will be particularly useful for you when you are coaching.

If the coach is working out the next question while the coachee is speaking, the coachee will be aware that he is not really listening. Far better to hear the person through and then pause if necessary while the next appropriate question comes to mind.

John Whitmore, *Coaching for Performance* (2002)

Coaching is not an exam where you get only one chance. If a question does not work, ask another. When you are in a good relationship it does not matter. There is only one mistake that you can make in coaching and that is to irreparably damage the relationship.

Myles Downey, *Effective Coaching* (2003)

Language in successful coaching is the disciplined simplicity that comes from trusting clients to tap into their own resources. It is about paring down to the essence – having the questions but understanding that you don't need to have the answers.

Jenny Rogers, *Coaching Skills: A Handbook* (2008)

We develop our questioning skill best by developing our capacity for curiosity. Encourage yourself to wonder, about all kinds of people and all kinds of situation. Ask yourself lots of questions, and you will become better at asking them of other people.

Alison Hardingham, *The Coach's Coach* (2004)

Simple questions often have the greatest impact, because they allow the coachee to use energy for forming their response, rather than trying to understand the wording of the question. In addition, they often get 'to the heart of the matter' more easily, simply because of their direct nature. We obviously need to balance 'direct' with a need to maintain rapport, and that is still possible. When asking questions, being clever just isn't clever.

Julie Starr, *The Coaching Manual* (2011)

5

PLAYING BACK

Introduction

In the last two chapters we have looked at the two key skills you need to manage coaching conversations – listening to understand the client and asking mainly open questions to help them explore their world. In my own coaching conversations I frequently use a third conversational skill – playing back to the client my understanding of what they've been saying or maybe communicating non-verbally. Accurate play back helps both to manage the conversation and to build the coaching relationship.

In this chapter we begin by looking at three ways in which you might play back your understanding – summarising, paraphrasing and reflecting back using the client's own words. We then consider some of the benefits of playing back your understanding. We go on to explore the idea of clean language – that is, using the client's exact words. We then look at a number of types of reflecting back, drawing on ideas from a technique known as Motivational Interviewing. We end by considering the play back of emotions and of non-verbal communications.

Three ways of playing back

There are three main ways in which you can play back to your client your understanding of what they've said. First, you might **summarise** to play back your appreciation of the key points raised by the client. You might, for instance, say something along the lines of *You seem to be saying that there are four issues here ...* . Summary is usually used to cover an extended piece of conversation.

Second, you can **paraphrase** what the client has said, turning their words into a different formulation. For instance, if your client says *It feels like I'm banging my head against a brick wall*, you might respond with *It sounds as though you're feeling very frustrated and perhaps a bit angry.*

Third, you might **reflect back** to the client what they have said, repeating their exact words. We'll look later in the chapter at why it might be important to repeat the specific words used by the client. In the previous illustration, you might reply *Tell me more about what it's like to be banging your head against a brick wall.*

You may sometimes sense that a single word or phrase used by a client seems charged with significance, perhaps indicated by their tone of voice. For example, the client might say *I'm really disappointed with my boss's response*, with a strong emphasis on the word *disappointed*. A simple reply, such as saying in an inquisitive tone *Disappointed?*, may be enough to encourage the client to think more deeply. Or you might respond with a question such as *And what's behind 'disappointed'?*

EXERCISE 5.1

WHAT MIGHT YOU PLAY BACK?

You might like to try out these three ways of playing back within some meetings that you take part in over the coming weeks. Summarise where the meeting is up to, or paraphrase what someone is seeking, or reflect back some of the exact words used by someone – and notice what happens. You might make some notes after the meeting on the effect of your play back, perhaps identifying what seems to work best in different contexts.

The benefits of playing back

Jenny Rogers notes these key features of a genuine summary:

- It does not contain any judgement of your own.
- It does not interpret.
- It uses the client's language.
- It ends with a question – *Have I got that right?* or *Is that a fair summary of where we seem to have got to?*
- It is genuinely a summary and therefore brief. (Rogers, 2008)

Julie Starr lists a number of benefits of summarising briefly. Timed well, a summary:

- Gives the coachee a rest.
- Demonstrates accurate listening by the coach.
- Enables the coachee to hear for themselves what they've been saying, and check for themselves how they feel hearing that now.
- Enables the coachee to form links in the information they have expressed.
- Creates a natural 'pause' which enables both the coach and the coachee to reconsider progress and decide the best way forward.
- Might 'prompt' the coachee to surface additional, relevant information or insights. (Starr, 2011)

I find that I use summary as one of the main ways in which I manage a coaching conversation. For example, I often use it when the client has set the scene, perhaps having ranged over a number of aspects of their situation. If my summary captures the main points reasonably accurately, this lets the client know that they've been understood and enables them to move forward in their thinking.

A summary also gives me time to think, and I sometimes use a summary when I'm not sure what to do next in the conversation. I might end such a summary with a question inviting the client to choose what they want to look at next by asking, for example, *What would you like to focus on now?*

At times a summary is enough to enable the client to identify what they want to do. In terms of the equation

Awareness + Responsibility = Performance

it is sometimes the case that awareness is all that's required for the response to be obvious to the client. Or, in the words of Tim Gallwey, 'awareness is curative'.

Myles Downey writes of these three ways of playing back:

> In using these skills something special can happen. As the coach repeats what has been said, summarises, or paraphrases, the player often has a new insight or idea. I can only guess as to why that might happen. I think it is that, as the player hears the issue played back, it is possible to get a little distance … from the issue, to be not so attached, and in seeing it differently to have some new thoughts. (Downey, 2003)

Playing back helps to check your understanding of the client's situation. It is a useful way for the coach to punctuate and manage the conversation. There is one other benefit in playing back your understanding, and it is probably the most important reason why play back is important in coaching. Playing back an empathic understanding to the client shows them that they've been listened to, understood and hopefully accepted – this helps to build rapport and trust in the relationship between the client and the coach.

On numerous occasions I've felt an almost tangible shift in a client when they realise that they've been understood and accepted.

Paraphrasing, reflecting back and clean language

When you paraphrase a client's words, you change them into a different expression. This is sometimes helpful for the client – for instance, hearing their words played back in a different formulation might expand their understanding. As an illustration, let's return to an example used earlier.

Client: *It feels like I'm banging my head against a brick wall.*

Coach: *It sounds as though you're feeling very frustrated and perhaps a bit angry.*

Client: *You're right. I am angry. I hadn't realised that till now.*

However, there is a danger when you change the client's words that you distort their meaning. In this illustration, the client might respond to the coach's paraphrase by saying:

Client: *No, I'm not at all angry.*

In the early 1980s a New Zealand trauma therapist called David Grove developed the idea of **clean language**. In his work with clients he used only their exact words and metaphors, and he considered that paraphrasing unhelpfully distorted the client's reality. He would reflect back not just their exact words but sometimes also their non-verbal expressions.

Wendy Sullivan and Judy Rees suggest that:

Using a person's own words in your question indicates that you have really been listening in a non-judgemental way. Don't paraphrase – parrot-phrase instead! People's words are important to them, and using their words tends to help them feel respected and acknowledged. (Sullivan and Rees, 2008)

In the pure form of working with clean language, questions are asked in very particular ways so as not to introduce ideas from the coach. Sullivan and Rees go on to list a dozen basic clean language questions, those that are used most often by practitioners. Two common clean language questions – where X represents the client's exact words – are:

- What kind of X is that X?
- And is there anything else about X?

Nancy Kline also emphasises the importance of working with the client's own words:

> The best wording is the Thinker's own: their mind has specifically chosen and uttered those exact words for a reason. Those words mean something to the Thinker. They come from somewhere and are rich with the Thinker's history, culture, experience and any number of associations in the Thinker's life. (Kline, 1999)

In my own practice, I adapt some of the ideas of clean language without confining myself to the form of questions used by clean language practitioners. For example, sometimes a client uses a word or a phrase that seems significant, employs a striking metaphor, or repeats the same term a number of times. I might then reflect back to them their exact words, maybe with a questioning intonation in my voice. For example:

Client: *I'm dreading seeing him again.*

Coach: *Dreading?*

Or I might simply invite them to explore a vivid term further. For example:

Client: *I think I'm at the end of the road.*

Coach: *Say a bit more about being at the end of the road.*

Or I may use something akin to a clean language question to encourage them to develop their metaphor. For example:

Client: *Yes. Alarm bells are ringing for me.*

Coach: *What kind of alarm bells?*

Client: *Alarm bells that sound a warning.*

Coach: *And what kind of warning do the alarm bells sound?*

In this video clip, which is taken from the interview that Christian van Nieuwerburgh did with Lina after my coaching conversation with her, Lina talks about her experience of having her own words played back to her.

Link to Video 5.1
Playing back the client's own words

EXERCISE 5.2

REFLECTING BACK AND PARAPHRASING

The difference between reflecting back and paraphrasing is that the former uses the precise words used by the client whereas the latter changes their words.

As an exercise, write down how you might respond, first, to reflect back and, second, to paraphrase these statements.

1. I haven't a clue what my boss wants me to do with this project.
2. When I think about my future career I feel all tingly inside.
3. What I really need is someone to organise my diary.

Different types of summary and reflection – some ideas from Motivational Interviewing

In Chapter 17 we will look at an approach called Motivational Interviewing. This is a therapeutic approach which seeks to help people with problems such as alcoholism or drug addiction to change their behaviour. These individuals often feel ambivalent about change. MI is based on the idea that exploring and resolving the client's ambivalence – *I want to change, but I don't want to change* – is the key challenge in facilitating change. MI practitioners use play back considerably in their work.

William Miller and Stephen Rollnick (2002) describe three kinds of summaries that are useful in MI:

- A **collecting summary** is a short statement that gathers in a few sentences the key ideas that the client has been expressing – like collecting flowers and presenting them back as a bouquet – and invites the client to continue. The coach is likely to end a collecting summary with an open question, which is some version of *What else … ?*
- A **linking summary** relates what the client has just been saying to earlier material, perhaps even from a previous session, with the intention of inviting the client to consider the relationship between the two items. This can be particularly useful in helping the client to explore ambivalence – the pros and the cons of change, for example.
- A **transitional summary** is useful when the coach wishes to move the conversation on from one focus to another, or to wrap up towards the end of a session. It is useful for the coach to signpost that they are about to offer a transitional summary – for instance, they might say *Let me try to pull together what you've said today*. In summarising a session, the coach inevitably selects what to include or exclude, and it is important to invite the client to modify or add to the summary.

Another idea from Motivational Interviewing that I find particularly helpful when a coaching client is feeling ambivalent or seems to be stuck is the notion of a **double sided reflection**. This simply means playing back both sides of the client's dilemma, giving equal weight to both aspects. MI practitioners believe that when you appear to argue for one side of a possible change, the client is likely to respond with arguments for the other side. *Yes, but … .*

As an illustration, you might say to a client who is unsure whether or not to accept a job offer:

On the one hand, the new job means more money and a fresh challenge. On the other hand, you feel that you're just beginning to make a real difference where you are now.

Note that it's important that these arguments accurately represent the client's views.

Playing back non-verbal communications

It is also possible to play back some of a client's non-verbal communications. Sometimes a client's gesture or a facial expression, especially if it's repeated a number of times, strikes me as significant. I then have a choice as to whether or not to mention this to the client. If I do choose to play this back, I need to do so with great care to ensure that I don't damage the relationship by, for instance, embarrassing the client.

I would not, therefore, do this at an early stage in a coaching relationship. However, if I felt that we'd built a good level of rapport and trust, I might ask a client about a particular gesture or even, if I think the client will be receptive, simply copy their gesture. As an example, a client might open their arms wide as they speak and I might mimic the gesture as I play back some of their words.

We mentioned above that David Grove extended his idea of clean language to include non-verbal expressions. In Chapter 16 we'll look at a Gestalt approach to therapy and coaching. One of the key ways in which a Gestalt therapist or coach will work with a client is by attending to what is happening here and now in the room. For example, Marion Gillie describes how she works with what happens in the moment to help a supervision client:

> Typically, the supervisor pays close attention to the supervisee's movements, breathing pattern, changes in skin tone (red patches, going pale, etc) and tracks patterns that emerge over time. The supervisor would then share these observations and invite the supervisee to note his or her own 'here and now' reactions, which might be sensations, feelings, images or thoughts. (Gillie, 2011)

A Gestalt practitioner will not seek to interpret or pass judgement on what these data might mean or signify. As an illustration, suppose that as a client is speaking about a difficult relationship with their boss their face reddens and they bang their fist on the table. You could play back to the client – in a sense, paraphrasing their body language – something like *It sounds like you're really angry with him.* If, however, you wish to avoid any interpretation then you might simply play back what you've observed by saying, for instance, *I notice when you talk about your boss that your face goes red and you bang your fist on the table. I wonder what that might mean?*

Communicating empathic understanding

In his book *The Skilled Helper*, Gerard Egan sets out this stylised formula to play back to a client your empathic understanding of them and their situation:

> **You feel** …. [here name the correct emotion expressed by the client]

> **Because** …. [here indicate the correct thoughts, experiences, and behaviors that give rise to the feelings] (Egan, 2007)

He notes that the basic formula needs suitable modification and personalisation in practice. He then offers some illustrations:

- You feel furious because he keeps failing to hold up his part of the bargain.
- You feel troubled because you believe that you're being left in the dark.
- You feel bad, not so much because of the pain, but because your ability to get around – your freedom – has been curtailed.

To communicate an empathic understanding, you need to recognise with some accuracy both the key emotions expressed by the client and also the crucial experiences, thoughts or behaviours that gave rise to these emotions.

In conveying your understanding of a client's emotions, you need to use the correct **family** of emotions and the right **intensity** of emotion. Egan writes that, 'The words *sad*, *mad*, *bad*, and *glad* refer to four of the main families of emotion, whereas *content*, *quite happy*, and *overjoyed* refer to different intensities within the *glad* family.'

Who summarises?

We noted above that a coach using a Motivational Interviewing approach would invite the client to add to their summary at the end of a session. In my own practice I always ask the client to summarise at the end of a coaching session. I use different formulations, each of which has a carefully chosen emphasis. Here are two examples of what I might say:

- As we draw to a close, tell me what you're taking from our conversation today.
- Summarise please what you intend to do following today's session.

I would use the first formulation when the client has deepened their awareness of their situation but has not yet decided what action they want to take. I would use the second formulation when the client has been discussing what they will do to address their situation.

I find that clients are sometimes surprised when I ask them to summarise rather than me doing it. However, I think it's important that it is the client – not me – who summarises at the end of the conversation. And at times I'm surprised at what they consider most important – my summary would have been less accurate and less useful for the client.

I occasionally ask a client to drop me an email which captures their thinking or the actions they intend to carry out. This may be simply because we've run out of time in the session, but more usually it's because my sense is that the client needs to do a bit more thinking before they're ready to commit to action. My intention in asking them to write things down is that I think it will be of benefit to them to articulate explicitly their thoughts or plans. It's certainly not to enable me to check up on them.

Inviting the client to summarise

This clip is the end of my coaching session with Lina. I invite her to summarise what she is taking away from the conversation. I also reflect back her exact words *This is in your head*.

Link to Video 5.2
Inviting the client to summarise

EXERCISE 5.3

SUMMARISING THIS CHAPTER

As we end this chapter, what are the main ideas from it that you might use in your own coaching conversations?

6

LEARNING HOW TO COACH

Introduction

Tim Gallwey, an American coach whose ideas on coaching we'll look at in more detail later in the book, writes that:

> Coaching is an art that must be learned mostly from experience. (Gallwey, 2000)

The title of this book is *How to Coach*. My aim in writing the book is to help you learn how to coach or, if you already coach, to become an even more effective one.

Coaching is a practical activity. Reading this book will help you to learn *about* coaching. But, to learn *how to* coach, you'll need to try things out in practice. It is rather like learning how to drive a car. You need to know some basics, such as how the accelerator, brake and clutch work. But then you need to get behind the wheel and start driving, hopefully in a fairly safe setting. When you first drive, it feels a bit awkward and you initially have to think hard about what you're doing. But with practice you become more fluent and eventually drive the car without apparently thinking much about, for example, which gear to be in.

To develop your competence as a coach, therefore, you need progressively to gain experience – and to reflect upon and learn from this experience. I encourage you, therefore, to find opportunities to try out in practice the various ideas set out in the book. This chapter describes two very useful activities for doing this – working with one or two colleagues to coach each other, and working with a practice client.

We begin, however, by discussing the cycle of learning from experience that provides a framework for learning how to master a practical skill – such as coaching.

Learning from experience

In the words of Kurt Lewin, 'There is nothing more practical than a good theory.' Here is a brief summary of a theory of learning from experience which underpins my own approach to helping people learn how to coach.

Deep and sustained learning – becoming able to do something you couldn't do before – only comes through experience. Experience on its own isn't enough, however. You need to reflect upon and make sense of your experience to create knowledge, and this knowledge deepens when you apply it in practice. The process can be viewed as a learning cycle (Figure 6.1).

Figure 6.1 The learning cycle

The learning cycle in the diagram is my rewording in simpler language of the learning cycle set out by David Kolb. He offers this definition:

> Learning is the process whereby knowledge is created through the transformation of experience. (Kolb, 1984)

To see if this notion of learning from experience makes sense to you, you might try Exercise 6.1.

EXERCISE 6.1

THE EXPERIENTIAL LEARNING CYCLE

Think of something that you can do well, a skill that you have developed over time. Consider the various ways in which over the years you built up this skill. See if you can identify two or three activities at each of the four points of the experiential learning cycle that helped you develop this ability.

Coaching pairs or trios

Exercise 6.2 is one that is widely used on coaching skills programmes. It's a great way of practising and improving your coaching skills.

To do the exercise you'll need one or two other people who also want to develop their coaching skills. It can help too to work with different partners over time, which might be easy to arrange if you are on a formal coaching skills programme.

It is important that each of you has a real issue that you are willing to be coached on – the exercise is far less useful if you merely role play imaginary situations. A real issue is one which:

- Matters to you
- Is current – rather than a problem you had some years ago or might hypothetically face in the future
- Where you are central to the issue – it's not a problem that a friend has
- Where you are not sure how to proceed – if you know what you're going to do, the exercise doesn't work
- Isn't something that's bothered you for years and years – that would be too difficult

I'll describe the exercise on the assumption that there are three of you working in a trio. Each person has the opportunity to coach, to be coached and to observe a coaching session. If you are working with just one other person in a coaching pair, then there is no observer in the exercise.

EXERCISE 6.2

EXERCISE 6.2

COACHING TRIOS

Step one: 30 minutes

Agree who will be coach, client and observer first time round. The coaching session will last for 20 minutes. This will be followed by a 10-minute feedback session.

The observer acts as time keeper. Please limit the coaching session to 20 minutes – the objective is to practise and learn about coaching, not to complete the session.

Before the session starts it is useful for the observer to ask the coach about what areas of their practice they want feedback on. The coach might also indicate if they'd like a time signal from the observer – for instance, five minutes to go.

The coach then manages a 20-minute coaching conversation with the client on a topic chosen by the client. The observer is silent during this (apart possibly from a time signal).

The observer then facilitates a 10-minute feedback session, including feedback on the areas requested at the outset by the coach. Note that the client will have valuable information from their experience of being coached. If you are working in a pair, then you will need jointly to review the session without the help of a third party.

In the feedback session, avoid revisiting the content of the conversation, tempting though this may be. Rather, focus on the coaching process and on what the coach did well or less well, or on what they did that was helpful and what was less helpful. It's valuable to look at both positive and negative aspects.

Step two: 30 minutes

Swap roles so that *everyone* now takes on a different role. This will ensure that each of you has the chance to be the coach, the client and the observer.

Repeat step one.

Step three: 30 minutes

Swap roles again.

Repeat step one. This step isn't applicable when there are only two of you.

The coaching trios exercise provides an opportunity to learn at all four points of the learning cycle:

- To engage in the experience of coaching or being coached
- To reflect upon your experience, or to observe how someone else coaches
- To make sense of your experience and to refine your own views and theories of how to coach well
- To try out your ideas or to experiment with some of the concepts you are reading about

The trios exercise is akin to having a driving lesson – or perhaps three driving lessons. And, just as you wouldn't expect to be able to drive after just a few lessons, you can repeat the exercise a number of times to develop you capability and confidence.

Practice clients

If you are a reader who is learning to coach rather than someone who is already engaged in coaching, then the other activity that I encourage you to do to accompany your reading of this book is to work with one or more practice clients. A practice client is simply someone who is willing to be coached by you over a number of sessions. The benefit for them is that they receive free coaching to work through some of the real issues they face in their work or day-to-day life. The benefit for you is that you have a valuable learning opportunity to develop your skills and approach.

I recommend that you don't start work with a practice client until you're familiar with the material explored up to this point in the book.

If you do work with a practice client then you are likely to encounter some of the practical and ethical issues that we look at in the next few chapters. You will need to discuss with your practice client questions of where to meet, how often and for how long, and maybe you'll learn from first hand experience that half an hour in a busy coffee shop at lunchtime isn't ideal for coaching. You will also have the opportunity to work through issues such as contracting, reviewing progress and ending the relationship. You'll need to think about whether or not you will take notes during a session, what if anything you'll write up afterwards, and what you'll do to prepare for the next session. And you may have to think hard about issues of confidentiality and about whether you are working within appropriate boundaries. Wrestling with these kinds of questions as you encounter them with a practice client will help you to develop your approach to coaching and to clarify for yourself some of the practical and ethical questions involved.

The coaching trios exercise will help you learn how to manage a coaching conversation. Working with a practice client over a number of sessions will, in addition, help you to learn how to manage a coaching relationship over a period of time.

A coaching learning cycle

You will find that coaching trios or working with a practice client gives you a rich source of raw material to process and to learn from. Later chapters will also offer ideas that you might try out in practice. I hope that, as you create your own understanding of what works for you and your clients, you'll modify the ideas set out in the book and assimilate your own version of them into your practice.

You might view this as a learning cycle to develop your skills and confidence as a coach (Figure 6.2).

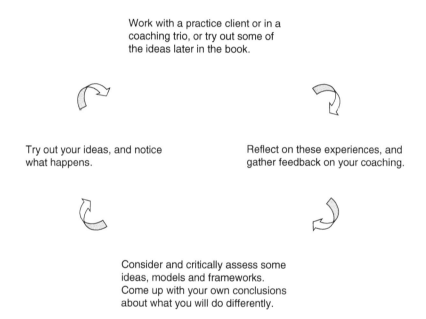

Work with a practice client or in a coaching trio, or try out some of the ideas later in the book.

Try out your ideas, and notice what happens.

Reflect on these experiences, and gather feedback on your coaching.

Consider and critically assess some ideas, models and frameworks. Come up with your own conclusions about what you will do differently.

Figure 6.2 A coaching learning cycle

Reflecting on your coaching experiences

We noted earlier that experience needs to be reflected upon to create knowledge. This can be done in discussion – and later in the book we'll discuss the value of working with a supervisor to reflect upon and develop your practice as a coach. It can also be done through writing reflectively about your coaching experiences. One way of doing this is by keeping a journal.

A journal isn't the same as a diary which records events. Rather, a journal is a place where you can record important experiences and how you thought, felt and behaved in response to what happened.

Madeline McGill writes:

> A journal is a place where we can be ourselves – where we do not have to pose – where we can remember and reflect on significant thoughts and events and so re-integrate them into the panorama of life ...
>
> It is a means of talking and listening to ourselves – a way of 'speaking our thoughts' – of having a dialogue with ourselves ... (Private communication)

In keeping a journal you may find that over time patterns emerge, and you understand more deeply your own motives and feelings and behaviour. For example, you might find on re-reading your journal that in a number of coaching sessions you encountered a similar situation and that on each occasion you responded in the same ineffective way. Reflecting on such a pattern might lead to learning and insight and an alternative way of responding when you next face a similar difficulty.

In their book *Reflective Writing in Counselling and Psychotherapy*, Jeannie Wright and Gillie Bolton say that, 'There is no right or wrong way to write a reflective journal.' They go on to say:

> There are many reasons why any practitioner or student in the talking therapies would benefit from keeping a personal reflective journal. Writing is like a form of mindful meditation. This kind of writing means slowing down, focusing in the here-and-now and accepting what is going on in your mind and body. The implications for self-care in an occupation which can be stressful are clear, and there are accompanying benefits for clients. (Wright and Bolton, 2012)

Helping a client to learn from experience

One of the main benefits many clients gain from coaching is that they learn things. They may, for example, learn how to:

- Acquire a skill
- Develop a new behaviour
- Modify an unhelpful habit
- Change how they think about an issue
- Perform more effectively

Through the conversations that a client has with you and through the actions they take outside the coaching room, they learn. As we go through the book you might like to consider how different ideas relate to helping a client to move around the experiential learning cycle. Table 6.1 offers some illustrations of how a client might visit each of the four points, either within a coaching conversation or outside the coaching room. As an exercise, you might like to add some more examples.

Table 6.1 Coaching and the four points of the learning cycle

	Within a coaching conversation	Outside the coaching room
Reflection	The safety of a coaching conversation offers a space for the client to reflect upon past experiences.	The client may think about what's emerged for them in a coaching conversation long after the session has ended.
Making sense of	The coach may share a model or framework which offers the client a useful way of understanding their situation.	Sitting in a business meeting, the client has an *ah-ha* moment where they suddenly realise what's going on.
Performing differently	A client might rehearse a difficult conversation or a presentation in the coaching room.	The client experiments with a new approach or tries out a new behaviour back at work.
Experience	The client's relationship with the coach may mirror how they engage with people more generally.	The client's day-to-day life between coaching sessions is providing them with fresh experiences and challenges every day.

Learning to coach – a lifetime journey

In the opening sentence of the preface, I wrote that, 'One of the joys of learning to coach is that it's a wonderful journey that doesn't end.' If you are already an experienced coach, these opening chapters may have been a reminder or refresher of things that you already know – though there might be some ideas or quotes that stimulate you to look again at some aspects of your practice. And later chapters will hopefully offer material for all readers to reflect upon or try out in practice.

In *Coaching Presence*, Maria Iliffe-Wood writes that:

Developing your coaching practice is a journey of self-discovery. Self-discovery is at the heart of being the best coach that you can be. It is a journey of challenge, richness and doubt. (Iliffe-Wood, 2014)

She adds, 'If you want to be a great coach, regularly practise your art.' Which takes us back to the words of Tim Gallwey with which we opened this chapter: 'Coaching is an art that must be learned mostly from experience.'

PART TWO:
DEVELOPING YOUR PRACTICE

7

CONTRACTING

Introduction

A very important aspect of coaching is agreeing a suitable contract at the outset of the engagement. In this chapter we begin by considering how you contract directly with a new client. We then discuss practical matters that need to be agreed, such as the time, place, frequency, length and cost of coaching sessions. Finally, in a situation where a third party has requested that you coach an individual, we look at three-way contracting with both the individual client and the organisational sponsor.

Contracting with a new client

Allard de Jong writes that:

> Coaches are responsible for ensuring that coachees are fully informed of the coaching contract, terms and conditions, prior to or at the initial session. These matters include confidentiality and the cost and frequency of sessions. It is your responsibility to generate a frank discussion around what this potential coachee may or may not expect and respond to her requests for information about the methods, techniques and ways in which the coaching process will be conducted. This should be done both prior to contract agreement and during the full term of the contract. (de Jong, 2006)

Contracting well is important to coach effectively. Anne Scoular (2011) writes that, 'On the rare occasions that something goes wrong in coaching and people come to me for help, 99% of the time it was a failure of *contracting*.'

The Global Code of Ethics for Coaches, Mentors and Supervisors, which is signed by the Association for Coaching, the European Mentoring and Coaching Council and other bodies, 'sets the expectation of best practice in coaching, mentoring and supervision'.

In regard to contracting it states:

> Before starting to work with a client, members will explain and strive to ensure that the client and sponsor know, and fully understand, the nature and terms and conditions of any coaching, mentoring or supervision contract, including financial, logistical and confidentiality arrangements.
>
> Members will be open about the methods they use, and on request be ready to supply the client with information about the processes involved.
>
> www.associationforcoaching.com/general/custom.asp?page=AboutCodeEthics

The purpose of contracting is to establish clearly at the start of a coaching relationship what the client can expect from coaching and from you as the coach and, on the other hand, what you expect of the client. This clarity is vitally important whether you are an external or an internal coach.

Geoff Pelham explains that 'proper contracting is fundamental to the success of coaching', and highlights that this is not really about creating a detailed written contract. Rather, it is 'the fundamental process of setting up the coaching relationship – agreeing how we are going to work together and the conditions under which this can happen'. He adds:

> Contracting 'frames' the relationship, and like a picture frame it sets up a space that is different from everyday life. It sets the boundaries of the coaching relationship, demarcating a separate and distinct protected arena where a different kind of conversation can take place. (Pelham, 2016)

In my own practice I always say two things explicitly to a new client about how I work. First, I reassure them that our conversations will be confidential on my part. Unless I judge that the client is likely to do something dangerous – which includes the risk of suicide or a breakdown – or seriously illegal, I will not reveal anything about what they tell me to anyone else. I have never, in fact, had to break confidentiality for either of these reasons. But, to give an extreme example, if a client were to tell me that they'd planted a bomb in a supermarket, then I'd break confidentiality.

The one exception is that I might discuss a coaching relationship with my supervisor, who in turn will treat what I tell them as confidential. And, it may occasionally happen that the client and I agree explicitly that it would be useful for me to share something with another party.

The second thing I mention to clients at the outset is that I work primarily non-directively. I say that I am very unlikely to give them advice and will seldom offer suggestions. And, if I do make a suggestion, then I'll signal clearly that I'm doing this. I also say that I might share with them a model or concept that may offer a useful perspective on their situation. (I'll give three examples of these in Chapter 15.)

Working non-directively means that the client sets the agenda for our conversations. I tell them that I'm likely to ask a question near the beginning of each coaching conversation about what they'd like to talk about in today's session. Hence, they will find it useful to consider in advance of each session what they want to cover.

I find that sometimes a client says that they would like advice or suggestions from me, or would welcome my views on what they are doing. I generally decline to offer advice, but will agree to offer suggestions or comments to a moderate degree.

The key point here in terms of contracting isn't about working non-directively. Rather, it is the importance of giving the client some idea of your approach to coaching, and the implications for what they can expect and what they themself need to do to collaborate effectively with you.

Similarly, I'm not saying that you have to handle confidentiality in the same way that I do. However, I do think you need to be clear in your own mind what your position is, and to share this with your client. To take a practical example, which we'll look at shortly, what is your position regarding giving feedback to the client's line manager or organisation?

Having agreed an initial contract about how you will work together, this may need to be reaffirmed or modified as the coaching relationship develops over time and as the client possibly becomes clearer about what they want from coaching. Clients often don't know exactly what to expect from coaching, and their understanding of the process develops as they experience it at first hand. As someone once said, *You don't know what milk tastes like till you've tasted milk.*

Erik de Haan writes:

> time after time, it proves impossible to plan coaching in advance. Sometimes it takes a number of sessions before a coachee gathers sufficient confidence and trust to say what is really the problem. This doesn't mean it is a bad idea to draw up an explicit coaching contract or even to plan coaching meetings, but it does appear at the same time to be essential to keep refining or adjusting the contractual relationship on an ongoing basis. (de Haan, 2008)

Here is an illustration of how a coaching contract might evolve in the light of the unfolding relationship. It sometimes emerges that a client needs help from a counsellor or therapist – instead of, or perhaps as well as, coaching. If this happens, then it's vital to talk explicitly about this with the client, and reach an agreement about whether you will continue to coach them or whether they will find support elsewhere. You might, for instance, be able to continue to coach a client about work-related issues while they also see a counsellor about deeper or historical issues that are affecting their emotional wellbeing. While the topics of boundaries and of referral might have been a hypothetical possibility covered at the time of initial contracting, it may feel very different to both client and coach in the immediate reality of their encounter with one another.

Time, place, frequency, length and cost of coaching sessions

Another area to cover during contracting are the practical arrangements for holding sessions. How long do you expect the coaching relationship to last? How much time will be given to each session? How many weeks or months will there be between sessions? And where will you meet?

In my own practice, I expect the client to come to me, and we talk in my office at Warwick Business School. I generally work in 90-minute sessions, which occasionally run over and which end early if we've come to a natural conclusion for that day. I set aside two hours for each of these sessions in case we don't start on time or run over. The frequency with which I meet with clients is more variable, and is driven by the needs of – and maybe time pressures on – the client. I see some clients for just a one-off session; I see others for four or five conversations over a period of months; and I have some clients whom I've worked with for several years. It may be that early sessions are more frequent – to build up momentum, as it were – and then the gap between sessions increases. I also find that some clients come back a few years later, sometimes for a one-off conversation and sometimes for a number of sessions.

As an internal coach, I do not have the same commercial pressures on me as external coaches charging fees to clients. This gives me the freedom not to have to agree in advance with every client how many times we will meet. It also means that I don't need to have a written contract covering other commercial terms such as the fee to be paid and charges for cancelled or missed appointments.

However, if you are running your own coaching business or working as a coach or an associate for a coaching firm, then it is important to agree these arrangements and the various costs explicitly and in writing. You may set – or the firm employing you may have – a standard set of terms and conditions. Or you may negotiate different terms with different clients. In any case, it is vital to agree in writing the commercial terms of the coaching arrangement.

If you are coaching a client and the payment is being made by the sponsoring organisation, it is preferable to have conversations about money with someone from the organisation rather than the client being coached. Negotiation of fees, dealing with cancellations or resolving problems of late payment can cloud the relationship and are best dealt with outside coaching sessions if possible. This, of course, isn't possible if you are coaching an individual who is paying for the coaching themself.

Anne Scoular offers a useful reminder about establishing appropriate commercial terms to any new coach seeking to establish their business:

> Nevertheless, many coaches in training still have to be reminded about this piece – they get so absorbed in the thrill of actual coaching, they need to be gently reconnected with the standard business 'hygiene factors' they had temporarily forgotten. (Scoular, 2011)

Apart from commercial arrangements, another important practical matter is the venue for coaching sessions. Does the client come to you, or do you go to them, or do you meet in a neutral venue such as a hotel lounge or room? There are pros and cons in each of these, and it's important that you identify what will be suitable for you and your clients. This will be influenced by, among other things, where you live, where your clients are based, the premises that are available at home or nearby, what you can afford, the expectations of your various clients, and the emotional depth at which you may be working.

My own view is that it is preferable for the client to come to the coach. I remember Robin Linnecar, one of the founding partners of the executive coaching firm Praesta, telling me that one of his clients regarded coming to the Praesta office as like entering a haven. Moreover, if the client has to travel to and from the coaching appointment, this gives them time to think about the upcoming session and to reflect upon the conversation afterwards. It also reduces the likelihood of being disturbed on their premises by phone calls or so-called pressing matters.

On the other hand, the client or the sponsoring organisation may expect the coach to come to their offices. This may be unavoidable, but it does mean that the coach has much less control over things like room layout and interruptions. It may mean too that the coach has to deal with the stress of travelling and unforeseen delays, interferences which can get in the way of coaching well.

A final practical matter to consider is the role of telephone and email support. In my own small private practice as a supervisor of independent coaches, I tell my supervisees that I'm happy for them to contact me by phone or email when necessary. While my supervision clients do this from time to time, it has never become excessive and so hasn't been problematic. Again, the key point is that you agree clearly with the client the basis on which you work and how available you are for phone or email contact.

A growing trend within coaching is to replace face-to-face sessions with telephone or Skype conversations. These bring clear advantages in terms of saving time and costs in travelling. You can coach someone who is literally on the other side of the world. On the other hand, the nature of the conversation is inevitably affected since there is reduced or no visual contact, so that there is a trade off between practicalities and quality of conversation. Of course, it is possible to use a combination of both face-to-face and remote conversations. As an illustration, I met one of my supervision clients who lives a considerable distance away for an initial face-to-face session, and all of our subsequent sessions have been lengthy telephone conversations.

EXERCISE 7.1

CONTRACTING WITH A PRACTICE CLIENT

One of the ways in which you may be developing your coaching skills is by working with a practice client. If so, it is important at the outset that you contract clearly with them. A contract with a practice client might contain – in addition to the items normally contracted for – points about feedback from the client or joint review with the client to help you to learn from the coaching practice.

As an exercise, produce your own checklist of areas that you intend to cover when you start a new relationship with a practice client.

As your experience of managing coaching relationships develops, you may wish to amend your checklist in the light of this experience.

Three-way contracting – who is the client?

It may be that a third party has initiated coaching for someone. For instance, an organisation may arrange external coaching for one of its executives. Or, a line manager or HR professional might set up internal coaching for an employee of the organisation. In this case, there are three parties involved – the coach, the client and the individual or organisation setting up the coaching.

It is useful to distinguish between the **sponsor** – that is, the organisation who commissions the coaching – and the **client** – that is, the individual being coached. The expectations and needs of the client may not be the same as those of the sponsor. For me, a guiding principle for the coach here is clarity – being absolutely clear in your own mind about what you expect, and being absolutely clear in your conversations with both the sponsor and the client.

In my own work as an internal coach, I take the view that my prime duty is to the person being coached, the client. As discussed above, I tell them that I treat what they tell me as confidential unless we explicitly agree otherwise or if I think they may do something illegal or dangerous. The client sets the agenda. However, I may have been briefed by the client's line manager or by their HR contact about the background that has prompted the request for coaching. If there are issues that the sponsor wishes to be addressed, I ask the sponsor to discuss these explicitly with the client. The client and I can then agree an agenda, which incorporates both the expectations of the sponsor and the needs of the client. I don't provide feedback to the sponsor or report anything other than a vague statement such as *the coaching seems to be going well* – unless there has been an explicit agreement by the client that I will.

Anne Scoular takes a very different view from mine. She writes:

> There is also the sometimes tricky contractual matter that the real client is not the person sitting in front of you, it's the organisation paying the bill. Some people, usually former therapists who in my view haven't properly switched to operating under the rules of business, disagree, and maintain that the 'client' to whom they have primary and sole responsibility is the person sitting in front of them. I feel quite passionately that this is wrong: ethically, and indeed legally, if the coach is contracted with the organisation, then the organisation is the client. (Scoular, 2011)

As you can see, opinion diverges considerably here. The vital point is that you, the client and the sponsor are clear and explicit about what the agreement is.

An issue that sometimes happens is that the client does not actually want to be coached, but is going along with the arrangement to satisfy in some way the sponsor – or perhaps as a way of keeping their job. As you might imagine, this is not a good basis for a coaching engagement. Anne Scoular writes:

> Typically the coach's first contact is with the corporate 'buyer' or initiator of the coaching. When the coach is briefed by them, there are some questions about the prospective individual client so simple that it might seem naïve, even a bit embarrassing, to ask – usually these are of course the most important! Does the person actually want to be coached? Did anyone ask them? What is the purpose of the coaching? (Scoular, 2011)

It may well be that coaching isn't the appropriate intervention. Perhaps the individual needs some specific training, or focused and honest feedback, or performance management. Identifying the appropriate response would be far more effective than setting up a coaching assignment in the hope that a message gets through to the client.

Another possibility is that the individual is taking part in a development programme, which involves a number of workshops and other activities, including coaching. They want to take part in the programme, but don't want to be coached – or perhaps they are anxious about what a coaching conversation might uncover. In this situation, a useful starting point is for the coach and client to talk this through together.

EXERCISE 7.2

THREE-WAY CONTRACTING

Coaches differ in how they handle contracting when there is a third party, an organisational sponsor, involved. Make some notes on how you would like to handle a three-way coaching contract. In particular, what is your stance on:

- Agreeing an agenda with the sponsor that is not fully shared with the client
- Providing feedback to the sponsor from the coaching conversations
- Reporting the results of an assessment of the client using psychometric instruments or 360 degree feedback
- Confidentiality

PRACTICAL ISSUES

Introduction

In working with clients there are a variety of practical considerations that you need to have thought through and clarified what you personally will do in your practice as a coach. In the previous chapter we looked at the important issue of contracting. In this chapter we consider the following topics:

- Making notes during coaching sessions
- Keeping records
- Use of between-session tasks and assignments
- Reviewing progress
- Evaluation
- Ending a coaching assignment

Making notes during coaching sessions

An issue which learner coaches often worry about is whether or not to make notes during a coaching conversation. They may reason that writing something down will break eye contact with the client and so they may come across as not giving full attention. On the other hand, it can be useful to make some notes to keep track of the conversation. I find that learner coaches often go to extremes, either making no notes or making extensive notes, often of specific facts and details.

In my own practice I generally make a few sketchy notes during the conversation. Sometimes the client says something that I want to explore with them but don't want to interrupt the flow of the conversation – I'll jot down a word or two to remind me to come back to this. On other occasions the client may say a word or phrase that strikes me as particularly vivid or significant, and I note this down in their exact words. As we considered in Chapter 5 when we looked at clean language, there may be a power in the precise words or metaphor used by the client and it is important to preserve their exact phrasing.

One thing which I usually note is the client's answer to any question about the objective of the session or what they'd like to take away from the conversation. I find it useful to refer back to this as the conversation unfolds or as we draw to a close.

Another time when I'm likely to make notes is when the client is producing a list. As an illustration, I may have asked a question about the pros and cons of a course of action, and notes are helpful both for me to keep track and also to play back to the client their list when they've finished talking. Sometimes, rather than me making the list, I will ask the client to write down their list themself.

Another example of when I may make notes is when I'm trying to understand who is who in a set of relationships or in an organisational structure. But beware of the danger of capturing detailed information that isn't essential, rather than focusing on what the client really wants to talk about. Moreover, since the client already knows this information, repeating it to you usually does little or nothing to raise their awareness.

There are times when the client is talking about something highly sensitive and it just feels inappropriate to write anything down. There are other occasions when I make a point of reassuring the client that I will destroy the notes at the end of our session. And sometimes the client asks if they can take away my scribblings containing, for example, a list of key points or a model that I've sketched.

These are simply my own practices, and you need to work out what will suit you and your clients. You might like to monitor some of your coaching conversations and see what, if anything, feels different when you make lots of notes, when you make few, and when you make none.

Keeping records

Another issue where you need to decide how you will operate is in keeping records of coaching conversations. Moreover, it may be that you are working in a field or in an organisation where there are rules about record keeping that you must follow.

The Global Code of Ethics for Coaches, Mentors and Supervisors states:

> Members will keep, store and dispose of appropriate and accurate records of their work with clients, including electronic files and communications, in a manner that ensures confidentiality, security and privacy, and complies with all relevant laws and agreements that exist in their country regarding data protection and privacy.

www.associationforcoaching.com/general/custom.asp?page=AboutCodeEthics

There are a number of reasons why you might wish to keep a record of your work with clients. These include:

- To note explicitly the objectives of the client and, if relevant, the organisational sponsor for the coaching assignment
- To record actions that the client intends to carry out so that these can be reviewed next time you meet
- To keep track of issues that are emerging and which you may wish to explore with the client in later sessions
- To monitor progress in achieving the goals of the assignment
- To note what your intuition tells you might be going on
- To draw from in your own supervision sessions
- To protect yourself if in some way the coaching goes wrong and you are required to account for what you have done
- To keep a simple record of how many sessions have taken place for billing purposes

Jenny Rogers (2008) states unequivocally that, 'As a coach you absolutely must keep and file notes on each client.' She goes on to add, 'A professional coach spends time before a session reviewing notes from the earlier sessions as a way of getting in the right frame of mind to work with a client.' She then lists some useful basic principles about making client notes, including:

- Keep notes short and simple: a page and a half of bullet points is usually more than enough.
- Keep judgements out of your notes – limit them to the factual and descriptive.
- Always write notes in a way that would not embarrass you if they were seen by clients – which clients have a legal right to do.
- Store the notes in a secure, locked cupboard or filing cabinet.
- It is best practice to keep the client's contact details separate from the actual notes of each session. (Rogers, 2008)

In keeping records you need to consider whether there are any issues arising from the General Data Protection Regulation. Clients are entitled to see the notes that you keep on them and so – as Jenny Rogers recommends – it is important to write up your notes in a way that would not be embarrassing if the client saw them.

Having listed these sound reasons for keeping records and noted the explicit requirement of the Global Code of Ethics, I have to admit that I generally don't keep records of sessions. I take each session as a fresh encounter, asking the client what they want to cover today. I'm assuming that the client will bring up anything that's important to them. I realise that my practice in this regard might seem sloppy, but I find that it is fit for purpose.

One thing that I sometimes do is to invite the client at the end of a session to make notes on key points that have arisen for them or on what they intend to do following the session. The notes are for them to keep, and my hope is that they will find them a useful aide memoire. I also might ask a client to send me an email after a session with some bullet points pertinent to what we've been working on. In particular, I may ask a new client at the end of our initial session to email me a summary of what they see as the objectives of our coaching work together. This can provide a useful reference for both of us to review the progress of the coaching.

I see two main advantages in asking the client to record the key points. First, this is more likely to encourage them to take responsibility. Second, their perception of the key points is more important than – and may differ from – my perception. There is a third, practical advantage for me of saving time, but I regard that as a bonus and not a valid reason for operating as I do.

Julie Starr takes a different point of view, and advocates that the coach sends the client a short written record after a session:

> The coach will have been taking a few notes during the session. It is a simple matter for the coach to draft a quick e-mail soon after the session as a record of agreements. As well as a courteous professional gesture, it has the following benefits:
>
> - It creates an accurate mutual record of what's been agreed.
> - It can be used as a start-point in the next session.
> - In the e-mail you might also check if they're still happy after the session, maintain rapport, etc. (Starr, 2011)

Having described my own practice in regard to keeping records, and having noted what others have to say, I invite you to decide what you will do in your own practice. If you choose to keep records of each coaching session, you may like to create a simple template for your notes of each conversation based on aspects you consider important.

In this video clip, I discuss my own practice in taking notes with Christian van Nieuwerburgh after my coaching session with Lina.

Link to Video 8.1
Taking notes

Template 8.1   Coaching review sheet

You might use some of the prompts below to make notes following a coaching session. The final three questions invite you to reflect upon and learn from the session, which you may find useful after a session with a practice client. Please modify these to suit your own practice.

- Name of client:
- Date and venue of session:
- Main topics covered:
- Agreed next steps:
- Tools or reading recommended to client:
- Issues that might need to be explored at the next or later sessions:
- What did you do during the session that seemed to help?
- What did you find difficult to handle?
- What might you do differently next time?

EXERCISE 8.1

NOTES AND RECORDS

The aim of this exercise is simply to help you to clarify what you will do to make and keep notes of coaching sessions.

- What is your stance on making notes during coaching sessions?
- If you do keep notes, what will you do to store them safely and securely?
- If you do keep notes, what will you do to review them before the next coaching session?

As your practice evolves, you may wish to amend this in the light of experience.

Use of between-session tasks and assignments

One of the things which you are likely to do at the end of many of your coaching sessions is to agree with the client what they are going to do before you next meet.

The use of between-session tasks and assignments is a feature of many approaches to coaching. As we shall discuss in Chapter 15, it is a particularly important aspect of cognitive behavioural coaching where between-session tasks are used to help a client modify unhelpful ways of thinking or behaving. However, I don't think you have to be practising from a cognitive behavioural perspective to see the potential value in a client carrying out actions between sessions.

Erik de Haan draws lessons from research into how psychotherapy works to produce a view of how coaching works. We look at this in detail in Chapter 12. He points out that:

> In most cases the time spent outside therapy is more than 99% of the time available, so it is not surprising that much happens there that is of greater importance in terms of change than what takes place in or what is said during the therapy. (de Haan, 2008)

Different types of between-session actions might be useful. Here are three possibilities:

- Practical steps towards achieving a goal. As an illustration, a client seeking to change jobs might decide to register with two recruitment agencies and to update their CV before the next session.
- Behavioural experiments. As an example, a client who wishes to be more assertive might set themself the challenge of having a difficult conversation with a colleague.
- Monitoring performance or progress. For instance, a client who lacks confidence in group situations might use a scale of 1 to 10 to assess how confident they are feeling at different times in team meetings. Simply giving themself a rating may raise their awareness of how they are feeling and also of the factors that influence how they feel.

As we considered in the previous section, one advantage in having a written record of actions agreed is that this can be revisited near the start of the next coaching session.

Reviewing progress

If you are working with a client over an extended period of time, it is useful to review progress. How often, how formally and in what way are questions to consider in your practice.

Alison Hardingham emphasises the importance of the coach recognising early on if things are going awry in a coaching relationship. She recommends that the coach uses their feelings as a guide here, and that small adjustments by the coach can set things on course again. She writes:

> In fact, if the coach can recognise early that a mismatch is occurring between his behaviour and his coachee's needs, it may allow him to put things right that could otherwise spiral out of control. (Hardingham, 2004)

As well as the coach making small 'course corrections', it is also helpful to review progress explicitly with the client. Lucy West and Mike Milan suggest that:

> Normally, halfway through the contract (in terms of either time elapsed or number of hours spent together), a formal progress review with the client is desirable. ... By the end of the halfway review session, the coach should undertake to re-contract for the remainder of the work with the client. (West and Milan, 2001)

As the coach, you too will have your views on how well the coaching is going and on how it may be improved, and you might share some of these in the review. Such a mid-term review may then lead to some revision of the coaching contract.

In the next chapter and in Chapter 21 we shall look at the important topic of supervision of coaching. Reviewing coaching assignments – particularly the more challenging or problematic ones – with a supportive supervisor is a powerful means of improving the service you offer to your clients. It is also an important way to develop your capability as a coach.

Template 8.2   Reviewing progress of a coaching assignment

You might ask some of the questions below of a client to review progress midway through a coaching assignment. Please select or modify the questions to suit your own practice.

- How useful are you finding these coaching sessions?
- What in particular are you finding useful?
- What aspects of this coaching are you finding less helpful?
- How would you characterise our relationship?
- To make the coaching even more effective, what would you like me to do differently?
- To make the coaching more effective, what will you do differently?
- What feedback will you give following this review to the organisational sponsor (if there is one)?

Evaluation

As coaching continues to grow in popularity, questions to evaluate its effectiveness will increasingly be asked, particularly by those who are funding the coaching. Glenn Whitney (2001) notes that, 'Although development coaching is increasingly enjoying widespread acceptance, it will be progressively more challenged by its clients to *prove* its added value.'

As you develop your own coaching practice, you need to consider how you will evaluate your effectiveness as a coach and assess the benefits that your coaching brings to your clients and their sponsors.

The type of mid-term review that we've just been considering can also take place at the end of a coaching assignment. Feedback from the client and, if there is one, the organisational sponsor can help all parties concerned to gauge how effective the coaching has been.

Gil Schwenk (2007) offers a useful caution to anyone who reckons that the value of coaching can be measured precisely. He writes that, 'I believe trying to establish a rock solid quantitative ROI [return on investment] for coaching is a rogue argument that will tie HR departments in knots as calculations will often be based on qualitative feedback and spurious assumptions.'

The outcomes of a coaching relationship can be far and wide reaching. The client may find years later that they have an insight which had its roots in a coaching conversation much earlier. You can't measure these things, and you can't quantify their monetary value. In the words of Albert Einstein: 'Not everything that can be counted counts, and not everything that counts can be counted.'

However, you can gather feedback – from the client or their manager or organisational sponsor – to describe in qualitative terms what the client has gained and the benefits to their organisation. You may also be able to compare these with the objectives agreed in the contracting phase at the start of the coaching relationship, although it may be that the client has learnt things through the coaching experience that they didn't envisage at the outset. Gathering such feedback can paint a picture of how successful the coaching has been. I think this is realistic, though it may disappoint those who seek a precise financial measure such as a return on investment.

EXERCISE 8.2

EVALUATING YOUR COACHING

This exercise invites you to set up a process to evaluate your effectiveness as a coach and to assess the benefits that your coaching brings to your clients and their sponsors.

- What will you do to establish how satisfied your client is with the coaching assignment?
- If there is an organisation sponsor, what will you do to establish how satisfied they are with the coaching assignment?
- What will you do to distil your learning from each of your coaching assignments?

As your practice evolves, you may wish to amend this in the light of experience.

Ending a coaching assignment

Lucy West and Mike Milan write that:

> The end of a development coaching contract is a significant event. If the work has been meaningful and effective, both coach and client are likely to regard their relationship as a significant one and therefore to have strong feelings about its ending. (West and Milan, 2001)

Jenny Rogers (2008) recommends that, 'In general, managing and marking the ending is a lot better for both sides than letting it peter out.'

There are a number of aspects to ending a coaching assignment well. First, as we have just been considering, it is important to evaluate the effectiveness of the coaching and to provide appropriate feedback to the various parties involved – the client, the sponsor and the coach.

Second, it is useful for the client to consider how they will continue to develop after the coaching has ended. You might, for instance, help them to identify further development goals and associated action plans that they will carry out without ongoing support from you. Or, you could encourage them to reflect on their experience of coaching and identify how they can coach themself in future. There is a sense in which the role of the coach is to make themself redundant.

Third, it is important to acknowledge that the coaching relationship is indeed at an end. Beverly Brooks writes:

> This is a difficult area for all concerned, not least because it involves negotiating loss. It is hard for coaches because they inevitably have an attachment to the client and for clients because they have an attachment to their coach. However, it is an ethical way to proceed which allows true growth for both. (Brooks, 2001)

9

ETHICAL ISSUES IN COACHING

Introduction

In this chapter we shall consider a number of ethical issues that you need to bear in mind as you practise as a coach. In various places we shall refer to the Global Code of Ethics for Coaches, Mentors and Supervisors that has been agreed between the Association for Coaching, the European Mentoring and Coaching Council and a number of other coaching organisations. You can access the Code via this link:

www.associationforcoaching.com/general/custom.asp?page=AboutCodeEthics

While codes of ethics and practice contain useful reminders about what you should be doing, it is ultimately up to you as an individual to choose how to behave. Allard de Jong (2006) emphasises that, 'At the end of the day, only you can ensure your integrity in your moment of choice.'

We begin by looking again at the importance of establishing and honouring a clear contract with your client and, if relevant, the sponsor of the coaching engagement. We then consider confidentiality and when you as a coach might break confidentiality. We move on to look at questions of competence and the necessity to work within appropriate boundaries. This leads naturally on to discussion of continuing professional development and the importance of supervision for practising coaches. We end with a consideration of cultural and diversity issues in coaching.

Contracting

In Chapter 7 we looked in some detail at contracting, the purpose of which is to establish clearly what the client can expect from you and what you expect of the client. Contracting needs to cover both practicalities, such as charges and the time, place and frequency of sessions, and also how the coaching process will work. Where there is a third party involved, such as the client's line manager or an HR person representing the organisation for whom the client works, it is important too to establish a clear understanding of shared goals for the coaching and how feedback to the organisation, if any, will be handled.

The Global Code of Ethics contains the following points under the heading of Contracting:

- Before they start working with a client, members will make this Code available to their client, and explain and make explicit, their commitment to abide by this Code. Members will also make their clients and sponsors aware of their respective bodies' complaints procedures.
- Before starting to work with a client, members will explain and strive to ensure that the client and sponsor know, and fully understand, the nature and terms and conditions of any coaching, mentoring or supervision contract, including financial, logistical and confidentiality arrangements.
- Members will use their professional knowledge and experience to understand their clients' and sponsors' expectations and reach agreement on how they plan to meet them. Members will also try to take into account the needs and expectations of other relevant parties.
- Members will be open about the methods they use, and on request will be ready to supply the client and sponsor with information about the processes involved.
- Members will ensure that the duration of the contract is appropriate to achieve the client's and sponsor's goals and will actively work to promote the client's independence and self-reliance.
- Members will ensure that the setting in which any coaching, mentoring, supervision or training takes place offers optimal conditions for learning and reflection and therefore a higher likelihood of achievement of the goals set in the contract.
- Members should always put their client's interests first but at the same time safeguard that these interests do not harm the interests of the sponsor.

In *Values and Ethics in Coaching*, Ioanna Iordanou writes that:

Contracting is the part of the coaching relationship that has the potential to minimise several ethical pitfalls that you might fall into as a coach, especially as a novice coach. (Iordanou et al., 2017)

Confidentiality

Confidentiality is very important in coaching. The client needs to believe that they can explore their thoughts and feelings, their hopes, fears and concerns, with someone who will not reveal any of this to another party. This is essential to build a relationship of trust.

However, while confidentiality is very important, it isn't absolute. As mentioned in Chapter 7, in my own practice I tell clients that I will break confidentiality if I think they are doing something dangerous or seriously illegal. I sometimes, though not always, add that I might discuss what has taken place in our conversations with my supervisor.

These views are reflected in the Global Code of Ethics, which includes the following points:

- When working with clients, members will maintain the strictest level of confidentiality with all client and sponsor information unless release of information is required by law.
- Members will have a clear agreement with clients and sponsors about the conditions under which confidentiality will not be maintained (e.g. illegal activity, danger to self or others) and gain agreement to that limit of confidentiality where possible unless the release of information is required by law.
- Members will inform clients that they are receiving supervision and identify that the client may be referred to anonymously in this context. The client should be assured that the supervision relationship is itself a confidential relationship.

An important practical matter concerning confidentiality arises when there is a three-way contract between coach, client and the sponsor who has commissioned the work. There needs to be agreement about what, if anything, will be fed back by the coach to the sponsor. Jenny Rogers states her own position very clearly:

> Where organizations ask me for progress reports on a client as a condition of the work, I will refuse the work. … I know how impossible it will be to create trust if the client believes that the coaching is about *assessment* – a completely different process. … I suggest that client and boss agree among themselves how to satisfy the boss's need to know what is going on. (Rogers, 2008 – italics in original)

Not all coaches operate in this way, however, and some will agree a contract which includes their giving feedback on progress to the sponsor. This may extend to giving a view on whether the individual is suitable for promotion or retention within the organisation. This inevitably creates a different relationship between coach and client, limiting the client's willingness to be fully open with a coach who is to a greater or lesser extent assessing the client.

Beverly Brooks (2001) considers this question of whether the coach is accountable to the sponsor or the client. She too recommends clear contracting between the three parties at the outset, and adds that, 'In my experience the sophisticated buyer [of coaching services] will usually insist that the coaching objectives are shared ('the what'), but not expect that the meat of the individual sessions will be ('the how').'

I think it's important that you work out your own position on how you will handle this in your own practice.

One other aspect of confidentiality concerns the keeping of records. It is essential that you keep all records and client data safe and secure, and this continues to apply after the coaching relationship has come to an end. Under the General Data Protection Regulation clients have a right to see what you have recorded, and you need to be mindful of this when creating your records.

Competence

Beverly Brooks (2001) writes that, 'A strong coach, in my view, is one who "knows what he or she doesn't know" and has a strong enough ego to admit it.'

The Global Code of Ethics states explicitly that as a coach you must be competent to work effectively with your clients, and that you need to recognise where the client requires the support of another professional. It states:

- Members will have the qualifications, skills and experience appropriate to meet the needs of the client and will operate within the limits of their competence. Members should refer the client to a more experienced or suitably qualified practising member where appropriate.

This emphasises the importance of referring the client to a more suitable person when they need support that is beyond your competence or perhaps simply just beyond the boundary of what is suitable for coaching. As an illustration of the latter point, in my work as an internal coach with staff of the University of Warwick it would not be appropriate for me to explore marital issues in any depth with a client – even if I were trained and competent to do so.

In this video clip, I talk about staying within boundaries of appropriateness and competence in a discussion after my coaching session with Lina.

Link to Video 9.1
Staying within boundaries of
appropriateness and competence

Case study

You are coaching a client who works within the same organisation as yourself. By the third session you feel that you have established a good degree of rapport and trust with the client. The focus of the coaching is their relationship with their line manager. The client wishes to behave more assertively and confidently in their conversations with their manager, whom you know to be a forceful character.

In the third session the client becomes tearful as they reveal that they are concerned about losing their job, and that their problems with their boss are causing them sleepless nights and considerable anxiety. They also share that they recognise that they have a problem with authority figures which goes back to their childhood in a household dominated by a powerful father. They saw a counsellor about feelings of low self-esteem and depression last year.

- What issues does this raise for you as a coach?
- How might you handle these?

EXERCISE 9.1

BOUNDARIES AND REFERRAL

1. Make a list of topics which a client might raise which you would decline to coach them on because they are beyond the boundary of your current **competence** as a coach. This list might change over time as you become more experienced and confident as a coach.
2. Make a second list of topics which a client might raise which you would decline to coach them on because they are beyond the boundary of what is **appropriate** in the context in which you are coaching.
3. Identify some people or organisations that you might refer a client to in order to help them deal with:
    - Deep-seated emotional problems
    - Financial worries
    - Running a business
    - Presenting themself with greater impact

Continuing professional development and supervision

The Global Code of Ethics emphasises the importance of continuing professional development in order to enhance your competence as a coach, noting that:

- Members will develop their level of coaching and/or mentoring competence by participating in relevant and appropriate training and/or continuing professional development.

The Code also underlines the importance of supervision in maintaining and enhancing a high quality of practice and in operating ethically:

- Members will engage in supervision with a suitably qualified supervisor or peer supervision group with a level of frequency that is appropriate to their coaching, mentoring or supervision practice, the requirements of their professional body and the level of their accreditation, or evidence engagement in reflective practice, ideally with peers and/or more experienced colleagues.
- Members will discuss any ethical dilemmas and potential, or actual, breaches of this Code with their supervisor or peer supervision group for support and guidance.

The importance of supervision is mentioned by most writers on coaching. For instance, Peter Shaw and Robin Linnecar (2007) write that, 'A key factor in ensuring high-quality coaching is rigorous professional supervision. This must not be skimped. Quality professional supervision is crucial for any good coach to be really effective.' Beverly Brooks (2001) goes further when she says that, 'I think it naïve at best, and dangerous at worst, if the coaching is not supervised by another professional with some psychological expertise.' Ioanna Iordanou sees

> supervision as a fundamental prerequisite for an ethical coaching practice. This is because it provides a safe space for coaches to reflect on their practice and their relationship with their clients and other stakeholders that are involved in the coaching process. (Iordanou et al., 2017)

She emphasises the importance of reflection on practice when she writes that

> in order to develop a fruitful coaching relationship, coaches need to reflect on it constantly. Coaches who work from an ethical perspective do not only rely on their instinct but also keep asking themselves what seems to be working in the relationship and what needs to be addressed further, in order to maintain an effective coaching practice. (Iordanou et al., 2017)

The topic of supervision is such an important one that we will devote Chapter 21 to it. We also look at continuing professional development in Chapter 22.

Cultural and diversity issues

Throughout the book we have emphasised that coaching is first and foremost a relationship between coach and client. To be effective as a coach implies that you can create appropriate relationships with a wide range of people. It follows, therefore, that you need to be able to create coaching conversations with people who are different from you in terms of gender, colour, class, ethnicity, and so on. The Global Code of Ethics states that:

- Members will avoid knowingly discriminating on any grounds and will seek to enhance their own awareness of possible areas of discrimination.
- Members will be cognisant of the potential for unconscious bias and seek to ensure that they take a respectful and inclusive approach, which embraces and explores individual difference.

This becomes even more important if you are working internationally, in a multinational organisation or in an organisation such as a university where staff and students come from all over the world.

Helen Baron and Hannah Azizollah emphasise the importance of being aware of your own cultural assumptions and biases, particularly if you are a member of the dominant culture within a society. They write that:

If the coach is not aware of making cultural assumptions, it is unlikely that a coachee with a different set of assumptions will develop the degree of trust required to really engage with the coach and in the coaching process. ...

To be effective in a coaching relationship, coaches must continuously reflect on their own cultural assumptions and biases and how these may distort their perspective and the way they work with clients. (Baron and Azizollah, 2007)

Lucy West and Mike Milan (2001) suggest that it is important to be less directive when working with someone from a different culture. They say that, 'the more a coach works across cultures, the less directive he or she can afford to be as it is very likely that the coach's advice or guidance will not be appropriate for the different culture'.

While it's valuable to be aware of cultural difference, it's useful too to remember that everyone is unique and that someone's individuality often overrides their cultural background.

I find two things are particularly helpful when coaching an individual from another country. The first is to listen with great attention to try to understand their perspective. This is true in all coaching, but I think it takes more effort when there is a difference in native languages. And, as we considered in Chapter 3, if your listening helps the client to understand then it doesn't actually matter if you don't fully understand what the other person is thinking or saying.

The second thing that seems to me vital is to have unconditional positive regard for the client – one of Carl Rogers' core conditions. It can be easy to think mistakenly that someone struggling to express themself in a second language is less intelligent or sophisticated, and to feel somehow superior or perhaps to slip into – in Transactional Analysis terms – some form of Nurturing Parent. And, of course, that is unhelpful.

The type of coaching that we are exploring in this book is a Western, even British, notion. In Chapter 20 we shall consider how coaching might be adapted for use in some very different national cultures.

EXERCISE 9.2

DIVERSITY

Here are some questions to prompt some self-reflection in relation to cultural and diversity issues.

- What cultural biases or prejudices do you recognise in yourself?
- What aspects of your language or non-verbal communication might be problematic for someone from a different cultural background to you?
- What types of people do you feel in some sense superior to?
- What types of people do you feel in some sense inferior to?

10

TOOLS YOU MIGHT USE IN COACHING

Introduction

Coaching generally occurs through a series of conversations. In earlier chapters we explored the key skills of listening, questioning and playing back that you use to manage coaching sessions. There are other things you can do in a coaching conversation, and in this chapter we'll look at a number of tools you might introduce in a session to help a client think through their situation. I shall illustrate the use of tools within a coaching conversation by discussing five that I myself use regularly with clients:

- Scaling
- Rich pictures
- Metaphor
- Reflective writing
- The empty chair

These are simply some of my own favourites, and it is by no means an exhaustive list. As you develop your own practice you will probably identify other tools that you like to use. One of the advantages of working with the tools covered in this chapter is that they don't cost any money.

Scaling

The idea of scaling is simple, flexible and potentially very useful in coaching. The coach merely asks the client to rate something on a scale of 1 (or 0) to 10. Here are some examples to illustrate different aspects that the client might rate:

1. On a scale of 1 to 10, how committed are you to carrying out this action – where 10 means totally committed and 1 means not at all committed?
2. How confident are you that you will be able to do what you've said on a scale of 0 to 10 – where 10 means you are certain you will succeed and 0 means that you think it will be impossible to succeed?
3. You've said you're currently at a 6 on your scale. What would it take to get to a 7?
4. I'd like you to monitor how assertively you behave in your meetings with your boss over the next few weeks. At the end of each meeting, simply rate your assertiveness on a scale of 0 to 10, and keep a record of your scores till our next coaching session.

As these examples illustrate, scaling can be used to measure performance or confidence or commitment or many other aspects. It can be used to measure past, current or future behaviour. Since the client assesses their own performance, it can be very useful in raising awareness and encouraging responsibility.

You can combine an initial scaling question with a follow-up question, as in example 3, inviting the client to consider how to move one point higher on their scale. Note that asking the client what it would be like to be at 10 may not be helpful as operating at 10 could be far beyond their capability.

You might also combine the idea of scaling with a physical action – for instance, you could ask the client to imagine that the scale from 1 to 10 runs across the room, and invite them to stand at the point where they've assessed themself. As they stand there, ask questions to help them explore what this is like. You might then invite them to move one point higher on the scale in the room, ask them what it's like in this new position, and encourage them to talk about what it would take in reality for them to move to this higher position. The physical acts of standing and moving may lead to deeper insights than the scaling on its own.

As example 4 above suggests, you can also use scaling as part of an assignment that invites a client to monitor their performance between sessions on an issue that's important to them.

Scaling is a tool which fits easily into many approaches to coaching. We'll look at it again in Chapter 16 when we discuss solution-focused coaching.

In this short clip from my coaching conversation with Lina, I ask her to rate her level of competence on a scale from 1 to 10.

Link to Video 10.1
Scaling

After discussing with Lina how she rated herself on five aspects, in this clip I invite her to consider what would need to shift within her for her to rate these attributes at a 9.

Link to Video 10.2
Moving up the scale

Rich pictures

A technique which I use fairly often in coaching conversations is simply to ask the client to draw a picture which illustrates some aspect of their situation. I use the term *rich picture* to capture the notion that their drawing might contain a wealth of ideas and information. People usually sketch a series of images rather than just one picture.

Some clients protest that they're no use at drawing. I try to reassure them that artistic skill isn't important – matchstick people are fine. If a client is really uncomfortable about drawing, however, I don't insist and instead find another way to take the conversation forward.

I use one ground rule for the exercise – the picture mustn't contain any words. I'm hoping that the exercise will surface ideas that might not have emerged if, for instance, I'd asked them to list the key aspects of their situation. As the client draws, and later as they talk about the images in their picture, they may make connections, gain insights or think laterally.

We noted in Chapter 4 that it is important to choose your words carefully when asking a question. A crisp question – simply expressed – helps to focus the client's thinking. Similarly, it is important to phrase crisply the theme of the rich picture. *Draw a picture which represents your life today* has a very different focus than *Draw a picture of what you'd like to be doing in five years' time*. I choose the focus which reflects where we are up to in the conversation, selecting what I think will be most useful for the client to think through next.

I sometimes leave the client for five minutes to do the drawing, possibly making them a drink while they work. I prefer to give them a sheet of flipchart paper and a selection of coloured pens. There's something about drawing on a large sheet of paper that can be liberating. But you can simply use A4 paper, though it is helpful to have different coloured pens.

When the client has finished drawing, I invite them to talk about their picture, encouraging them to consider in more depth what lies behind the images they have sketched.

I love the simplicity and openness of the exercise. Within the given focus, it is entirely up to the client to choose what to depict. It is a great illustration of how the coach can be directive about the structure of the conversation and non-directive about the content. I also like the way in which fresh ideas emerge in the client's thinking as they explore their images.

I once worked with a woman who drew something like the picture in Figure 10.1 to illustrate her life situation. When I asked her what the image meant to her she was silent for some time – a deep, thoughtful silence – and eventually said: *My husband is coming between me and the kids.* The drawing had helped her see something that she'd never realised before. It was a profound moment of insight for her.

Figure 10.1   A rich picture

EXERCISE 10.1

DRAWING A LIFELINE

Here is a drawing exercise which you might like to try yourself.

- Take a piece of flipchart paper and draw a line which represents your life to date. Mark and label those events in your life which you consider significant.
- Reflect upon what you were thinking and feeling at each of these times. Reflect too on how you made decisions at these times. Add some notes to your lifeline which capture these reflections.

(Continued)

You can also use the exercise with a client at the start of a coaching relationship – it's a quick way of finding out a lot about a new client. If you ask them questions to explore aspects of their lifeline, it can help them to spot patterns in their life or to reflect upon how they made key decisions.

When I ask a client to draw their lifeline I deliberately do not offer them an example as I want them to be free to draw whatever kind of line they wish.

Metaphor

In Chapter 5 we saw how the therapist David Grove developed the idea of clean language, which uses the exact words, metaphors and non-verbal expressions of the client. He found that the more he used clean language, the more his clients were able to use and develop their own metaphors to explore their world, often leading to profound and lasting change. Clean language practitioners consider that as a person's metaphor changes so too does their view of the world, the decisions they make and the actions they take.

In everyday language each of us continually uses metaphors to express our thoughts and ideas. However, metaphor is much more than just a matter of language. The language we use shapes the frames through which we view the world. And how we see the world affects how we behave and the actions we take. In other words,

- We speak in terms of metaphors
- We think in terms of metaphors
- We act in terms of metaphors

Gareth Morgan (1996) writes that, 'The use of metaphor implies a way of thinking and a way of seeing that pervade how we understand our world generally.'

Any metaphor offers a partial way of looking at something. Like looking at a mountain from different sides, different metaphors offer different perspectives. Thus any metaphor is incomplete, and potentially misleading.

A metaphor is neither true nor false. Rather, the usefulness of a metaphor depends on the richness of the insights it generates. This is particularly significant when we consider the use of metaphor in coaching.

When coaching, I sometimes find that a client uses a metaphor that seems particularly vivid or meaningful. If this happens, I encourage them to explore their metaphor further. A simple phrase such as *Say a bit more about ...* is often all that's required to allow them to think more deeply.

Clients vary in how comfortable they feel exploring metaphors. If a client finds the idea of working with metaphor odd or difficult, I choose another way of working with them. Here is an example, taken from my book *Don't Just Do Something, Sit There*, of how I was able to work with one client who was happy to develop her metaphors.

> I explored with one client a metaphor that she introduced to describe how she felt about being in conflict situations. She likened this to being attacked physically on the head. She was well aware that this described her situation metaphorically, not literally. She then identified the notion of putting on a mask – like a welder's mask – to protect herself. She considered how a mask could help her to behave effectively when in a conflict. When she tried this out in practice, she found that mentally putting on her mask did indeed enable her to behave effectively when faced with conflict situations. She took this notion further and deliberately chose her dress and make up – her mask – at the start of each working day to ready herself for any conflict that might arise through the demands of her role. (Thomson, 2009)

Another way of working with metaphor is to ask the client to come up with a comparison that encourages them to think laterally. For example:

- If your organisation was a high street store, which would it be and why?
- If your job had a theme tune, which piece of music would it be?

You might like to come up with some of your own examples.

This kind of comparison often generates some real insights for the client. And, on other occasions, it does nothing for them!

I sometimes find when coaching that a metaphor occurs to me, generally spontaneously, to capture what a client is saying. Depending on the nature of the relationship, I may choose to share this with the client. For example, I was working with one client who felt he was holding himself back at work. I said, 'It's like you're confining yourself to the A roads when you could be driving on the motorways.' 'That's right', he confirmed.

Here is another example from *Don't Just Do Something, Sit There* of a metaphor which occurred to me that I shared with a client.

> I was working with one client who found herself having to take a role within her organisation that was not what she really wanted to do but which enabled her to continue working there. I introduced the notion of finding a place in a lifeboat to enable her to survive until she moved to where she really wanted to be. She found this a helpful image, and brought it up again in subsequent conversations over a period of months. Then in one conversation she began to talk about being in a life raft. After she'd used the term several times I pointed out that *lifeboat*

had given way to *life raft*, and we explored what was different for her in being in a life raft rather than a lifeboat. One difference she identified was that a life raft seemed to her to be a craft that is drifting without a rudder. (Thomson, 2009)

Note that the metaphor of a lifeboat would certainly not be regarded as clean language since it was I, not the client, who introduced it.

EXERCISE 10.2

EXPLORING METAPHORS

As an exercise, how would you answer some of the following questions? You might need to modify some of them to reflect your own situation if, for example, you work for yourself.

- If your organisation was a high street store, which would it be and why?
- If your boss was an animal, which animal would they be?
- If your team was a sports team, what team would it be?
- If your job had a theme tune, which piece of music would it be?
- If you and a particular colleague were going to a fancy dress party together, what would you be wearing that captures the nature of your relationship?

You might like to devise some of your own questions to help a coaching client use metaphor to explore their situation or their relationships.

EXERCISE 10.3

METAPHORS FOR COACHING AND THE ROLE OF A COACH

Here is another exercise to help you explore your own approach to coaching and how you see your role as a coach. Remember that a metaphor is neither true nor false – what matters is the insights that it generates.

- Think of two metaphors for coaching. Which words or behaviours do these metaphors suggest?
- Think of two metaphors for the role of coach. Which words or behaviours do these metaphors suggest?

Reflective writing

A tool that I am increasingly using in coaching conversations is to invite the client to write. One way of doing this is simply to ask the client to write for six minutes on whatever is in their mind. There is something about specifying six minutes that seems to free people up to write – it's longer than five minutes but not daunting.

You can also give a more specific focus to what you'd like the client to explore. For example, you might ask them to write about:

* Their thoughts and feeling about their current role
* What they'd like to be doing in five years' time
* What they're going to do following the coaching session

As with a rich picture, I choose a theme which I think will be of most value for the client. For example, here is an exercise I might use when the client wants to explore their future career direction. I ask them to pick a point in the medium or long term – for instance, in five years' time or their fiftieth birthday or the day they retire. I also ask them to choose someone who is, or was, significant in their life. They then write a letter to this significant person dated at this future point. The theme of the letter is what they achieved and are proud of between today and the date of the letter. The letter is thus about aspirations for the future rather than past achievements.

I find that this exercise is richer when the client writes prose rather than just bullet points. I usually leave them on their own for five or ten minutes to write the letter and then ask them to read it out. We then explore what is significant for them in what they've written.

EXERCISE 10.4

LETTER TO A SIGNIFICANT OTHER

You might like to try the exercise about writing to a significant other person. You may wish to give the letter a particular focus, such as your future career as a coach.

* Choose a date some time in the medium or long term.
* Choose someone who is – or was – significant in your life.
* Write a letter to that person from this future point. In the letter, outline what you have achieved between today and that point.
* Take some time to reflect upon what your letter means to you.

Another exercise that's useful when the client is speaking a lot about another person – maybe their boss or a difficult colleague, for example – is to ask them to write from the perspective of the other person. As with the empty chair exercise that we'll look at in a moment, this sometimes really helps them to appreciate the other individual's viewpoint.

You can set up different expectations about what the client will share with you. In the six-minute exercise, for instance, I might say that I don't expect the client to share anything of what they write, so their reflections can be as deep and personal as they wish. Or I might say that I'd like them to share whatever they wish, which leaves them free to choose how much or how little to share with me. Or I might say at the outset that I'd like them to read out loud all of what they write.

Another reflective writing technique to be used outside rather than within a session is the use of a journal that is written over time. We discussed this in Chapter 6. Jeannie Wright and Gillie Bolton say that:

> Journal writing has the power to help people understand themselves, each other, their relationships with each other and their world better. It draws on the imagination and deep memory as well as logical cognitive thought. (Wright and Bolton, 2012)

These are all aspects that might be very useful for some of your coaching clients. And you yourself might find that keeping a journal is a simple and inexpensive way of reflecting upon and learning from your coaching experiences.

Nine words self-reflection process

In *Coach Yourself First* Mark Bisson (2017) describes his modification of an exercise developed originally by Margaret Chapman-Clarke. (See www.coaching-at-work.com/2015/10/30/toolbox-the-nine-words-process/ for her original presentation of the exercise.)

The exercise invites the client to write about a dilemma or problem they are facing. Ask them to write for three minutes on the topic. Encourage the client to write freely without crossing things out or worrying about spelling, punctuation and grammar. Then ask them to circle three words that stand out for them. Repeat the process two more times. This produces nine minutes' worth of writing and nine highlighted words. You can then help the client to explore what they have written with questions such as:

- What do you observe about what you've written?
- What surprises you?
- What realisations have you had?
- What feelings have been generated?

He goes on to note that he has used the exercise on himself. He writes that:

> I have been surprised at the topics and dilemmas I have chosen to write about and how easy it is to write for three minutes 'in the flow'. I have used it to consider my own wellbeing as a coach and thorny ethical dilemmas. (Bisson, 2017)

Reflective writing

Please watch this clip from my coaching conversation with Lina. In this I invite Lina to do some writing to capture advice she could give herself when she may be slipping into impostor syndrome and her version of herself as *Hot Mess Lina* is coming to the fore. Lina wrote for over two minutes with me silently watching on – we've edited this out.

Link to Video 10.3
Reflective writing

The empty chair

I sometimes use an approach called the empty chair exercise in a coaching session when the client is speaking a lot about someone else, such as their boss or a difficult colleague.

You can set up the exercise in different ways. One way is to place an empty chair near the client and ask them to sit in it. Explain that when they are sitting in that chair you'd like them to speak as if they were the other person, using terms such as *I think …* rather than *He or she thinks …* . Then ask them a number of open questions to explore how things look from the perspective of the other person. Inviting the client to sit in the chair of the other and look at the situation from that different perspective often helps the client to deepen their understanding of what is going on and what they need to do.

Another way of doing the exercise is to ask the client to imagine that the other person they have been speaking about is sitting opposite them in the empty chair. Invite them to speak 'directly' to the other person, saying the things that matter or need to be said.

You can combine the two ways by asking the client to swap chairs a number of times, in a sense encouraging a conversation between the client and the other person. When I use both chairs I sometimes finish by asking the client to stand up, look down on these two 'people' and tell me what they see going on between them.

Once the conversation is over, you can help the client to process the experience by asking them what they found significant or surprising in the exercise. Some clients find the exercise really useful, opening up fresh insights, while others report that nothing new emerged for them.

You can also use the empty chair when a client describes themself as behaving very differently in different situations – perhaps they are confident in some circumstances and very hesitant in others. It can be helpful to ask the client to give a name to the two selves that they are describing – for example, *Assertive Anne* and *Anxious Anne*. You might then ask the client to move between two chairs, setting up a conversation between their two selves. As an illustration, you might begin by asking *Assertive Anne* what she'd like to say to *Anxious Anne*, and then invite *Anxious Anne* to respond.

The empty chair exercise is used in psychotherapeutic settings and in approaches to counselling such as Gestalt or psychodrama. It can be a very powerful experience. In a coaching context, it is important that you are clear about how you are using the exercise and that you don't stray beyond boundaries of competence or appropriateness.

I hope you find that some of the tools described above help you in your coaching conversations. You may already have tools that you find useful, and you will probably come across others – for example, in your reading, conversing with other coaches, attending workshops, or in supervision – as you develop your coaching practice. For instance, I recently heard a coach describe how he used an ordinary pack of playing cards to invite a client to explore how he viewed the different people in his organisation.

The decision to introduce a tool, and which one to use, is based on your judgement about whether it's likely to help the client to explore their agenda. Tools like these are not a substitute for the basic coaching skills of listening, questioning and playing back. Rather the skills and the tools complement one another, enabling you to create meaningful conversations that help your clients to become more aware and to respond more effectively as a result of their increased awareness.

EXERCISE 10.5

REFLECTIVE WRITING

Here is an exercise you might like to do as we close this chapter. Spend six minutes writing down your thoughts, feelings and questions about how you could use these and other tools in your coaching practice.

11

FEEDBACK AND PSYCHOMETRIC INSTRUMENTS

Introduction

In the previous chapter we looked at some tools you might use in coaching conversations. Another thing you can do in a coaching session is to offer feedback to your client. We begin this chapter by noting that a coaching engagement offers an ideal context for a client to receive feedback. We then look at how to give feedback effectively and invite you to create your own guidelines. We go on to consider the idea of generating rather than giving feedback, helping the client to assess their own performance or behaviour. We then note the importance of gathering feedback from your clients to assess your own effectiveness as a coach. We end the chapter by looking at two widely used approaches to help a client become more aware of their behaviour – 360 degree feedback and psychometric instruments.

Coaching provides the opportunity for feedback

Jenny Rogers writes:

> Coaching is one of the few occasions where anyone is permitted, even encouraged, to comment on the immediate behaviour of the other person. Being able to do

this with the honest intent to help the other person learn and with no wish for self-aggrandisement endows the act of giving feedback with enormous power. (Rogers, 2008)

She goes on to emphasise that feedback isn't the same as criticism, which is often experienced as some form of attack.

Alison Hardingham also reckons that a good coaching relationship offers a special opportunity for feedback. It is special because:

- The client has confidence that the feedback is being offered with the sole intent of helping them achieve their goals – there's no hidden agenda
- The coach has considerable direct and indirect experience of the client's behaviour
- The coach is skilled at giving feedback and helping the client interpret it. (Hardingham, 2004)

Julie Starr regards giving constructive feedback as one of the fundamental skills of coaching:

One of the great things about a coaching relationship is that it helps the coachee to experience a different view of themselves and their situation. ...

Effective feedback can accelerate a coachee's learning, inspire them, motivate them, help them feel valued and literally catapult [*sic*] them into action. (Starr, 2011)

Giving feedback effectively

Compare these three pieces of feedback that might be given to someone after a presentation:

- Your PowerPoint slides are no good
- Your PowerPoint slides are great
- The font size on your slides is too small, which makes them difficult to read at the back of the room

The first two items of feedback are unhelpful, although the second might be nice to hear. The third piece of feedback is useful because it is specific, it describes the impact of the behaviour, and it is possible to do something to improve things.

Jenny Rogers offers these guidelines for giving feedback effectively:

- Ask permission every time
- Stick to factual descriptions of what you have seen

- Don't interpret – describe what you have seen without attributing a motive
- Describe the impact on you
- Link the feedback to the client's goal
- Ask for the client's view of what you have said
- Agree how you will work on the material generated
- Look for opportunities to offer more positive than negative feedback
- Choose your words carefully. (Rogers, 2008)

Let's develop some of these points.

If your approach to coaching is primarily non-directive, it is vital first to ask the client if they would like to hear your feedback. Myles Downey emphasises this point:

> If the session has been run in a non-directive fashion and, suddenly and uninvited, the coach comes out with some feedback, it can be very disruptive to the session and can damage the relationship. And without relationship, coaching cannot happen. (Downey, 2003)

In Chapter 2 we noted Downey's guidelines on how to give advice, make a suggestion or offer feedback. He recommends that, when giving feedback, you first check that the client wishes to hear your feedback and then, once you have given your feedback, you move immediately back to the non-directive end of the spectrum, avoiding the temptation to defend or justify your view.

A common recommendation on giving feedback is to begin with something positive, move on to the negative, critical feedback you wish to give, and finish with another piece of positive feedback. In the States this is sometimes called an Oreo sandwich after the biscuit which is a cookie with a filling in the middle.

I myself am not keen on this tactic as it may be insincere and it might well dilute the message. I prefer the guidelines which I've heard from Elspeth May, an executive coach. She suggests:

- Say what you notice
- State the impact on you
- Shut up

The intention behind her third point is to avoid the risk that the coach gives a lengthy explanation of their feedback, possibly because they are feeling uncomfortable or because they want to justify it. The explanation, however, is likely to dilute or muddle the feedback.

In Chapter 16 we shall consider a Gestalt approach to coaching. One thing that a Gestalt coach might do is to feed back to a client what they are noticing here and now in the room without any interpretation or judgement on what this might mean. It seems to me that there are two risks in interpreting. First, you might be wrong. Second, you might be right. And being right might not be helpful to this client at this moment in time. Let them work it out for themself.

EXERCISE 11.1

GUIDELINES FOR FEEDBACK

It is useful to be clear about your own views on how to give feedback effectively to your coaching clients.

Take a few minutes to produce your own guidelines on how you will give feedback.

You may find it useful to monitor how this works out in practice and, if appropriate, to modify your guidelines in the light of experience.

Generating feedback

Recall the basic equation:

Awareness + Responsibility = Performance

A risk in giving feedback is that, even when the other person apparently accepts what you are saying, they do not really grasp the point. Moreover, even if the person fully understands the feedback they may not be committed to doing anything as a result. In other words, giving accurate feedback will not necessarily enhance performance.

An alternative to *giving* feedback is *generating* feedback. Your role – using your listening and questioning skills – is to encourage the other person to generate their own feedback on how they performed. A client who generates their own feedback will be more aware of what they did and more likely to take responsibility for performing differently next time.

John Whitmore writes that:

Generating high-quality relevant feedback, as far as possible from within rather than from experts, is essential for continuous improvement, at work, in sport and in all aspects of life. (Whitmore, 2002)

To help someone generate their own feedback, all you need to do is to ask them a few open questions, helping them to explore their answers. It is worth asking both about what went well and what didn't go so well. For example, you might ask:

- What are you pleased about in this piece of work?
- What are you less pleased about?

If after reviewing a piece of work the client is still missing something important, you might wish to point this out. This is best done after the client has made their own assessment. You may well find that there is no need for you to add anything because the client identifies all the key points themself.

EXERCISE 11.2

GENERATING FEEDBACK

This is an exercise to generate your own feedback on a piece of work that you have done. Choose a project that you have done recently or are currently engaged on. It might be work-related but equally it may be something outside of work. It could also be a coaching assignment or even a single coaching session.

To generate your own feedback, write down your answers to some of the following questions:

- On a scale of 1 to 10, how satisfied are you with this project? What would have made this one point higher?
- What are you pleased about in this piece of work?
- What are you less pleased about?
- What would you do differently next time?
- What have you learnt from doing this project?

You might draft your own set of questions to use on a regular basis to generate your own feedback on the work that you do.

Feedback to the coach

If feedback is valuable for clients, it is also valuable for you as the coach. You may wish to ask your clients for their views on what you do as a coach. Some coaches do this regularly at the end of each session, some do it from time to time, and I imagine some never do this.

My own preference is to ask for feedback from time to time, either as part of a review of how the coaching engagement is going or at the end of a coaching relationship.

Template 11.1   Coaching feedback sheet

Here are some questions you might use or adapt to gather feedback – from time to time – from your clients or practice clients.

Ask your client to spend a few minutes capturing their thoughts in response to the following questions. Then spend some time with the client clarifying your understanding of what is meant.

Resist the temptation to become defensive or to justify your actions. You do not need to agree with the client's views but it is important to understand them.

- What does the coach do that helps you?
- What does the coach do that does not help you?
- What might the coach do differently?
- Any other reflections?

---

360 degree feedback

A potentially valuable tool in coaching is the use of 360 degree feedback. It is called 360 degree feedback because the feedback is given by people from all around the individual – their manager, their peers, people managed by the individual, and perhaps customers or suppliers. The person also assesses themself.

360 degree feedback is generally gathered via a questionnaire, which is usually distributed and returned via email and the internet these days. Questionnaires may be tailored to reflect an organisation's competency or values framework, or a more generic off-the-shelf instrument may be used.

Another option is to gather the feedback through interviews with relevant people. This is expensive – in terms of time or money – and is more likely to be used in executive coaching. Peter Shaw and Robin Linnecar (2007) write that in their experience oral feedback gathered by the coach 'is the most powerful device for getting to the bottom of important issues that need to be resolved'. Face-to-face interviews are preferable, but time and cost may dictate the use of telephone interviews.

Helping the client work out what the feedback means for them is best done through a conversation in which the coach takes the client through their feedback. This enables the client, first, to digest the feedback and, second, to create an action plan in response to the feedback. Jenny Rogers says that the role of the coach in this debrief is to:

- Help the client look unblinkingly at the messages, positive, negative and middling
- Steady and reassure clients who only see the negative
- Challenge the clients who are unduly complacent
- Remind clients that feedback is not an instruction to change; they can choose what they take notice of and what they ignore
- Help the client make links to how they see themselves and to other feedback they have received over the years
- Help clients make links to their own perceptions of their learning agenda. (Rogers, 2008)

I often find that clients are to some extent anxious as we sit down to go through their feedback. I also notice that in most cases they find the feedback very useful, giving them both affirmation about things they do well and ideas on where they need to improve to be more effective.

Lucy West and Mike Milan (2001) write that although initial data gathering through psychometrics or 360 degree feedback or shadowing of the client by the coach can be very informative, it needs to be done with caution. It can, they suggest, get in the way of developing the relationship and can 'place the locus of evaluation externally and not enough within the executive' (that is, the person being coached). Clients sometimes consider that a psychometric report or 360 degree feedback carries an authority or precision that is more important than their own considered view. Feedback needs to be digested rather than swallowed whole.

Psychometric instruments

Another approach to develop a client's self-awareness is the use of psychometric tools. These range from simple questionnaires that you can download free from the internet (but note the points made below) to well-researched instruments that you need to purchase and perhaps be qualified to use. An example of the latter is the Myers–Briggs Type Indicator (MBTI), which 'is the most widely used personality instrument in the world, taken by more than 2 million people a year' (Scoular, 2011). We shall explore one dimension of the MBTI in Chapter 15.

You can find out about a wide choice of psychometric tools in *Psychometrics in Coaching*, edited by Jonathan Passmore (2008), which is a comprehensive guide to the subject. In the opening chapter he and Elizabeth Allworth write:

> Coaches have an expanding range of psychological assessment tools from which they can draw to assist coachees build the self-awareness that is necessary to identify new career and life goals, and to enhance their performance at work. The burgeoning psychological testing industry has produced a myriad of measures enabling coaches to support coachees to better understand their behaviour, their preferences and their capabilities as they relate to work and life. Personality tests, aptitude tests and questionnaires assessing values, interests, leadership and motivational needs represent some of the kinds of tests currently available on the market internationally. (Allworth and Passmore, 2008)

They offer these guidelines for ethical and best practice in the use of tests:

- Testing should be evidence-based
- Tests should be selected carefully to address the referral question
- Only tests with adequate psychometric properties should be used
- Test users should be competent to administer and interpret tests
- Test users should respect the privacy of the test taker. (Allworth and Passmore, 2008)

In an article entitled 'Using psychometrics in coaching', Alan Bourne writes:

> The clients who gain the greatest benefit from psychometric tools are likely to be those who are open in their responses when completing them, open-minded and curious to understand themselves better and who do not take a defensive attitude to feedback which may challenge how they see themselves. (Bourne, 2007)

In *The Psychology of Executive Coaching*, Bruce Peltier offers these words of caution:

> Most testing tools are proprietary, and the seller of the instrument cannot be counted on as a valid source of information. Testing companies hype their products. There are hundreds of inventories that are, at best, a worthless and whimsical distraction, and at worst, a source of distorted information accompanied by the patina of technical or scientific truth. Coaches, at the very least, should try the instrument out on themselves before using it with clients. (Peltier, 2010)

Jenny Rogers offers some words of warning about the possible impact of using a psychometric tool on the relationship between coach and client:

In using psychometric questionnaires you are potentially disturbing the balance of power in the client-coaching relationship. In the normal run of a coaching conversation, the client has the information and you have the questions – in pursuit of a shared understanding. With psychometrics, you have the expert information about the questionnaire. This could disadvantage the client and probably explains why many clients will express nervousness about completing a questionnaire with whose purpose they are unfamiliar: 'Will it tell you something about me that could be uncomfortably revealing?' (Rogers, 2008)

If you decide to use one or more psychometric instruments in your coaching work, it is important to be clear about why you are using them. Psychometric instruments can act as a catalyst to stimulate a conversation between you and your client, potentially offering a vocabulary to make sense of the client's thoughts, feelings and behaviour. They can help the client to compare aspects of themselves against how other people have been assessed. Used appropriately, they can enhance the client's self-awareness and invite them to consider how they will respond as a consequence.

It is also important to realise that no psychometric instrument tells the whole story. Most are self-report instruments – that is, the client answers a number of questions about themselves – and so the reported results may be affected by the mood the respondent was in when they completed the questionnaire or by their blind spots. And any psychometric instrument necessarily focuses only on certain aspects of personality, behaviour, motivation, or whatever.

Jenny Rogers emphasises the value of allowing the client to make their own sense of what the results are telling them. She writes:

> One of the most important questions in the debriefing discussion is, 'How does this seem to you?' or 'How does this tally with how you see yourself?' The client's answer here has to be the best and last word on the topic. (Rogers, 2008)

Alison Hardingham points out that all diagnostics, including psychometric tools and 360 degree feedback, need interpreting. She is referring here to 'the work that allows a recipient of feedback to work out what it all means for him. Only when that work has been done can there be the possibility of an increase in self-awareness.' She offers these points about diagnostic tools:

- They can be a useful starting point for developing self-awareness
- To be useful, there must be extensive 'interpretation' of the raw data they provide
- 'Interpretation' means the active exploration by the coachee, with the coach's help, of what he 'makes of' the data
- The coaching environment is an ideal environment for such interpretation to take place, because it provides time, support, and psychological safety. (Hardingham, 2004)

12

COACHING AS A RELATIONSHIP

Introduction

Throughout the book we have been using this definition of coaching:

> Coaching is a relationship of rapport and trust in which the coach uses their ability to listen, to ask questions and to play back what the client has communicated in order to help the client to clarify what matters to them and to work out what to do to achieve their aspirations.

The choice and order of these words is significant. I see coaching as first and foremost a relationship between two people. In this chapter we shall explore the nature of the coaching relationship from a number of perspectives. We begin by looking at Erik de Haan's views on the importance of the relationship in coaching. We then summarise the key ideas of Carl Rogers, the originator of a person-centred approach to therapy and counselling, which provide a foundation for non-directive coaching in particular. Next we briefly consider the idea of Parent, Adult and Child ego states, and how an Adult–Adult relationship between coach and client differs from one which is Parent–Child. We go on to consider the balance between support and challenge in coaching. We close by inviting you to reflect on the nature of your own coaching relationships with your clients.

The importance of the coaching relationship

I'd like to pose a simple, interesting and very difficult question. How does coaching work? Before reading on, you might like to spend a few minutes reflecting on your own experiences as coach or client, and on what made a difference to the effectiveness of the work.

I don't know the full answer to the question. However, I have some views about how coaching often, but certainly not always, helps a client. My beliefs are based in part on reading and reflecting on what other people have written, and in part on my own experiences as a coach, client, supervisor, facilitator and learner.

Academics and practitioners have begun to conduct research into how coaching works. Erik de Haan argues that as yet there isn't enough evidence from the coaching world to answer such a question. However, he draws on extensive evidence from the more established field of psychotherapy to summarise what makes therapy effective. He then goes on to suggest that similar factors are likely to be what makes coaching effective, though he recognises that we can't be certain that the evidence from therapy translates directly into the coaching arena.

His key findings from his survey of psychotherapy research can be summarised as follows:

- Psychotherapy often has a large and successful effect
- However, there is a negligible difference in effectiveness between different approaches
- The strongest factors affecting the outcome of therapy are:
  - The quality of the relationship
  - The person of the therapist
  - The client – probably the most important factor in therapy
  - The support, trials and tribulations experienced by the client outside the therapy. (de Haan, 2008)

De Haan goes on to argue that likewise the most important factor affecting the outcome of coaching is the client – how hopeful they are, how committed, and how much pressure they feel under to resolve their issues. Moreover, since the client spends at least 99% more time outside coaching sessions, what happens outside the coaching room is much more important than what takes place within sessions.

In his book *Essential Research Findings in Counselling and Psychotherapy: The Facts are Friendly*, Mick Cooper draws similar conclusions to de Haan from his review of the evidence. He writes:

Drawing these findings together, it seems reasonable to propose that, at the heart of most successful therapies, is a client who is willing and able to become involved in making changes to her or his life. If that client then encounters a therapist whom she or he trusts, likes and feels able to collaborate with, the client can make use of a wide range of techniques and practices to move closer to her or his goals ... the evidence suggests that the key predictor of outcomes remains the extent to which the client is willing and able to make use of whatever the therapist provides. (Cooper, 2008)

He concludes that the old joke seems to have got it right:

How many therapists does it take to change a lightbulb?

One, but the lightbulb has really got to want to change.

Stages of change

From their studies of people with an addiction, James Prochaska and Carlo DiClemente (1983) created a six-stage model of how ready people are to change their behaviour. This offers a useful template for assessing where a client stands in their willingness to make changes. The six stages are:

- Precontemplation – the client has no intention of changing, and may even be unaware that there is a problem
- Contemplation – aware that there is a problem, thinking about changing, but not ready to commit – possibly ambivalent
- Preparation – committed to changing; making plans and setting goals
- Action – plans have been put into action and changes made; this may be uncomfortable
- Maintenance – changes have been consolidated and reinforced
- Termination – changes have become part of the individual's identity

---

De Haan reckons that, 'Although we can't demonstrate that there is one specific approach that works better than others', it is nevertheless really important to be committed to and to believe in the approach you do adopt. He writes, 'commit yourself heart and soul to your approach but resist the temptation to believe that it is truly superior' (de Haan, 2008).

This leads him to propose 10 commandments for an executive coach:

1. First, do no harm
2. Have confidence
3. Commit yourself heart and soul to your approach
4. Feed the hope of your coachee
5. Consider the coaching situation from your coachee's perspective
6. Work on your coaching relationship
7. If you don't 'click', find a replacement coach
8. Look after yourself, to keep yourself as healthy as possible
9. Try to stay fresh and unbiased
10. Don't worry too much about the specific things you are doing. (de Haan, 2008)

He goes on to write:

> My view of coaching now is that coaching is predominantly an exercise in *self-understanding* and *self-changing* on the part of the coachee. This exercise takes place only partly in collaboration with an outside professional, the coach. The ability of the coachee to bring about the intended understanding and change is many times greater, however, than the ability of the coach to bring about change by means of a considered choice of interventions. Coachees do the actual work all by themselves, and the only thing that coaching can do is to help them find and activate their natural, inherent abilities. (de Haan, 2008 – italics in original)

He then says that, 'The only thing the coach can actually influence ... is the *relationship* between coach and coachee.'

Julie Starr describes how she sees the special nature of a coaching relationship:

> A coach will focus solely on an individual's situation with the kind of attention and commitment that the individual will rarely experience elsewhere. ...

> A coaching relationship is like no other, simply because of its combination of objective detachment and commitment to the goals of the individual. (Starr, 2011)

Myles Downey encapsulates the vital importance of the coaching relationship when he writes that:

> Effective coaching rests on a solid relationship between coach and player. ... As a practising coach and a supervisor of other people's development as coaches, I notice that almost every unsuccessful coaching intervention is a result of a ropey relationship. ...

Without a relationship there is no coaching. In fact the only real mistake that a coach can make is to damage the relationship irreparably. Everything else is recoverable. (Downey, 2003)

Carl Rogers and a person-centred approach

We turn now to consider (Rogers, 1961) the views of Carl Rogers and his person-centred approach to psychotherapy, counselling and teaching which, for me, provide the philosophical foundations of non-directive coaching. Rogers was an American who was born in 1902 and died in 1987. He was one of the leading figures in the humanistic psychology movement which emerged in the 1950s as a third approach distinct from both the psychodynamic and the behaviourist approaches. Humanistic psychology affirms the inherent value and dignity of human beings. It views people as striving to find meaning and fulfilment in their lives. It has a hopeful, constructive view of people and of their capacity to grow and to shape their own lives.

In an article published a year before he died Rogers states briefly his central hypothesis:

It is that the individual has within himself or herself vast resources for self-understanding, for altering his or her self-concept, attitudes, and self-directed behavior – and that these resources can be tapped if only a definable climate of facilitative psychological attitudes can be provided. (Quoted in Kirschenbaum and Henderson, 1989)

He goes on to add that his approach 'depends on the actualizing tendency present in every living organism – the tendency to grow, to develop, to realize its full potential. ... It is this directional flow that we aim to release.'

In the article Rogers describes the three conditions that he says are both necessary and sufficient to create an effective relationship that lets the other person grow, whether that's in the context of therapy, education, management, parenting, or coaching. To provide Rogers' 'definable climate of facilitative psychological attitudes', the facilitator (described as the therapist in the quotes below) needs to have and to demonstrate to the other person three things.

The first element is genuineness, realness, or congruence. ... Genuineness means that the therapist is openly being the feelings and attitudes that are flowing within at the moment. There is a close matching, or congruence, between what is experienced at the gut level, what is present in awareness, and what is expressed to the client.

> The second attitude of importance in creating a climate for change is acceptance, or caring, or prizing – unconditional positive regard. ... Acceptance involves the therapist's willingness for the client to be whatever immediate feeling is going on – confusion, resentment, fear, anger, courage, love, or pride. It is a nonpossessive caring. When the therapist prizes the client in a total rather than a conditional way, forward movement is likely.

> The third facilitative aspect of the relationship is empathic understanding. This means that the therapist senses accurately the feelings and personal meanings that the client is experiencing and communicates this acceptant understanding to the client. ... Listening, of this very special, active kind, is one of the most potent forces for change that I know. (Quoted in Kirschenbaum and Henderson, 1989)

Translating these ideas into coaching practice, then, the basic assumption is that the client has the capacity to shift their understanding, their sense of self and their behaviour. Or, as de Haan (2008) suggests, 'coaching is predominantly an exercise in *self-understanding* and *self-changing* on the part of the coachee ... the only thing that coaching can do is to help them find and activate their natural, inherent abilities'.

To help the client to work out what they want and how they will set about achieving this, the coach needs to offer a relationship that demonstrates to the client that they are genuine in the conversation, that they have unconditional positive regard for the client as a person, and that they have an empathic understanding of the client's experience. For me, this is the essence of an effective coaching relationship.

In *The Psychology of Executive Coaching*, Bruce Peltier writes:

> The person-centered approach can be viewed as the sine qua non (or ultimate prerequisite) for the successful executive coach. It is a set of threshold skills. These skills and conditions must be in place before other interventions are attempted. Without them, other coaching interventions are unlikely to make a difference. (Peltier, 2010)

Erik de Haan notes the similarity between his own views and those of Rogers. However, for him it doesn't follow that the coach has to work only at the non-directive end of the spectrum. He reckons that the coach might also

> just as easily make use of more directive, suggestive and confronting interventions, precisely because I assume that the coachee can take it; or in fact that even the strongest confrontations, prescriptions and provocations are generally not powerful enough to unbalance the ability of coachees to change themselves, or to establish it if this is lacking. (de Haan, 2008)

EXERCISE 12.1

CARL ROGERS' CORE CONDITIONS

This exercise invites you to assess how well you demonstrate Rogers' core conditions in your coaching relationships. On a scale of 1 (poor) to 10 (excellent), rate yourself on your ability to:

- Be genuine with your clients
- Accept your clients unconditionally
- Convey an empathic understanding of the client's world
- Trust your clients

Take some time to consider what leads you to give yourself these ratings.

Coaching as an Adult–Adult relationship

In Chapter 15 we shall summarise briefly the idea from Transactional Analysis of Parent, Adult and Child ego states. This offers a perspective for making sense of relationships in general and the coaching relationship in particular. The theory suggests that each and every one of us spends time in and switches between three psychological or ego states – Parent, Adult and Child. This, in turn, can lead to patterns of transactions or interactions between people, such as Parent–Child or Adult–Adult.

The Parent and Child ego states are subdivided in Transactional Analysis. When you are in Critical Parent state, you may be looking to correct the behaviour of the other person, whereas in Nurturing Parent you may be seeking to take care of them. When you are in Free Child, you are likely to be in a playful or creative mode, whereas in Adapted Child you are compliant and conforming to the wishes of others. The Adult ego state is not subdivided within TA.

I find the idea of Adult–Adult transactions a useful way of conceptualising the conversation between coach and client. My own intention in coaching primarily non-directively is to create Adult–Adult relationships, trusting that the client knows what is best for them and has the resources to establish their own goals and ways of achieving these. I think that one danger in operating from the directive end of the spectrum, offering advice or suggestions, is that with some clients it may lead to a Parent–Child pattern of communication between coach and client. And, if the client is in an Adapted Child ego state, they are less likely to be aware of what they really think and feel, or to take full responsibility for actions to achieve the goals that matter to them.

However, I occasionally catch myself offering suggestions or solutions in a coaching conversation when I regard the client in some way as less competent. I sometimes realise that I have done this several times with a particular client. I then wonder if I am in some sense interacting as a Parent – perhaps a Nurturing Parent – and regarding the Client as being in some type of Child ego state. So, I need to consider what is going on that makes me behave in this way with this individual when my usual style is to operate in an Adult–Adult way, being predominantly non-directive and leaving the client to work out their own way forward. And, having noticed that I've been in a Parent ego state, I have to move back into Adult and resume coaching from there.

EXERCISE 12.2

COACHING FROM AN ADULT OR PARENT EGO STATE

Think of the conversations you have had recently with some of your coaching clients.

- With which clients do you generally stay in an Adult ego state, inviting them to respond from their Adult?
- With which clients – or at what times – do you move into a Nurturing or Critical Parent state? What do you do? And how does your client respond?
- What is the difference that makes the difference in determining which ego state you are in when you're coaching?

Rapport and trust

In our definition we describe coaching as a relationship of rapport and trust. If you are able to listen to the client with great attention, accept them unconditionally, and play back to them your empathic understanding of their world, then it's likely you'll be building rapport in the relationship. I think these behaviours are much more significant in establishing rapport than more superficial notions such as mirroring body language or using words that are similar to the client's.

Recall the words of Meg Wheatley that we quoted in Chapter 3:

Why is being heard so healing? I don't know the full answer to that question, but I do know that is has something to do with the fact that listening creates relationship. (Wheatley, 2002)

When you can create rapport in this way it becomes more likely that the client will trust you and be more open in what they share with you in your conversations. And, as they share their thoughts and feelings, their hopes and fears, they are likely to become more deeply aware of what matters most to them, what they really, really want, and what they will do to realise their dreams or resolve their difficulties.

Rapport creates trust. And trust deepens rapport. Both develop over time. The client will tell you things in the fourth session that they didn't in the first.

Not only is it vital that the client trusts the coach, it is also important for the coach to trust the client, having faith in the client's ability and wisdom to know what is right for them.

In *The Coaching Relationship in Practice*, Geoff Pelham discusses how the coach needs to make 'the situation safe enough' for the client to explore deeply. The client may feel anxious about this, and worried that they will be judged. He asks how the coach can invite the client 'to look at their part in what happened' without coming across as critical or judgemental. He writes:

> if I can connect with the coachee then something shifts in my manner and the relationship. A kind of intimacy and closeness builds, bringing with it care and concern for the coachee and a pleasure in the work we are doing together. Then my whole manner becomes appreciative of the other person, and judgements I make are set within this context. (Pelham, 2016)

He adds that the coach can't simply switch this on – this level of care and concern isn't possible when first meeting the client.

Support and challenge

An important issue to think through in your own coaching practice is *What kind of mix of support and challenge do you wish to offer your clients?* I take it as self-evident that the coach needs to support each client, and to be perceived by the client as being supportive. A more complicated question is *What role do you see challenge playing in your coaching practice?*

John Blakey and Ian Day argue that executive coaching, which is their focus, needs to incorporate a high degree of challenge as well as support. They consider that in their own training to be coaches, in many coaching books and in the accrediting standards of professional coaching bodies, there is a bias towards support rather than challenge. In their experience of coaching executives, these clients welcome and thrive on challenging interventions. They write that:

a healthy challenge, when delivered from a relationship of trust and mutual respect, serves to stretch people's thinking and drives them to dig deeper into the reality of their situation and the true potential of the future. (Blakey and Day, 2012)

Alison Hardingham argues that a coach plays a variety of roles at different times to help their clients. The key roles she describes (which is not an exhaustive list) are:

- Coach as sounding board – listening and responding to the coachee as they talk through different ideas and possible courses of action.
- Coach as conscience – when the coachee asks the coach 'to remind him, make sure he doesn't forget, stop him doing something, check whether he has done something, and so on'.
- Coach as challenger – this is 'invaluable when there is something highly relevant to progress on the coachee's goals that they either haven't thought of or are avoiding thinking about'.
- Coach as teacher – when the coach 'has some experience or knows something or someone that the coachee could benefit from knowing too'.
- Coach as 'safe container' – when the coachee has intense feelings that they need to express to someone who will hear, understand, take seriously and 'not think any the less of them for what they have heard'.
- Coach as 'professional friend' – a friend with a specific purpose who is an equal and who can be relied upon to behave professionally. (Hardingham, 2004)

Writing of the challenger role, she says that:

Deciding how often, and when, to take the role of challenger is one of the key things a coach must pay attention to. She needs to observe carefully the effect her challenging has. Does it liberate the coachee from some behaviour he had got stuck in? Or does it mire him in uncertainty and passivity? (Hardingham, 2004)

Challenging a client

In this video, I challenge Lina during our coaching session. I ask her first, 'What needs to shift within you?' I then ask her, 'Who are you really trying to please?' The clip shows this part of our conversation, followed by Lina's reflections during her debrief with Christian on the effect on her of the second question.

Link to Video 12.1
Challenging a client

This raises the question of what we mean by challenging. Blakey and Day (2012), who regard accountability to the organisation and its various stakeholders as vitally important, write that '*Challenge* refers to interventions that compel the individual to confront current reality … and to meet the changing expectations of all stakeholders.'

I think it is possible to combine challenge with operating mainly non-directively. For example, you might use the technique of double sided reflection – where you play back both sides of a client's dilemma, giving equal weight to both sides – to challenge a client to face up to contradictions or tensions in their position. As an illustration, you might say to a client: *You tell me that you really want a new job, and that you've not made any job applications since we last spoke. I wonder what's going on.* This could be a strong challenge to the client, but it leaves it open to them what – if anything – they wish to do about their situation.

Myles Downey (2003) describes a number of behaviours, such as giving feedback, making suggestions and challenging, as skills which a coach might sometimes use to **propose** some kind of input to the client. For him the purpose in challenging is to raise the client's awareness. He considers that 'true challenge comes from a belief in the other's potential'.

When he has something to propose to a client, Downey asks himself four questions before going ahead:

- Will it raise awareness?
- Will it leave responsibility and choice with the player?
- Is the relationship strong enough to withstand the intervention?
- What is my intent? (Downey, 2003)

Only when he can answer *Yes* to the first three questions and when his intent is in the service of the client does he go ahead to make a proposal.

EXERCISE 12.3

CHALLENGING A CLIENT

Take some time to reflect on your coaching conversations and on these questions:

- In what ways do you challenge your clients?
- What happens when you challenge them?

Your own coaching relationships

In this final section I'd like to invite you to pull together your own views about some of the ideas we've been looking at in this chapter. Here are a number of questions which you might like to spend some time thinking or writing about in order to reflect upon the nature of your coaching relationships with your clients. You may find some questions more useful for you than others.

EXERCISE 12.4

YOUR OWN COACHING RELATIONSHIPS

- How do you think coaching works?
- What are the different roles that you play with your clients?
- What words or phrases illustrate the nature of your coaching relationships with your clients?
- Reflecting on the ideas explored in the chapter, what will you do differently with your coaching clients?

13

THE USE OF SELF IN COACHING

Introduction

Throughout the book we have taken the view that coaching is first and foremost a relationship between the coach and the client. We looked at this in more detail in the previous chapter, and noted the view of Erik de Haan that the only thing the coach can actually influence is the relationship.

In this chapter we shall explore various aspects of how the coach can use themself in the conversations they have with their clients.

Michael Frisch offers this working definition:

> Use of self: A coach's thought or feeling reaction to a client that the coach is both aware of and will use, either directly or indirectly, in the service of the coaching. (Frisch, 2008)

We begin by considering how the coach might share examples from their own situation or history with a client, which Frisch would not consider as use of self in the above definition. We then look at how the coach might feed back things that they observe in the client. We go on to explore how the coach can utilise what they notice within themself as the conversation unfolds, considering how this will impact on the quality of the coaching relationship. This is a much deeper and more advanced way of using yourself in coaching. We then look at the ideas of Maria Iliffe-Wood on how a coach can operate in four modes of presence to share themself in different ways in the service of their clients. We end by discussing how you might enhance your self-awareness of what is going on within a coaching conversation.

Self disclosure

Near the start of my first coaching session with a new client I ask them to tell me about how they got to where they are today. This question is deliberately a little vague as I'm interested in what they choose to share. I usually follow this question up by asking them about their interests outside work. I then take a few minutes to tell them something of my own career history, my current role and my interests outside work. I often find that there are some points of connection between us – maybe we've both worked for the same organisation, or lived in the same part of the world, or have a common interest, or have children of a similar age.

In saying a little about my own background, I hope that the client will see that there is a real person sitting in the role of coach. And, if there are some points of connection, it can help to build rapport between us.

As the relationship develops, I may occasionally share something which has happened to me that has some similarities with the issue that the client is exploring. Maybe they're going through an organisational change which has echoes from my past, or perhaps they're faced with a decision on whether or not to accept a new job. My intention in doing this is not to suggest to the client that what I did or have experienced is in any way a guide to what they should do. Rather, I am simply trying to show my understanding of their situation.

If you do choose to share some of your own story with a client, it is important to do this selectively and briefly. Self-disclosure is in the service of the client, and a lengthy monologue from the coach doesn't help them. Moreover, stories which imply a way forward may be, to a greater or lesser extent, directive. If you share such a story, it is important to be clear about your intent and to consider the likely effect on the client.

Because they do not wish to direct the client in any way, some therapists, counsellors or coaches would say that it is utterly inappropriate for the coach to reveal anything about themselves or their history. Not only might this influence the client, but it could also be felt as some kind of judgement. As an illustration, some coaches who meet clients in their own office ensure that there are no family photographs on display which would indicate that they were married or had children.

EXERCISE 13.1

SHARING YOUR OWN EXPERIENCES

This exercise invites you to consider when and how you will disclose information about yourself with a coaching client. Under what circumstances do you – or might you – share your own experiences with a coaching client?

(Continued)

> If you do disclose some of your own background to a client, notice what happens when you do this in your coaching conversations. You might like to make some brief notes after the session, and over time see if there is any pattern in what happens when you self-disclose.

Sharing observations with a client

A second way in which you might use yourself in a coaching conversation is to share what you notice with the client. As an illustration, imagine that your client is describing a new role they've just taken on. They tell you several times how pleased they are to be in the new job. However, as they speak you notice that they are slumped in their chair, their tone of voice is low, and they are wringing their hands continually. You haven't observed them displaying this type of body language in previous conversations. In short, their words seem inconsistent with their body language.

Take a moment to consider what you might say or do in this scenario.

There are a number of possibilities. You might choose to do nothing, and move on with the conversation. You might make a mental or even written note of what you've noticed, and wait to see what emerges as the conversation unfolds. You might say something to focus the client's attention on their new role – for instance, *Tell me more about the pros and cons of your new job*. Or, you might simply play back to the client what you've observed.

In Chapter 16 we shall consider how a Gestalt therapist or coach will use what is happening 'here and now' in the room during a coaching conversation as a cornerstone of their work with clients. Note that a Gestalt practitioner won't offer an interpretation of what this might mean, but will invite the client to consider what it could represent. In this example, the Gestalt practitioner would not say something along the lines of: *Although you say you're pleased with the new job, I don't think you really are.* This might be accurate, but it is an interpretation of what the client's body language signifies. Rather, to avoid interpreting, they might comment, *As you talk about how pleased you are in your new job, I notice that you're slumped in your chair and your voice is low. I wonder what that could mean.*

Another time when you might share observations with a client is when you recognise a pattern over time. As an illustration, imagine you have a client who is exploring how to be more influential with the senior people in their organisation. They tell you that they find it difficult to say what they really think when in conversation with the directors. You recall that in the previous coaching session they described how they found it hard to say *No* when colleagues asked them to take on various tasks that were not properly part of their role. And in an earlier conversation they had spoken of being unable to ask their boss for resources that were essential to carry out a project. You realise that all three situations are examples of the client being unable to behave assertively. You might link these three observations in a summary statement, inviting the client to consider what this means for them. For example, you could say to the client:

> As you speak about your difficulty in being influential with the directors, I am reminded of our last conversation where you described how you were unable to say No to your colleagues. And also of the occasion when you found it hard to ask your boss for more resources. I wonder what might link these situations.

Alternatively, you might end a summary like this with a direct comment such as:

> It seems to me that you find it difficult to be assertive in these three situations.

I think it is important that when you draw the client's attention to a possible pattern you do so in a way that leaves it up to them to agree or not. The preliminary phrase *It seems to me …* in the last statement is intended to indicate that you are offering this merely as your view of what might possibly be going on.

EXERCISE 13.2

SHARING YOUR OBSERVATIONS WITH A CLIENT

You might imagine a spectrum of ways in which you could feed back your observations to a client, ranging from the Gestalt practitioners' stance of making no interpretation at one end to the opposite end where the coach interprets what they notice in the client.

- In your own practice where do you typically operate on this spectrum?
- Under what circumstances do you – or might you – offer an interpretation?
- What preliminary phrases do you use to make your comments more tentative?

Sharing what is going on within you

We move now to a deeper and potentially riskier way of using your self in coaching conversations and relationships. This is to point out to the client what is happening for you within the session. This is a way of working that a Gestalt coach will use with their clients. Since they regard what happens within the session as representative of the client's life outside of the coaching room, they reckon that how the coach experiences the client may be similar to how other people encounter them. As in a hologram, the part is representative of the whole.

You don't have to operate from a predominantly Gestalt position to use the idea of sharing your felt experience with your coaching clients. As an illustration, I once had a supervision client whom I'd known for a very long time and with whom I had a strong relationship. I noticed during one of our supervision sessions that my mind had twice drifted off and I'd stopped paying attention to what he was saying, which was unusual in our conversations. I shared this with the client, inviting him to speculate on whether this might be significant. He replied that he felt he'd been talking about things that weren't that important in regard to the issue he'd brought to supervision that day.

In this example, it was important that I already had a strong relationship with this particular client. For me, to share an experience like this at an early stage in a coaching relationship would be very risky and inappropriate.

Marjorie Shackleton and Marion Gillie, who practise from a Gestalt perspective, offer some guidelines on if and when to disclose something that has emerged within you. They suggest that:

- The key question that guides your decision is always 'how will your disclosure serve the client?' (For example, will it heighten the client's awareness?)
- If you are unsure then wait, and by delaying you may get further clarity about your internal data which might well be of use to the client at a later point in the session.
- If a feeling, image, etc. *has* persisted with this client during the session or over the time you have known him or her, it is important you choose to disclose when it emerges once more in the current session. (Shackleton and Gillie, 2010)

If you do decide to share what is happening for you, then your choice of words is very important. Shackleton and Gillie emphasise the importance of owning what you say (using *I* rather than *You*), of not interpreting, and of being non-judgemental. They recommend 'offering your self-reflections lightly, with curiosity and wonderment'. Imagine, for example, how a client might react to these two statements:

- This all seems a bit irrelevant and boring.
- I notice my attention has drifted, and I wonder what's happening for you as you talk about this.

Shackleton and Gillie (2010) also suggest that if you find yourself frequently working on the same issue with every client, then that's probably about you, and should be taken to supervision.

Another way in which I share what is going on for me with a client is when a word or metaphor or image occurs to me as the client is speaking. Depending on how well established our coaching relationship is, I may or may not share this with a client – 'lightly and with curiosity'. Shackleton and Gillie give an example where one of them shared with a client the image that had come to them of a bird skimming along a hedgerow. This led to client and coach engaging at a deeper level rather than, as they had been doing, skimming the surface.

If you do share something that is going on for you with a client and it doesn't seem to hold any meaning for them, it is important simply to let this go rather than persist. If it's really significant, it will come up again.

A person-centred perspective – being genuine

I mentioned above that you don't have to be working from a Gestalt perspective to utilise what is going on for you within a coaching session. In the previous chapter we looked at the three core conditions which Carl Rogers regarded as necessary and sufficient to create an effective relationship that enables a client to grow:

- **Congruence**: being genuine, being real, sharing feelings and attitudes, not hiding behind a facade
- **Unconditional positive regard**: non-judgemental acceptance and valuing of the other, in a total not conditional way
- **Empathy**: understanding the other's feelings and experience, and also communicating that understanding

Rogers' condition of congruence is akin to the coach using what is going on in their self. 'Sharing feelings and attitudes' with a client can be risky. If what you are sharing is somehow critical of the client or overly challenging, you may damage the relationship. I think that your ability to be genuine depends on you first having unconditional positive regard for the client. If you find yourself being judgemental of the client, it's probably better to keep your genuinely held but critical thoughts and feelings to yourself.

It follows that if you can unconditionally accept a wide variety of people, then you will be able to share your 'feelings and attitudes' with a greater range of clients. I suspect that one of Carl Rogers' great qualities was his ability to non-judgementally accept so many clients. If, on the other hand, you are someone with a host of prejudices, you may have to work very hard indeed to create effective coaching relationships with some potential clients.

Link to Video 13.1
Sharing an impression
with a client

Sharing an impression with a client

Please watch this clip from my coaching session with Lina. In the first part I feed back to Lina my impression of her enthusiasm and vitality that came through to me in our conversation. In the second part, which is taken from her reflections afterwards with Christian van Nieuwerburgh, she explains the effect on her.

An advanced skill

The use of self at this deeper level of sharing genuinely with the client what is going on within you as you coach is an advanced skill. However, the ability to use your self in the interest of the client is potentially a very valuable asset.

Peter Bluckert writes:

> I regard the use of self as the highest order coaching skill. It can be the key difference between good and great coaching. …

> In my view techniques have their place but the most important tool of all is yourself. Your self. In the search for toolkits many aspiring and practicing coaches miss this fundamental point. (Bluckert, 2004)

Katherine Long argues:

> That who I am as a coach is connected to who I am as an individual

> That gaining congruence and authenticity brings greater effectiveness to my practice.

> Therefore …

> to be more effective to my clients there needs to be congruence between who I am as a person and who I am as a coach. (Long, 2011)

At the risk of oversimplifying matters, you might summarise these views in the phrase: *Who you are is how you coach.* As a coach, you bring yourself to the relationship. And, as we noted at the start of the chapter, coaching is first and foremost a relationship.

Marion Gillie (2011) emphasises that how you 'show up' informs, not necessarily consciously, what the client chooses to reveal. She highlights two aspects of this. The first is your ability to engage in I–Thou dialogue with the client, openly and respectfully sharing what is important without trying to impose your will on the other person. The second is your presence. She writes:

> Presence is much more than how 'professional' you are as a supervisor. It includes how 'grounded' you are in yourself and your work, how able you are to 'contact' the client, even when they are difficult to reach. It is the ability to *be in the here and now*, ie to tune into what is going on within yourself (your reactions to your supervisees, what they evoke in you, what images come to mind, what sensations are stimulated) as you are impacted by them, and to disclose some of this in order to 'make contact'. (Gillie, 2011)

Myles Downey talks about how each of us brings something unique to what we do, including coaching. He writes:

> Whatever your uniqueness might be, your brand of humour, your particular intelligence or your type of professionalism will show up in your coaching. Best to understand what it is and also to understand how it can influence your coaching, positively and negatively. (Downey, 2003)

EXERCISE 13.3

WHO YOU ARE IS HOW YOU COACH

Myles Downey suggests that whatever your uniqueness might be will show up in your coaching. Take some time to list your own distinctive qualities that you can usefully bring to your coaching.

- Which of these qualities do you display in your coaching conversations?
- Which of them will you use more in your coaching practice?
- Which will you use less in your coaching?

Self-experience

In *The Coaching Relationship in Practice*, Geoff Pelham uses the term *self-experience* to 'refer to the thoughts, feelings and behaviours that arise in the coach in relation to the coachee'. He notes that:

for many people new to coaching, self-experience has no place at all. Initially the proposition that my own feelings are relevant to the work seems strange and rather alarming. (Pelham, 2016)

He agrees with his colleague, Peter Bluckert, that 'the capability to use that self-experience, that felt sense, is the highest of coaching skills'. He goes on to distinguish two strands. The **technical** aspect is 'to do with the power and impact of such disclosure and how to do it in practice'. The **relational** aspect 'concerns the impact of use of self on the quality and depth of the relationship'.

In regard to the technical aspect of use of self, he offers these guidelines (which have many similarities with those we noted earlier from Shackleton and Gillie):

- It is something that arises unbidden in the session – a feeling, image or intuition. (It's not advice, guidance or suggestions.)
- It's more often a background sense that might easily be overlooked, especially if it's discomforting.
- It's often not clear what the feeling means.
- Work with the proposition that it may be about what is happening in the relationship.
- Share whatever it is in a way that invites curiosity and interest about its meaning and relevance to the session.
- Find the words that the coachee can connect with and use rather than being confused or put off.
- It often feels risky. If the coachee discounts it, don't pursue it. If it's significant it will persist or return.

In regard to the relational aspect of use of self, he writes:

My own experience has been that the more I allow myself to enter fully into the relationship the greater the depth of the work. The more I care for the coachee the more they matter to me, and the more I show this is the case the better the work tends to be. As I enter more deeply into the relationship the use of self tends to shift from 'technique' to a genuine sharing of what is going on for me. (Pelham, 2016)

Modes of presence

This section is based on the ideas of Maria Iliffe-Wood, which she sets out in her book *Coaching Presence: Building Consciousness and Awareness in Coaching Interventions*. Coaching presence 'is a way of being (which) will set the tone for the coaching'. It creates 'an enabling space' to help the client to learn.

She notes a range of things that contribute to this way of being:

- You are 'in the moment' with your client.
- You are both equal in the relationship and you value the diversity between you.
- With compassion and empathy you hold a safe space for the client to express and deal with any difficult or uncomfortable issues.
- You are fluid. You are flexible, adaptable and responsive to your client's needs. Your intuition and creativity come to the fore to help the client.
- It is purposeful and deliberate. (Iliffe-Wood, 2014)

She then describes four levels of awareness which the client might access:

- Level one awareness: what is obvious to the client – what is right in front of their eyes
- Level two awareness: what clients know at a deeper level – accessible but harder to reach and recall
- Level three awareness: what clients don't realise they know, or have forgotten, or are trying to avoid
- Level four awareness: what clients don't know, or are unconsciously avoiding

She goes on to describe four modes of presence. 'Each mode of presence relates to how much of *you* is in the approach or intervention: how much you allow your thoughts, beliefs, opinions, judgements, feelings, etc to influence your work with the client.' These broadly translate across to the four levels of awareness, as in Table 13.1.

Table 13.1 Modes of presence

Client's level of awareness	Coach's mode of presence	Key words to describe mode of presence	Metaphor for mode of presence
One	**Invisible Coach mode**	Silence, listen, trust, patience, brevity, simplicity	*You trust the driver and enjoy the ride.*
Two	**Emergent Coach mode**	Stimulate, elevate, expand, magnify, detachment, creativity, perseverance	*You offer the client a new map.*
Three	**Evident Coach mode**	Share, inform, prompt, highlight, intuition	*You highlight different routes on the map.*
Four	**Visible Coach mode**	Steer, incite, probe, challenge, provoke, courage	*You read the map and give the driver directions.*

Here is an illustration of each of the modes which draws on ideas discussed earlier in the book:

- Invisible Coach mode: You ask questions to help the client work through the stages of the GROW model.
- Emergent Coach mode: You introduce a tool – for example, inviting the client to draw a rich picture or to sit in the empty chair.
- Evident Coach mode: You share, in Geoff Pelham's words, your self-experience.
- Visible Coach mode: You offer the kind of challenge discussed by John Blakey and Ian Day – one which compels the client to confront reality.

Iliffe-Wood explains how to use the model in a coaching session:

> The choice of mode of presence requires a deliberate decision. Each time you leave a mode you make another deliberate choice. Throughout the coaching regularly ask yourself two questions: 'Which level of awareness am I trying to facilitate in the client?' and, 'Which mode will help the client most in this moment?' Be definite about your choice. Once you have chosen the mode of presence, this will inform your interventions. It will immediately narrow or expand the options available to you or inform how you continue with an existing intervention. (Iliffe-Wood, 2014)

She devotes a separate chapter of her book to each of the four modes of presence. Here are some of the key points she makes on each.

- **Invisible Coach mode**

You are not the invisible coach. The invisible coach is found with the client: the invisible coach is the client's own inner wisdom.

It will often be the starting point of any coaching and it is the mode you keep returning to throughout the coaching.

You use the bare minimum and simplest of interventions. *Less is more* when using this mode.

- **Emergent Coach mode**

You provide a means for clients to continue their exploration of a topic. You can use your most creative interventions, tools or techniques. You still do not add anything of yourself in the interventions.

Your intention is to help clients access new information, to explore in more detail, to see beyond the edges of their current vision.

You may need to explain interventions or tools before clients can use them.

- **Evident Coach mode**

You are now sharing aspects of yourself in the coaching. You are most likely to be using your intuition to aid their exploration.

Your intention is to help clients to expand, deepen and heighten their own exploration. You are helping them to empower their own invisible coach. You want to draw aspects to their attention that will help them to either think about the topic in a different way, or pay attention to something they have not been attending to so far.

You may share your feelings, emotions, words and images, certain aspects of your experiences, knowledge and observations – in the interests of the clients' learning. You do not share your ideas or solutions.

You provide the information but the client is free to decide whether to take it on board or disregard it.

- **Visible Coach mode**

Your presence is more overt. You are steering the coaching session in some way.

Your intention is to incite a response in clients. You want to help them to access information that is in their level four awareness. Your intention may be to take them out of their comfort zone, because that is where the potential for transformational learning lies.

You press clients more in this mode, particularly when they appear to be avoiding certain aspects or interventions. Ultimately clients can decline the invitation to explore the suggested route.

You may need to have strong resolve, to have the courage of your convictions, to hold your nerve.

Like Emergent and Evident Coach modes, you do not stay in Visible Coach mode for long. Once the client is going ahead with the intervention you go back into Invisible Coach.

Thinking back over recent coaching conversations, how often do you work in:

- Invisible Coach mode
- Emergent Coach mode
- Evident Coach mode
- Visible Coach mode

Which mode(s) will you seek to use more frequently?

What might inhibit you from doing so?

Developing self-awareness and intuition

Peter Bluckert (2004) describes the coach's use of self as 'the ability to put words around those intuitive moments when we believe we know something but struggle to describe it'. He adds that, 'We all have these moments though we may not always trust them enough to risk articulation.'

I don't think you can teach this use of self or intuition. It is, however, possible to reflect continually upon your coaching practice, seeking to be more aware of what's happening in your coaching conversations and relationships and using your awareness skilfully to enhance your coaching craft.

One way of developing your awareness of your self is to cultivate the habit of mindfulness. We shall look briefly at this in the next chapter on the inner game within the mind of the coach.

A useful way of reflecting upon and learning from your coaching practice is by seeking feedback from your clients. In Chapter 11 we listed some open questions that you might ask of your clients to do this. Their feedback might help you become more aware of what you do that is helpful and less helpful.

Another way of reflecting on your practice is to record – with the client's permission, of course – some of your coaching sessions on video or audio tape. You can play the tape back, and through a process of recall become more aware of the factors and dynamics which influenced your behaviour in the coaching session.

A very useful means of developing your ability to use your self in coaching is by working with a supervisor. We shall look at this in some detail in Chapter 21. Working with a good supervisor is invaluable in developing your coaching capability and clarifying who you are when you coach.

14

THE INNER GAME OF COACHING

Introduction

In this chapter we look at the inner game that is going on within the mind of the coach as they converse with a client. We begin by summarising the ideas of Tim Gallwey, who introduced the term in the 1970s in his classic book *The Inner Game of Tennis*. This includes the notion of interference – that is, the things that get in the way of our performing at our best. We then look at some practical matters that can be handled in advance of a coaching session to avoid some potential interferences. We go on to consider the interferences that might arise for the coach during a conversation, interferences which can test the skill, experience and confidence of the coach. We then discuss how giving great attention to the client, and being mindful of all that is going on, are ways of managing these mental interferences. We end by looking at the importance of trust within the coaching process.

Tim Gallwey and the inner game

The ideas in Tim Gallwey's book *The Inner Game of Tennis*, which first appeared in Britain in 1975, have been hugely influential in shaping the type of coaching explored in this book. Gallwey was a talented tennis player in his youth, and later became an educationalist and also a tennis coach.

Reflecting on how he handled tennis coaching lessons, Gallwey realised that he was giving too many instructions and thereby causing confusion. He concluded that 'he had to teach less, so that more could be learned'. Gallwey suggests that:

> There is a far more natural and effective process for learning and doing almost anything than most of us realize. It is similar to the process we all used, but soon forgot, as we learned to walk and talk. It uses the so-called unconscious mind more than the deliberate self-conscious mind. (Gallwey, 1975)

The idea that people learn best by tapping into their own natural learning processes has similarities with Carl Rogers' notion of the self-actualising tendency. These are views which are fundamental underpinnings of a non-directive approach to coaching.

He also noticed that in a tennis lesson the player being coached spent a lot of time talking to themselves, criticising their own performance. He postulated that within each player there were two selves – Self One who seems to give instructions to Self Two who carries out the actions. Self One then evaluates how well or badly Self Two has performed.

Myles Downey describes Self One and Self Two as follows:

- Self One is the internalised voice of our parents, teachers and those in authority. Self One seeks to control Self Two and does not trust it. Self One is characterised by tension, fear, doubt and trying too hard.
- Self Two is the whole human being with all its potential and capacities including the 'hard-wired' capacity to learn. It is characterised by relaxed concentration, enjoyment and trust. (Downey, 2003)

The outer game of tennis is the game played against the opponent on the other side of the net. Gallwey writes that the inner game is:

> the game that takes place in the mind of the player, and it is played against such obstacles as lapses in concentration, nervousness, self-doubt and self-condemnation. In short, it is played to overcome all habits of mind which inhibit excellence in performance. (Gallwey, 1975)

Gallwey describes the negative thoughts of Self One as interference. It is this interference that prevents the player from performing to the level of their potential. He summarises this in the equation:

Performance equals Potential minus Interference

It follows that someone who can minimise unhelpful interferences will perform at a higher level, closer to their potential. If you can help a client to tackle inner obstacles such as lack of confidence or fear of failure, then they will be more effective or successful. This is one way of framing what you are doing when using a cognitive or cognitive behavioural approach to help a client think and act differently.

It also follows that if you can minimise the interferences that you yourself experience when you are coaching then you will improve your performance as a coach.

Preparing for a coaching session

One fairly straightforward way of eliminating some of the interferences that may get in the way of you coaching well is to give yourself enough time to prepare for the session. A basic consideration is to have everything you need to hand – for example, things such as pen and notepad, a box of tissues and a clock. If you keep notes on your clients, make sure you've allowed time to read these through and to consider what this means for the session ahead. Do you need to visit the loo, and have you switched off your mobile phone?

You can also arrange in advance the layout of the room, placing chairs and tables where you want them to be. This may not always be possible, however, if the venue is the client's premises or a local hotel.

Consider too how relaxed you are as you prepare to coach. Arriving in a breathless rush from a previous meeting isn't a good way to start. On the other hand, a few minutes of peace and quiet before you meet the client may help you to leave behind your various concerns, to still your mind and to concentrate on the conversation ahead. Taking a few minutes to ground yourself like this helps you to start the coaching session relaxed and focused on the client.

EXERCISE 14.1

PREPARING FOR A COACHING SESSION

This exercise invites you to consider the things that you can manage before a coaching session so that you can start the session free from interferences.

- What items do you need to have at hand?
- What is your policy on keeping and reading records of previous sessions?
- How do you like the room to be laid out?
- What do you do to ground yourself before you greet the client?

Interference during a coaching session

We turn now to the more challenging issue of how you handle interferences that arise for you as the coach in the middle of a coaching conversation. Myles Downey writes some words that go to the heart of the inner game as it applies to coaching:

> The primary function of the coach is to understand, not to solve, fix, heal, make better or be wise – to understand. The magic is that it is in that moment of understanding that the coachees themselves understand for themselves, become more aware and are then in a position to make better decisions and choices than they would have done anyway. That is how coaching is profoundly simple and simply profound. But most of us struggle to get above our own agenda and want to be seen to be making a difference. (Downey, 2003)

I sometimes find when coaching that I start to feel some kind of responsibility for ensuring that the client solves their problem. This may happen when – generally 10 or 15 minutes into a session as the client has explained various difficulties facing them – I begin to think *How are we going to sort all this out?* I am, in Downey's terms, seeking to solve or fix or make better, wanting 'to be seen to be making a difference'. This is interference. It might also be viewed as my Self One telling me to try hard and make sure I do a good job. My guess is that it is an interference that is common, not least with those who are learning how to coach. It is important, when this happens, to notice it and then to remind myself that I am not responsible for coming up with solutions and that my role is to manage the relationship and the conversation in the service of the client. It really helps to focus on the process and not worry about the outcome. As Tim Gallwey says, 'The coach is not the problem solver.'

Another interference that arises, not least with newcomers to coaching, is to become concerned about what to say or do next while the client is talking or thinking. John Whitmore (2002) warns that, 'if the coach is working out the next question while the coachee is speaking, the coachee will be aware that he is not really listening'. So, in this situation, there is interference both for the coach, who is thinking of the next thing to say, and for the client, who perceives that they are not being fully listened to.

As a coach, how then do you quieten a Self One which is saying *I need to solve things* or *I must come up with a really good question*? A powerful way to do this is just to listen with respect, interest and empathy. Simply and continually pay attention to the client, seeking to appreciate their world. If you can focus on this, then you are less likely to be distracted by such Self One thoughts. As Nancy Kline (1999) says, 'The quality of your attention determines the quality of other people's thinking.'

Something else which happens to me from time to time is that my mind drifts off to think about something else as the client speaks. While this might be an indication that the client isn't speaking about what really matters to them, it is more likely just to be poor practice on my part. When it happens, I notice it, put it to one side, and focus back on the client.

One of the things that can happen in a coaching session or relationship is that the words or feelings or gestures of the client stimulate in the coach a memory of their own situation or past experience. It may even be that something in the unconscious of the client triggers something in the unconscious of the coach. In psychological terms, this is known as *countertransference*. These unresolved aspects of the coach's life – their baggage or unfinished business – can be another source of interference, getting in the way of coaching effectively. This is a suitable topic for the coach to take to supervision to help them either to process their own issues or at least to be able to recognise and put these to one side if they arise again in a session with a client.

In this video clip, I reflect on the interferences I experienced – and didn't experience – during my coaching conversation with Lina.

Link to Video 14.1
Interferences during a
coaching session

EXERCISE 14.2

INTERFERENCES DURING A COACHING SESSION

Take a little time to reflect on the interferences that arise for you during coaching sessions and get in the way of you coaching at your best.

- What are the unhelpful Self One thoughts that enter your mind in some of your coaching sessions?
- Under what circumstances are you tempted to 'solve, fix, heal, make better or be wise'?

Attention and mindfulness

We noted above that Self Two is characterised by relaxed concentration, enjoyment and trust. An analogy with driving a car may illustrate what relaxed concentration might feel like. As a learner, we don't expect to be able to drive a car after a couple of lessons – it takes time, practice and experience. A novice driver has to concentrate hard on individual aspects, such as steering, braking or changing gear. An experienced driver does these things apparently without thinking, and may sometimes arrive at their destination with little memory of the journey. However, there are times when the experienced driver has to respond intelligently and quickly to deal with a tricky situation on the road.

In a similar way, we coach best when we can bring a relaxed concentration to it. We are aware of things happening at a number of levels as we process various types of information. We are continually deciding what to do next, but this does not feel burdensome. And there are times which seem particularly significant and when we need to consider carefully the next step in the coaching session.

Self Two is also characterised by enjoyment. Downey writes that, 'one of the quickest ways of getting into Self Two is through enjoyment'. He notes, however, that, 'What is interesting in this is that you cannot make yourself enjoy something.' He suggests that the way into enjoyment is through awareness – simply noticing how you are feeling and rating your level of enjoyment. As you do this, you may find that your level of enjoyment rises. You might, as an exercise, like to reflect on the sessions or clients that you find enjoyable and those that you don't, and to consider which factors explain the difference.

Myles Downey writes:

> When I am coaching, whether it is a demonstration in public or a conversation in a client's office, I occasionally rise above my normal proficiency to another level of skill and insight where there is greater fluency and not a little joy. In Inner Game terms I am coaching from Self Two, a mental state that can be achieved in which one performs with excellence, where all one's faculties are available and where one's sensitivity is heightened. This is pure flow. (Downey, 2003)

Downey goes on to add that, 'In Self Two our observation is more acute, we pick up more of the messages and respond in an uninhibited and congruent manner.'

We noted earlier that a valuable way of reducing the inner thoughts that interfere with performance is to focus attention. By focusing attention, by simply noticing what is happening, you may enter this mental state of relaxed concentration that enables you to coach at your best.

An increasingly popular approach to this is the idea of mindfulness. Mindfulness is about being fully aware of what is happening – in your mind, in your body and all around you – while it's happening. It is about attending to what is going on here and now, rather than dwelling on what occurred in the past or worrying about the future.

Mindfulness is being used in a wide range of settings and for a variety of purposes. For example, in the health sector Mindfulness Based Stress Reduction (MBSR) is an approach to help people suffering from stress or chronic pain, and Mindfulness Based Cognitive Therapy (MBCT) is used to help patients with depression or anxiety related problems.

It is possible to learn the habit of mindfulness, and there are a growing number of books, courses and training materials available to help you develop. A key aspect is learning how to meditate. You may wish to use the mindfulness practice shown in Exercise 14.3 or find some other exercises to develop the habit of mindfully focusing your attention on what you are aware of in the here and now.

EXERCISE 14.3

A MINDFULNESS EXERCISE

Mark Williams and Danny Penman offer this one-minute meditation exercise that you might like to practise.

1. Sit erect in a straight-backed chair. If possible, bring your back a little way from the rear of the chair so that your spine is self-supporting. Your feet can be flat on the floor. Close your eyes or lower your gaze.
2. Focus your attention on your breath as it flows in and out of your body. Stay in touch with the different sensations of each in-breath and each out-breath. Observe the breath without looking for anything special to happen. There is no need to alter your breathing in any way.
3. After a while your mind may wander. When you notice this, gently bring your attention back to your breath, without giving yourself a hard time – the act of realising that your mind has wandered and bringing your attention back without criticising yourself is central to the practice of mindfulness meditation.
4. Your mind may eventually become calm like a still pond – or it may not. Even if you get a sense of absolute stillness, it may be only fleeting. If you feel angry or exasperated, notice that this may be fleeting too. Whatever happens, just allow it to be as it is.
5. After a minute, let your eyes open and take in the room again.

(Williams and Penman, 2011)

The importance of trust

A key to coaching from Self Two is trust. Tim Gallwey (2000) writes that, 'Perhaps the greatest benefit the Inner Game coach brings to the conversation is to trust clients more than the clients trust themselves. And having that trust in the client can be achieved only by having learned an increasingly profound trust in oneself.'

This issue of trust seems to me to be extremely important. To what extent do I trust the client to know, first, what is right for them and, second, to work out how to achieve this? To what extent do I trust myself to draw on my experience, intuition and care for the client to say or do what I need to say or do?

When I am coaching I also find it very helpful simply to trust the coaching process. If I find myself beginning to push for a solution, or starting to feel responsible for fixing things, or feeling under pressure to perform in some sense, I remind myself simply to trust the process, to be open to what is happening, and to wait to see what unfolds. This quietens my Self One and hopefully enables me to coach from Self Two.

Thus in coaching there are several aspects to trust. It is important that the client develops their trust in the coach. In addition, from the coach's point of view, you need to:

- Trust in the client to know what is right for them, and how they can achieve this
- Trust in yourself as the coach to draw on your experience and intuition to say or do what is required
- Trust in the coaching process – to let go of the desire to push for a solution or to fix things and, instead, to be open to what is unfolding in the conversation

Sometimes coaching is ineffective. Even a skilful coach, operating from Self Two, may at times be unable to help a client. While it is important for the coach to reflect on these occasions and to be open to learning about their coaching, it may be that the client wasn't in a place where they were ready to change. Gallwey (2000) offers some words of reassurance to the coach who might be prone in these instances to let their Self One criticise their ability. He writes that, 'Coaching cannot be done in a vacuum. If the learner doesn't want to learn, it doesn't make any difference if the coach is a great coach. Coaching is a dance in which the learner, not the coach, is the leader.'

PART THREE:
EXTENDING YOUR APPROACH

15

COGNITIVE AND COGNITIVE BEHAVIOURAL APPROACHES TO COACHING

Introduction

In Chapter 10 we looked at a number of tools you might use within a coaching session. Another thing you can do within a conversation is to introduce a model or framework to help your client to make sense of their situation. This may offer the client a fresh way of thinking about their circumstances and help to raise their awareness. You might then go on to explore what the client might do in response to their changed awareness.

You could regard working in this way as inviting the client to think and possibly behave differently. It reflects the basic coaching equation which we've looked at in earlier chapters:

Awareness + Responsibility = Performance

I think of this way of working as a cognitive approach. Offering the client a model to explore their situation is an example of working in Maria Iliffe-Wood's Emergent Coach mode, which we discussed in Chapter 13. In the first part of this chapter we shall consider three models that you might introduce into a coaching conversation to invite a client to think and behave differently.

There is, however, a much more comprehensive approach which takes ideas from the world of therapy and counselling and uses these systematically in a coaching context. Cognitive behavioural therapy (CBT) is based on the idea that our thoughts (or cognitions) affect our moods and feelings, on the one hand, and our actions and behaviour, on the other. Within the National Health Service, CBT is one of the preferred means of treatment for conditions such as anxiety and mild to moderate depression. In the second part of the chapter, we'll look at some of the key ideas that have been taken up within a cognitive behavioural approach to coaching.

In the final part of the chapter we shall discuss some of the key ideas in acceptance and commitment coaching. This seeks to help a client to accept rather than change unhelpful thoughts or feelings, and nevertheless to commit to action to achieve their goals.

Three concepts you might use in coaching

In this section we shall illustrate the use of models or frameworks by considering three that I myself regularly use with coaching clients. The three concepts are:

- Parent, Adult and Child ego states
- The Extravert–Introvert dimension of the Myers–Briggs Type Indicator
- The distinction between Urgent and Important tasks

Parent, Adult and Child ego states

In Chapter 12 we looked briefly at the idea of ego states. The concept comes from Transactional Analysis (TA), which is a psychological theory that seeks to explain how individuals think, feel, behave and interact with others, often in patterns that are repeated through life. Developed originally by an American, Eric Berne, TA uses a number of concepts that are expressed in simple and vivid language.

We develop our personality as we go through life, but much of it is shaped by our experiences in early childhood. Some aspects – our Child ego state – are like replays of how we ourselves behaved as young children seeking the love or approval of powerful figures in our lives, such as parents, older siblings or teachers. Other aspects of our personality – our Parent ego state – are based on feelings, attitudes and behaviours that we copied – or swallowed whole, as it were – from our parents or other authority figures. As we grow up we also integrate our experiences of healthy, cooperative relationships and of times when we coped well with difficulties – these emotional memories form our Adult ego state. Each of us spends time in and switches between these three psychological states – Parent, Adult and Child.

The Child and Parent ego states are subdivided in Transactional Analysis. When you were a young child you often had to adapt to the demands of your parents or carers. Later in life, when you are acting on the basis of these historic and often by now unconscious memories, you are in your Adapted Child ego state. However, when you were three or four years old you also spent time laughing, splashing water, playing with paint or glue or sand, and running around. When you are older you might somehow revert to these times, and you are then in your Free Child ego state.

If you find yourself in a conversation wagging your finger at the other person, speaking in a harsh tone, pointing out what they have done wrong and telling them how they should have behaved, then almost certainly you are in a Critical Parent ego state. However, when you were a young child your parents also looked after you and ensured that you were safe and well. When you find yourself years later looking to protect and look after one of your colleagues, then you may well have gone into a Nurturing Parent ego state.

The Adult ego state is not usually subdivided within TA. Thus there are five possible ego states – Critical Parent, Nurturing Parent, Adapted Child, Free Child and Adult.

One of the things which can happen in relationships is that we establish typical ways of interacting with one another. For example, the relationship between a manager and a subordinate may become one of mainly Parent–Child transactions. In general, however, an Adult–Adult relationship is more likely to be healthy and productive.

The key to breaking a pattern of unhelpful Parent–Child transactions is to consistently communicate from an Adult ego state and to continually invite the other party to operate from their Adult ego state. Note that there is no guarantee that the other party will respond from Adult state – all you can do is to remain in Adult yourself and keep inviting an Adult response. Changing such an established pattern of interactions may well be difficult, not least because it requires the other party to change their behaviour too.

There are a number of situations in coaching when I find it helpful to share the idea of Parent, Adult and Child ego states ideas with a client. A common one is when a client is working for a hard driving or even bullying manager. Such a manager is often operating from Critical Parent, and the client is responding from their Adapted Child. Framing the situation in this way raises the client's awareness of what is going on and how they are behaving. The challenge then for the client – and it may be a considerable one – is to respond differently by staying in their Adult ego state when their manager next addresses them from Parent.

Less frequently I find that it's my client who is unhelpfully adopting a Critical or Nurturing Parent ego state with one of their team whose refusal to take appropriate responsibility – which is Adapted Child behaviour – is hooking the client's Parent ego state. Once again the client's challenge is to remain in Adult and continually invite an Adult response from their team member.

A third example where the idea of ego states can be very helpful is in situations where someone is behaving passively when they would prefer to be assertive. Someone who behaves passively with another individual or in meeting situations is probably operating from an Adapted Child ego state. Encouraging them to explore how to operate from their Adult ego state is one way of identifying how they can behave more assertively and effectively.

The Extravert–Introvert dimension of the Myers–Briggs Type Indicator

The Myers–Briggs Type Indicator, or MBTI, is the most widely used personality questionnaire in the world. It was developed by two Americans, Katharine Briggs and her daughter, Isabel Briggs Myers, based on the psychological theories of Carl Jung. The underlying model proposes that each of us has an innate preference on four separate dimensions of personality.

I often introduce one of these four dimensions into a coaching session. I'll illustrate this by considering the Extravert–Introvert dimension, which is the one I share most often in coaching conversations.

This dimension refers to where someone gets their energy from and where they prefer to focus their attention. Extraverts are energised by being with other people whereas Introverts recharge their batteries, so to speak, by withdrawing into their inner world. For example, returning after a busy day at work to find a party going on at their home, an Extravert is likely to feel energised whereas an Introvert would rather have a quiet soak in the bath.

One way of caricaturing Extraverts and Introverts is that Extraverts speak first and maybe think later, whereas Introverts think first and maybe speak later.

I find that I introduce the Extravert–Introvert dimension mainly with Introverts and only occasionally with Extraverts. Being aware of their natural preference can enable an Introvert to modify their behaviour in meetings, for example. They may recognise that if they wait till they have fully thought through their position then the meeting will have moved on to another item and they have lost the chance to contribute. Hence they see the need to speak up sooner and more frequently in some situations.

The Extravert–Introvert distinction enables someone both to understand their own behaviour and to appreciate how other people behave. So, for example, an Extravert team leader may see the need consciously to create opportunities in team meetings for the more Introverted people – or perhaps those who are less experienced or confident – to contribute their ideas. Awareness of their own and other people's preferences on the Extravert–Introvert dimension of the MBTI can help the client to communicate or influence more effectively.

Urgent and important tasks

I sometimes invite a coaching client who is having difficulty managing their time effectively to make a list of the activities which make up their working week and then to put them into one of four boxes:

- Important and urgent
- Important and not urgent
- Not important and urgent
- Not important and not urgent

It is common to find that people view most of the things that they do as important. However, importance is a relative concept – some things are more important than others, and everything can't be top priority, by definition.

Having explored the distinction between urgent and important tasks, I suggest to the client that there are two basic things they need to do to manage their time:

- First, be clear about what their priorities are – that is, the things that are most important to them
- Second, spend their time in ways which reflect their priorities

This raises the question of who sets the priorities. While recognising that there may be real constraints on someone's freedom to choose their priorities, I think that ultimately the client is the decision maker about what their priorities are.

A very practical idea that often helps a client to spend their time on the important rather than the urgent can be summed up in the phrase *Schedule your priorities, don't prioritise your schedule.* Just because a meeting is in the diary or a task is on the to do list, that doesn't necessarily mean that it is important. On the other hand, putting things into the diary which are important but not urgent increases the likelihood that they will indeed invest time in these activities. A simple but highly effective technique is to book a meeting with themselves in their calendar. This might be time for planning or preparation or writing or simply thinking time. I encourage them to treat this meeting with themself as they would any other important meeting.

Cognitive behavioural coaching

We turn now to the more systematic use of a cognitive behavioural approach. Cognitive behavioural coaching has its origins in the therapeutic world. In his approach called Rational Emotive Behavioural Therapy Albert Ellis emphasised that our emotional response to an event is not caused by the event itself but by our beliefs about the event. And in Cognitive Therapy Aaron Beck highlighted the importance of our inner dialogue and its effect on our self-esteem.

The key idea that is central to a cognitive behavioural approach can be summarised in the words of the ancient Stoic philosopher Epictetus, who said that, 'People are disturbed not by things, but by the views which they take of them.'

Michael Neenan writes that:

What often blocks the way [to achieving their goals] are the coachee's self-limiting/defeating thoughts and beliefs (eg, 'I'm not good enough'), counterproductive behaviours (eg, procrastination) and troublesome emotions (eg, prolonged anxiety).

Cognitive behavioural coaching (CBC) helps coachees to identify, examine and change such thoughts and beliefs, develop productive behaviours and become more skilled at emotional management. (Neenan, 2006)

Helen Williams, Nick Edgerton and Stephen Palmer say that the main goals of CBC are to:

1. Facilitate the client in achieving their realistic goals
2. Facilitate self-awareness of underlying cognitive and emotional barriers to goal attainment
3. Equip the individual with more effective thinking and behavioural skills
4. Build internal resources, stability and self-acceptance in order to mobilise the individual to their choice of action
5. Enable the client to become their own self-coach. (Williams et al., 2010)

If we unpick these goals we can see that CBC needs to work at a number of levels. When coaching runs smoothly, the coach helps the client to clarify their goals and create plans to achieve these goals, and then the client goes off and implements these plans successfully. A behavioural approach, using the GROW model for example, might work well in this situation. 'There is no need to focus on psychological aspects if a simple problem-solving model will suffice' (Williams et al., 2010).

However, it is often the case that the client has some 'underlying cognitive and emotional barriers' which prevent them attaining their goals. The coach then needs to help the client to become more aware of these barriers and to develop their thinking or behaviour in order to overcome the barriers and successfully implement their action plan. Thus CBC is a twin-track approach, both practical and psychological. Michael Neenan writes:

The psychological track helps to remove the stumbling blocks to change such as procrastination, excessive self-doubt, indecisiveness, and self-deprecation, while the practical track assists coachees to develop an orderly sequence of goal-directed action steps. (Neenan, 2006)

As the work of the coaching progresses over time, the client develops not only new ways of thinking and behaving but also a new sense of self, enabling them in due course to become their own coach. 'The ultimate goal of CBC is for the coachee to become his or her own coach' (Neenan, 2006).

In her chapter in *Mastery in Coaching*, Helen Whitten writes that:

Changing thoughts, beliefs and behaviours requires hard work and reinforcement. I liken it to learning a new language – it takes repetition to build up a new vocabulary.

Similarly, changing habits requires repetition and can be uncomfortable. The neural pathways of mental and muscle reactivity have been well-trodden grooves for some time and, like driving a new car, helping clients 'reprogramme' their mind and body to respond in new ways can feel awkward at first. (Whitten, 2014)

In *The Psychology of Executive Coaching*, Bruce Peltier notes two cautions on using a cognitive approach:

First, not everyone seems to be able to notice the ways that they think. Their thinking styles, specific thoughts, and distortions are not readily available to them. Some of those clients can *learn* to access their own thinking, but others do not seem able to do this at all.

[Second] Many people feel insulted when their thinking is challenged. This is not hard to appreciate. Nobody really enjoys being told that the way they think is wrong. It is important to package cognitive methods in a positive frame ... and some form of positive rapport is an essential prerequisite. (Peltier, 2010)

In the following sections we shall look at some of the main ideas in the cognitive behavioural approach.

The ABCDE model

One of the key frameworks used in cognitive behavioural coaching is the ABCDE model, based on an approach originally devised by Albert Ellis.

A: Activating event

B: Beliefs and perceptions about this event

C: Consequences – cognitive, emotional, behavioural, physical or interpersonal

D: Disputing of self-limiting beliefs

E: Effective and new ways of thinking and behaving

The client reckons that some activating event, A, has caused or will cause the consequences, C. If an external event, A, really did cause C then there is little that can be done. Recall the words of Epictetus: 'People are disturbed not by things, but by the views which they take of them.' It is not A that causes C directly but rather it is the mental processing of A via the client's belief system, B, which leads to C.

When the client's beliefs, B, about A are irrational or unduly limiting or self-defeating, then the coach works to dispute, D, these unhelpful beliefs, seeking to help the client to develop new and more effective ways of thinking and behaving, E.

Let's illustrate this with an example. Suppose the client has an in-house interview in a few days' time for a job that they are well qualified for and which they'd really like to get. The upcoming job interview is the activating event.

The client is dreading the interview. They imagine becoming tongue-tied, stumbling to answer questions. They feel anxious, sleep badly, lose concentration at work and withdraw from some social situations – a raft of cognitive, emotional, behavioural, physical and interpersonal consequences.

Fortunately, they have a coaching session a few days before the interview with a cognitive behavioural coach. Through questioning, the coach helps the client to articulate the beliefs and perceptions that are relevant to the situation. Together they make the following notes about the client's thinking, which contains a number of unhelpful beliefs:

- I'm hopeless at interviews.
- There are bound to be better candidates than me.
- I don't deserve to get a job that I really want.
- If I don't get this job, then there's no future for me here.

The coach then helps the client to a more realistic statement of their position, which they capture as follows:

- While I do not enjoy interviews, I was recruited and subsequently promoted through interviews in this organisation. I can prepare as best I can and then give it my best shot on the day.
- There may be a more suitable candidate than me, and there is nothing I can do about that.
- I do deserve to get a job that I am qualified for, though there is no guarantee that I will.
- If I don't get this job, that will be unfortunate but other opportunities are bound to arise in the future.

As a result of this more realistic and helpful way of thinking, the candidate is able to relax, to prepare thoroughly, and to give a good account of themselves at the interview.

Performance interfering thoughts and self-limiting beliefs

In the above example the coach helped the client to identify and modify some of their performance interfering thoughts and self-limiting beliefs. Michael Neenan (2006) lists seven thinking traps which clients often fall into:

- All or nothing thinking – viewing events in either/or terms
- Overgeneralisation – drawing sweeping conclusions on the basis of a single incident or insufficient evidence
- Mental filter – only the negative aspects of a situation are noticed
- Catastrophising – assuming the worst and, if it occurs, your inability to deal with it
- Musts and shoulds – rigid rules that you impose on yourself and others
- Fallacy of fairness – believing in a just world
- Perfectionism – striving for standards that are beyond reach or reason

The cognitive behavioural coach will ask questions of the client, challenging their thinking and raising their awareness of how realistic their views and beliefs are. This technique is sometimes called Socratic questioning, after the ancient Greek philosopher Socrates. Typical questions might be:

- What is the evidence to support your assertion?
- How realistic is your belief?
- How often does this occur?
- If the thing you are concerned about did happen, what would be the impact?
- What are the pros and cons?
- Can you substitute I want to … for I should … ?

EXERCISE 15.2

DISPUTING PERFORMANCE INTERFERING THOUGHTS AND SELF-LIMITING BELIEFS

Think of a situation that you sometimes are in where you lack confidence, or of a situation that you deliberately avoid. Make a few notes to capture your thoughts on these aspects of the ABCDE model.

A: What is the situation?

B: What are your underlying thoughts or beliefs about this situation?

C: What are the possible consequences of being in this situation that concern you?

D: What is the evidence for and the evidence against the likelihood that these consequences will in fact happen?

E: What might you say to yourself or do differently to help you be more effective in this situation?

Imagery

There are a number of ways in which imagery can be used to help a client prepare and perform well. Gladeana McMahon (2010) describes an exercise to help a client increase their ability to deal with a challenging and potentially stressful situation. The client is asked to sit comfortably and then to imagine in lots of detail the difficult situation – the people, the room, the sights and sounds and smells, etc. The client then imagines some coping strategies they might use – such as the relaxation and breathing techniques described below. They then imagine using these to handle the challenging situation successfully. The degree of difficulty might then be increased – in the job interview example, for instance, the client might imagine how to deal with a particularly challenging interviewer. Working in this way – in the safety of a coaching session – affords the client a sense of emotional control over the challenging situation they are facing. They can then practise some more as part of a task assignment outside the coaching session.

Relaxation and breathing techniques

There are a variety of techniques that a cognitive behavioural coach might introduce to a client to help them to feel more calm and in control when they enter a potentially challenging and stressful situation. For these to be effective, the client needs to practise and become comfortable using them outside of the coaching sessions.

One approach to relaxation is to listen to a CD which takes you through a series of steps where you tense and then relax the different parts of your body, starting, for example, with your forehead and working down to your feet. The tape might last 20 minutes or so. If you do this regularly then you can develop the ability simply to tense and relax your muscles in a few seconds as you prepare to go into a potentially stressful situation.

Another approach is to do some deep breathing to help you relax. Simply take a long, slow breath in through your nose and then release this breath slowly out through your mouth, at the same time relaxing your shoulders. Do this three or four times, and repeat it at various points throughout the day. Once again, the idea is to practise this until you can call on it readily when you need to.

Task assignments

A cognitive behavioural coaching session will generally end with an agreement about what the client will do to practise new ways of thinking or behaving before the next session. Breaking long-established and unhelpful ways of thinking or changing beliefs that have arisen in childhood may take considerable effort sustained over time. The work of cognitive behavioural change is largely done outside of the coaching sessions, and requires commitment and persistence.

A cognitive behavioural coach will usually ensure that the tasks the client will do following the session are written down and agreed. Assignments are then reviewed at the start of the next session. The point of reviewing the task assignment is to identify what the client has learnt, not to determine success or failure.

Sometimes the task agreed is some kind of behavioural experiment. For example, a client in the example earlier in the chapter who is anxious about becoming tongue-tied at an interview might arrange a mock interview with a friend or colleague, and note what happens in this practice.

Some form of reinforcement – maybe a reminder on a Post-It note, keeping a journal, or asking a colleague to assist in some way – can be useful in carrying out assignments and in developing new habits.

Acceptance and commitment coaching

As we have seen, a cognitive behavioural approach seeks to help a client to change their thinking in order to operate more effectively. Acceptance and commitment coaching, in contrast, seeks to help a client to accept rather than change their thoughts and feelings, and nevertheless to commit to achieving their goals.

AC coaching is based on acceptance and commitment therapy, or ACT (which is pronounced *act* rather than *A. C. T.*). One way of summarising ACT is that it invites a client to focus on three areas:

- Accept your reactions and be present
- Choose a valued direction
- Take action

This section summarises some of the key ideas in AC coaching – it is based on a chapter by Tim Antiss and Rich Blonna in *Mastery in Coaching*. They write:

> Clients are guided and encouraged to notice the rise and fall of unpleasant thoughts and feelings, and to take these thoughts, feelings and sensations with them as they go about living the kind of life they want for themselves. AC coaches consider experiential avoidance – the struggle with unwanted thoughts and feelings, including attempts to control or suppress them – to be at the heart of many people's problems with living and the opposite of acceptance and psychological flexibility. (Antiss and Blonna, 2014)

We noted earlier the words of Epictetus which capture the essence of a cognitive behavioural approach: *People are disturbed not by things, but by the views which they take of them.* The essence of an AC approach might be summarised in these words: *People are disturbed not by things, nor by the views which they take of them. Rather, it is how they deal with things which shapes their quality of life and personal effectiveness.*

An AC coach will encourage a client to spend more time in contact with the present moment – to be mindful. 'Unhelpful and unwanted thoughts and images are commonly about the past or the future – not about what is happening in the immediate moment' (Antiss and Blonna, 2014). Four aspects of mindful moments are:

1. They focus on the present moment.
2. They are non-judgemental, accepting the present moment for what it is.
3. They are non-verbal. Adding speech to describe the present moment adds a level of interpretation and is one step removed from the here and now.
4. They are non-conceptual. During mindful moments nothing gets figured out, worked on, analysed, or solved. (Antiss and Blonna, 2014)

EXERCISE 15.3

UNHELPFUL AND UNWANTED THOUGHTS AND IMAGES

Identify a thought, belief, feeling or image that you sometimes have, one which isn't helpful and which tends to interfere with your performance or wellbeing. Write down in a sentence what this unhelpful thing is.

When this thought or feeling next occurs, simply notice this and focus your attention on what is happening in the moment.

- Focus on your breathing – notice your breath coming in and going out.
- Listen – pay attention to the sounds in the room, or from outside, or within yourself.

You might like to make some notes afterwards on what happened for you.

Three of the core concepts in AC coaching are experiential avoidance, workability and psychological flexibility.

Experiential avoidance

Much of what we experience inside our minds and bodies is unhelpful, unwanted, uncomfortable or painful. It is natural to want to avoid or reduce these experiences. This is experiential avoidance, and is considered the main issue which the client needs to focus on. Much of what the AC coach does is to help the client to reframe what needs to change.

> The AC coach helps the client to see that it is not their unwanted experiences per se that are the main cause of their frustration, difficulty, struggle or dissatisfaction, but rather the strategies and tactics they have been using to avoid or attempt to control or reduce these experiences, troubling thoughts and painful emotions. (Antiss and Blonna, 2014)

As an example, someone who feels sad or lonely in the evening may binge on food or consume too much alcohol to reduce these feelings.

Workability

Many clients will have tried – perhaps over many years – to address their issues, but the strategies they've adopted haven't worked, or perhaps worked briefly. The idea of 'workability' applies to beliefs as well as coping strategies. AC coaches are less interested in whether the client's beliefs are true, but 'whether their thoughts or beliefs are helpful to them living the valued life they want for themselves'. One technique here is to ask the client – with empathy and compassion rather than judgement – to what extent a thought, belief or action is helping them to achieve the life they want to lead.

In the example of the lonely person who is eating or drinking too much, this might have helped them to feel better in the evenings but at a cost to their health and wellbeing. An AC coach might ask them to consider how far their eating or drinking helps them to achieve what they really want from life.

Psychological flexibility

A lack of psychological flexibility is the main reason clients get stuck. An AC coach will seek to guide a client towards psychological flexibility in order to help them to:

- Live in harmony with their values
- Take effective actions towards their goals

- Distance themself from unhelpful thoughts
- Tolerate unpleasant feelings and sensations
- Pay attention to what is happening in the moment
- View the world from the perspective of an observing self

Returning to the example of the sad and lonely person, an AC coach would seek to help the client to recognise and accept these feelings, to choose how much food or alcohol they wish to consume, and to commit to a routine that achieves this. The coach would use 'a mixture of psychological education, metaphor, experiential exercises, Socratic methods, modelling of helpful attitudes and behaviours, practice assignments, goal setting, reflection and feedback' to help the client eat or drink less when they are on their own of an evening.

EXERCISE 15.4

INTEGRATING IDEAS INTO YOUR COACHING PRACTICE

Look back on the ideas explored in the three sections of this chapter.

- Which ideas might you use or modify in your own coaching practice?
- What specifically will you seek to do?

16

OTHER APPROACHES TO COACHING

Introduction

In the previous chapter we looked at cognitive behavioural and at acceptance and commitment approaches to coaching. In this chapter we look at some of the key ideas and techniques in three other approaches to coaching:

- Solution-focused coaching
- Neuro-linguistic programming
- Gestalt

All of these approaches are used by practising coaches, either as their main method or as part of a more eclectic or integrative style of working. If you find that one of these approaches particularly appeals to you, then I encourage you to find out more about it. Alternatively, you might find that one or two ideas from an approach seem useful and worth weaving into your practice. And the third possibility is that you don't consider the approach at all relevant or valuable to you. The choice is, of course, up to you.

Solution-focused coaching

Solution-focused therapy was developed by, among others, Steve de Shazer and Insoo Kim Berg who were working in the 1980s as family therapists in the Brief Therapy

Center in Milwaukee. They observed that their client families could easily become locked into unproductive arguments about what the problem was and who was to blame. They found that when they asked the families instead to focus on what they wanted to achieve and on the times when things were better, they made far more and faster progress. Since then the approach has been used in a variety of therapeutic and counselling settings, and has been taken up by coaches.

Here are some of the key characteristics of solution-focused coaching.

- **A focus on solutions rather than problems, and on the future rather than the present or the past**

A solution-focused coach is prepared to listen as the client talks about problems or things that happened in the past. This may help to build rapport with the client, and moving the client on too quickly may alienate them. However, the solution-focused coach will not want to dwell there, and will continually be looking to move the conversation on to explore solutions or to consider things that the client did successfully in the past when faced with a similar situation.

- **Use of the client's expertise and resources**

A solution-focused coach takes the view that the client is the expert about their own life. Clients understand their own hopes and fears, and know what has worked for them in the past and what they are prepared to do in the future. A couple of maxims that are useful for the client here are:

- If it works keep doing it.
- If it doesn't work stop doing it and do something else.

And a useful question to ask the client is some version of:

- What's the difference that makes the difference?

- **A focus on action, on clear goals, on positive change**

A solution-focused coach works with the expectation that positive change will occur, and will help the client to define clear and specific goals which can be stated in behavioural terms. The coach will also expect the client to work on their goals outside of the coaching session. They also reckon that change can often be achieved in a short space of time, which is in contrast to some approaches which rely on in-depth analysis and insight.

- **Use of reframing**

A solution-focused coach will try to help the client see the glass as half full rather than half empty, as the saying goes. Encouraging the client to focus on times when they've performed well or on their progress so far may enable them to see things in new and more positive and helpful ways.

- **A non-pathological approach**

A solution-focused coach does not regard a problem as an indication that the client is dysfunctional or ill, and does not spend time trying to diagnose an illness or find the root cause of a problem.

- **A collaborative, respectful relationship**

A solution-focused coach aims to build a relationship with their client which is both respectful and collaborative. The coach views the client as resourceful, capable of setting personal goals and of identifying ways of achieving these goals that will work for them.

I think these ideas fit very easily into the type of primarily non-directive coaching that we've been exploring in the book. I sometimes find it very helpful when a client has described a problematic situation simply to ask them if they can recall an occasion when they were able to behave as they would like to in this situation. Often they can, and we then explore what they could translate from their previous experience to the current context. For example, imagine you have a client who finds it difficult to speak up in team meetings. You might invite them to revisit in detail times when they were articulate in meetings, encouraging them to identify what they did that was helpful. This may enable them to identify for themself practical things – for instance, preparing well or asking a question early in the proceedings – that they can do to help themself to speak effectively at their next team meeting.

We shall now look at some of the tools that a solution-focused coach might use in a coaching session. These tools can readily be used or modified in other approaches to coaching too.

Scaling

The idea of scaling is simple, flexible and potentially very useful in coaching. We discussed it previously in Chapter 10. The coach simply asks the client to rate something on a scale of 1 to 10, and then goes on to explore with the client their self-assessment. An example of a scaling question is: *On a scale of 1 to 10, how clear are you about what success in this project looks like – where 10 means totally clear and 1 means not at all clear?*

Between-session assignments

Carrying out assignments between sessions is a potentially vital way in which the client can do the work they need to do in order to make the changes they seek. This helps to develop their capacity for self-directed learning. As we discussed in the previous chapter, assignments are also often used in cognitive behavioural coaching.

Within the coaching session the client articulates the goal they are seeking and identifies actions that they can take to achieve their goal. Outside the session they attempt to carry out these actions, monitoring and evaluating their success. They continue to do what is working and change what is not working.

One of the things I sometimes invite a client to do combines scaling and between-session assignments. As an illustration, I was working with a client who wished to be a better listener in meetings at work. I asked them to rate themself after meetings on a scale of 1 to 10 on how well they thought they'd listened during that meeting. I also asked the client to keep a simple record of their ratings to gauge whether their listening was improving over time. This helped them to become more aware of the quality of their listening, which in turn enabled them to listen to understand more often than they listened to disagree.

The miracle question

The miracle question, originally devised by Steve de Shazer and his colleagues, is intended to help the client to bypass problem talk and focus on how things would be if they had successfully implemented a solution. Bill O'Connell and Stephen Palmer describe its standard form:

> Imagine one night when you are asleep, a miracle happens and the problems we've been discussing disappear. Since you are asleep, you do not know that a miracle has happened. When you wake up what will be the first signs for you that a miracle has happened? (O'Connell and Palmer, 2007)

The timing of when to ask the miracle question is important. If the client is still exploring the problem, asking it too early may confuse the client, be ineffective and possibly damage the coaching relationship. Asking the miracle question when the client is focused on solutions and action is far more likely to engage them and produce useful ideas.

Some clients, even when in solution mode, don't like the wording of the miracle question or resist even the idea of a miracle. There are alternatives to the miracle question that the coach might ask, such *as If you could wave a magic wand and make things exactly as you'd like them to be, what would that look and feel like?*

One way in which I use a version of the miracle question is to ask the client to describe – or perhaps to draw a rich picture of – how things would be if everything worked out as they would like it to in relation to the issue they've been exploring.

When a solution-focused approach might not be appropriate

Michael Cavanagh and Anthony Grant write that:

> Of course, there are times when the solution-focused approach is not appropriate. Some clients may have causal stories about their situation which form a central and protected part of their worldview. Similarly, when clients have deeply felt needs to explore aetiology, attempting then to shoe-horn them into a methodology that feels incongruent is likely to be counterproductive. ... To force a solution-focused perspective onto an unwilling client runs counter to the core principle of respecting the client. (Cavanagh and Grant, 2010)

Bill O'Connell and Stephen Palmer note that a solution-focused coaching might not work with clients who:

- Are temporarily unable to tap into their resources
- Are looking for a 'quick fix' and are unwilling to put any effort into achieving the changes desired
- Have such poor levels of self-esteem that they are unable to appreciate their strengths and qualities
- Want a deeper understanding of the roots of their problem
- Want the coach to be directive and a problem-solver. (O'Connell and Palmer, 2007)

EXERCISE 16.1

A MIRACLE QUESTION

Imagine that you wake up one morning and you are coaching in a setting and in a style that is exactly as you'd like it to be. Describe in detail where you are, who you're with, what you're doing, and how you feel.

Neuro-linguistic programming

Neuro-linguistic programming, or NLP, is an approach to personal change based on the premise that there are crucial connections between:

- What is happening in a person's brain and body ('neuro')
- How they are communicating ('linguistic') – both verbally and non-verbally, and
- The patterns of behaviour they have learnt from their experiences ('programming')

Developed originally in the US in the 1970s by Richard Bandler and John Grinder, NLP assumes that the words, facial expressions and body language of an individual reflect their inner, subconscious beliefs and perceptions. If the client's beliefs and perceptions are inaccurate or limiting, this will cause problems in how they behave. An NLP therapist or coach carefully observes the client's verbal and non-verbal communications, and uses their observations to help a client to remodel their thinking so that they can behave in ways which help them to be more healthy, effective and successful.

In this section we'll look at some of the key ideas in NLP that you might use in coaching.

Building rapport

Bruce Grimley writes that:

> Before the NLP coach does anything with the client, rapport needs to be obtained. Rapport tells your client you understand their map of the world at a very deep level; only when they believe this will they give you 'permission' to lead them to their outcome. (Grimley, 2007)

One way in which a coach can build rapport is by **matching** the **representational system** of the client. Each of us represents the world to ourself through our five senses. For example, some people think and speak mainly in terms of **visual** images. A client who speaks using terms such as *perspective, view, clear picture, looking to the future, hindsight,* etc. is probably also using visual language in their thinking. If the coach adopts visual language when speaking to such a client, they are likely to build rapport more quickly with them.

Another client might have a preference for **auditory** terms – for example, they might use phrases such *as I hear what you're saying* or *it sounds like … .* The NLP coach will, to build rapport, seek to *tune into* their way of thinking. A **kinaesthetic** client might *feel out of touch* with reality, have a *gut feeling* that things are wrong, or feel that the conversation is only *scratching the surface*.

NLP suggests that a client's eye movements give clues to how they are thinking. So, for example, when a client looks up and to their right they are likely to be thinking visually and also to be constructing a new mental picture – perhaps of future possibilities – rather than simply remembering an image. A client looking horizontally and to their left will probably be recalling sounds from their past. While there are typical patterns, it is important that the coach seeks to observe carefully and **calibrate** their observations to each individual client.

Since NLP presupposes that the mind and the body are part of the same system, another way in which a coach can gain rapport is to match the body language of the client. You might observe this occurring naturally in a bar or restaurant by watching how when two people are in conversation they will often mirror the body language of one another.

A related notion is the idea of **pacing**. For example, if a client uses abstract words and talks mainly about the future then the coach who feeds back to the client in a similar fashion is pacing the client's way of thinking.

If the coach has successfully built rapport with the client through matching and pacing, and if the coach has established what the client is seeking to achieve, they may go on to **leading** the client. As an illustration, imagine that you have a client who is looking to find a new job in a different organisation. In response to your question about what they would find satisfying in a different role, they respond by telling you lots of things that they don't like in their current job and organisation. If you have successfully built rapport with them, you can more easily lead them to focus instead on the positive things that they are seeking in a new role and organisation.

EXERCISE 16.2

REPRESENTATIONAL SYSTEMS

If you glance through this book, you will see that I often use words and phrases that are visual – there are two examples in this sentence.

Think of the language that you typically use in conversation and in writing. Do you tend to use words and phrases that are visual, auditory or kinaesthetic?

Now think of a few people whom you know well. Which representational system does each of these people generally use? If you're not sure, you might like to listen carefully to their speech when you're next in conversation with them.

Well-formed outcomes

In all approaches to coaching it is important to establish what the client is seeking to achieve. NLP uses the notion of a well-formed outcome. Ian McDermott (2006) considers two key questions that an NLP coach will ask their client:

1. What do you want?
2. How would you know if you got it?

He says of the first question:

> Even in its simplest form it has extraordinary power. If you have been grappling with some problem this question will take you from the present state to the desired state. As you begin detailing what it is that you want, you make it more vivid. This has neurophysiological consequences. So often when coachees begin to focus on what they're really going for their state changes in palpably observable ways. (McDermott, 2006)

The second question encourages the client to become more specific in detailing how they will know if they have been successful. Depending on the client's representational system, the coach might ask them what they will see, hear, feel – or even smell or taste – when they have achieved their outcome.

Another aspect of a well-formed outcome is that it is stated in positive terms. If the client states their desired outcome in negative terms – *I don't want ...* – this creates an unconscious psychological barrier to achieving what they wish. A well-formed outcome has similarities to the well-known idea of a SMART objective – that is, one that is Specific, Measurable, Achievable, Relevant and Time-bounded. A well-formed outcome also needs to be aligned with the client's beliefs, values and identity.

Anchors

The mental and physiological state that you are in can have a profound effect on how you perform. Imagine turning up for a job interview or a game of tennis when you have flu – it's most unlikely that you'll do as well as you would normally do. You also carry around memories and associations from past events. Perhaps a particular song reminds you of the first time you fell in love. Maybe the sound of an electric drill takes you back to feeling anxious at the dentist'. Or you might associate the smell of newly mown grass with games lessons at school – which for some people will be a happy memory and for others an unpleasant one.

An **anchor** is simply a stimulus that generates a physiological response. These occur naturally in all of us, as the examples in the previous paragraph illustrate. Television commercials use appealing images, attractive people or popular songs to create a positive association in our minds with the product being advertised. Associations may also have been established through some kind of deliberate conditioning. In a classic case study Ivan Pavlov trained dogs to salivate at the sound of the bell which signalled the arrival of their food.

You can create an anchor to help a coaching client – or perhaps yourself – to access a resourceful state that will help them to perform well. As an illustration, I was working with a client who was anxious about giving presentations, which were something they had to do from time to time in their role. The client wanted to feel more confident as they stepped up to talk. I asked them to think back to a time when they did feel confident and gave a really good presentation. When they'd identified an occasion, I encouraged them to remember in detail what they saw in the conference room, to recall what they heard, and to describe how they were feeling. When they were immersed in their memories of this confident occasion, I asked them to come up with some words or images or simple physical actions that they could associate with feeling confident when presenting. They were able to anchor this confident state with the action of clasping their hands together and saying to themself the phrase *I'm good at this*. This gave them an anchor that they could access easily any time they stood up to present.

In the next chapter we look at a related idea in NLP, that of **collapsing anchors**.

NLP is like Marmite

Marmite is a food spread made from yeast extract which was invented by accident in 1902. It has a very distinctive flavour – some people love it, some people hate it, and some people have never tried it. Unilever, who produce Marmite, use the phrase *Love it or hate it* as a marketing slogan for the product.

NLP is like Marmite. I know people whom I respect in the world of coaching and management development who find NLP a very useful part of their tool box. And I know others who are scathing of NLP, regarding it as a pseudoscience and perhaps even a quasi-religion. They accuse Bandler and Grinder of taking three words which sound scientific – neuro, linguistic and programming – and putting them together to create their own psychological principles.

Although NLP has been around since the 1970s, there is little if any scientifically robust evidence to support the claims made by its practitioners. There are more reviews that have failed to find evidence for the assumptions or effectiveness of NLP.

Gestalt

Gestalt coaching evolved from its use in therapy and counselling where it was developed by Frederick 'Fritz' Perls and others in the 1950s and 1960s. The German word *Gestalt* has no exact equivalent in English. It embraces notions such as shape, form, configuration, pattern, whole. To form a Gestalt is to complete a pattern. This section considers some of the key ideas in Gestalt and how they might be used in coaching.

The three defining principles of Gestalt

There are three philosophical principles that are fundamental to Gestalt therapy, counselling and coaching – phenomenology, field theory and dialogue. Let's unpick what each of these three terms means.

- Phenomenology

Phenomenology is concerned with the study of objects and events as we perceive them. Julie Allan and Alison Whybrow write that, 'Phenomenology is the practice of seeking to understand situations through reference to the immediately obvious in-the-present phenomena.' They go on to say that:

> In a coaching setting, the coachee may expect the coach to pay detailed attention to the feelings, physical movements and postures and so forth that actually occur within the session and enquire into them or reflect them back. Gestalt coaching is lively and alive because the coach will always be seeking to uncover what has to be changed right here and now in this room so that change can happen effectively outside it and at another time. (Allan and Whybrow, 2007)

To focus on what is immediately present without interpretation or bias, the therapist needs to set aside – or bracket – their assumptions, prejudices and theories. This bracketing of preconceptions helps the therapist to encounter each client as they present themself uniquely at a particular time and place.

- Holism and field theory

Fritz Perls developed his ideas on human functioning from the work of Gestalt psychologists who studied how people organise their perceptions and experiences to make sense of the world. One key idea is the notion of **figure and ground**. When you look at the image in Figure 16.1 you will at some times see two faces and at other times a candlestick. When one is figure, the other is background.

Figure 16.1   A candlestick?

Julie Allan and Alison Whybrow write that:

> A Gestalt psychological view is that what we see and how we perceive things is not an objective reality but the result of who we are at one moment in time. What makes sense (becomes figure) in a particular context (ground) changes momentarily. In an attempt to organise the dynamic complexity of experience, we tend to arrange things in a way that makes sense according to our current thinking, prior experience or preoccupations. We are also predisposed to look for symmetry and equilibrium or 'closure'. (Allan and Whybrow, 2007)

Perls also drew on Kurt Lewin's idea of field theory. Each of us exists within a wider context or field, and we understand ourself in relation to that field. Marion Gillie describes how the totality of a person's context – their phenomenological field – includes their immediate situation, personal history, thoughts, feelings, conscious and unconscious beliefs, anxieties and fears, memories of past experiences, hopes and aspirations. In any situation what stands out for us, what we notice, what we hear, what we assume (i.e. what becomes *'figural'*) is a function of many things that are unique to us (Gillie, 2011).

One important consequence for coaching is that the coach is inevitably part of the client's field, which underlines the importance of the coach–client relationship.

- **Dialogue**

The philosopher Martin Buber distinguished between **I–Thou** interactions in which two people engage with each other in open, mutually respectful ways without seeking to impose their will on the other person, and **I–It** interactions where one or both parties treats the other as some kind of object to be shaped or manipulated. Much everyday conversation is appropriately of the I–It variety, perhaps involving the passing on of information, for example. I–Thou interactions are more intimate and intense, and so much less common. People engaged in I–Thou interactions will frequently slip back into I–It interacting.

Petruska Clarkson writes that:

> Gestalt recognises that from the first encounter onwards, client and counsellor exchange many moments of recognition of each other's real humanity. It is here that there is the most fertile ground for Gestalt work. (Clarkson, 1989)

The relationship between coach and client is important in all approaches to coaching, but it is especially important when the coach is working from a Gestalt perspective.

We look now at some of the other key ideas in a Gestalt approach that you might wish to integrate into your own coaching practice.

Awareness and response-ability

Julie Allan and Alison Whybrow say that:

> The goal of Gestalt coaching is to enable coachees to fully engage with their experiences (of themselves, others, their context …) in such a way that they are able to generate and carry forward what they want to be doing in a beneficial and satisfying manner. Awareness is key. (Allan and Whybrow, 2007)

In Gestalt, awareness is much more than being conscious of what is going on around you. Rather it means being fully present, tuning into whatever is most important for you at this moment. It is more like the total absorption that a child might bring to play rather than half-heartedly watching a television programme that you are vaguely interested in.

Allan and Whybrow go on to say that:

> The process of Gestalt coaching is to work to sharpen individual experience, to become aware of our assumptions and stereotypes and to challenge them in order to see what is taking place more clearly and therefore respond to what is actually happening, not what we think is happening. (Allan and Whybrow, 2007)

This sharpened awareness thus helps the client to respond differently. Gestalt very much takes the existential view that each individual is responsible for their own decisions and actions – or indecisions and inactions. The Gestalt approach reflects the basic equation that we've considered at various points in the book:

Awareness + Responsibility = Performance

In Gestalt the word *responsibility* is sometimes recast as *response-ability*. Our ability to respond arises from our awareness.

Unfinished business

Gestalt is a humanistic approach which believes that people are striving to achieve what they need and want – in other words, to self-actualise. However, blocks can get in the way to prevent them doing this. For example, an individual may have needs which they aren't fully aware of, or they may know what they want but are unable to take action to achieve this, or they take action which is unsuccessful in meeting their needs or goals. Gestalt uses the notion of **unfinished business** to describe a situation when we are unable to satisfy our needs.

Unfinished business reflects an incomplete Gestalt. This may reflect a current need – perhaps we are hungry and unable to eat just now. Or it may reflect experiences from the past – for example, the needs we had as infants that weren't satisfactorily met, or a bereavement that we haven't fully come to terms with, or the bullying we experienced at school but did not talk about. And this kind of unfinished business – this inability to obtain **closure** – consumes psychological and emotional energy.

An individual may repress memories and feelings out of awareness. Or they might hold a belief or way of thinking – for example, feeling inadequate or needing to please others – that arose originally from gaining closure in a distorted or pathological way. Or they might lock in their unmet needs in some physical manifestation such as shallow breathing or a tight posture or a repetitive gesture, which may become apparent in a therapy or coaching session. In these cases, some kind of closure was obtained but in an inappropriate way that did not properly or fully satisfy the original need.

A Gestalt coach will seek to help their client to obtain closure in order to satisfactorily deal with outstanding unfinished business.

A question that I sometimes ask a client when they seem to be hindered by past experiences is *What do you need to let go of?* It's important that the relationship is strong enough so that the client hears the question as an invitation rather than a judgement.

Working in the 'here and now'

One of the important ways in which a Gestalt therapist or counsellor or coach will work with a client is by attending to what is happening here and now in the room. Since the client's awareness is key, the coach invites the client to focus on the thoughts, images, feelings and bodily sensations that they are experiencing in the moment. This may help the client to be more fully in **contact** with whatever is most significant for them at that point in time.

Petruska Clarkson writes that:

> The quality of contact determines whether life 'passes by' or is lived and experienced to the full. ...

> Healthy contact is characterised by this whole-hearted and full-bodied engagement with that which is most significant for the person at a given moment. (Clarkson, 1989)

Note that a Gestalt practitioner will not seek to interpret or pass judgement on what they observe in the client. They might invite the client to exaggerate a gesture or to repeat something they have said to encourage them to gain greater clarity about what has emerged. This may then enable the client to become more fully aware, to move forwards and gain some measure of resolution.

Moreover, what happens in the coaching session is regarded as representative of how the client behaves more generally in the world. Each moment in the session can be regarded as a hologram for the client's life.

Another way in which a Gestalt coach might work with 'here and now' phenomena is to point out to the client what is happening for themself in the session. We looked at this in Chapter 13 on the use of self in coaching. As an illustration, imagine that your client is describing a challenging situation they are facing. You realise that you yourself have begun to feel somewhat anxious and you notice too that your shoulders are tense. You might share this with your client, without interpreting what it means but rather inviting the client to consider what it could mean.

In my own practice I sometimes become aware of an image or metaphor that comes into my head as I listen to the client. I then have a choice whether or not to share this. If I do, I offer my thoughts tentatively, without interpretation or suggesting what they might signify. Sharing with a client what is going on for you as the coach calls for sensitivity and requires that the relationship with the client is established securely.

Experimenting

As well as working in the 'here and now', a Gestalt coach might also use experiments in their work with a client. The coach encourages the client to try out new thoughts or actions within the safety of the coaching relationship.

We described one way of experimenting – the use of the empty chair – in Chapter 10. I used this recently with a client whose key challenge was that their manager was treating them unfairly and unreasonably. I invited the client to sit in another chair and then asked them some questions to answer from their manager's perspective. This helped them to appreciate what was important for their manager, and they were then able to use this awareness to decide how they would interact differently with their boss.

Here is an experimenting exercise that you might use with a client who is talking about the team that they lead or are a member of. Give the client a bowl of pebbles of different sizes, textures and colours. Ask them to choose individual pebbles to represent each team member, including themself, and place them on the table or the floor to represent where they see each individual. You can then explore with the client the thoughts and feelings that have led them to choose the particular pebbles and to place people where they did.

There are many possibilities for experimenting, and it is important that the coach is sensitive to the style, needs and comfort level of the client. It is important too to gain the client's consent before setting up an experiment, and not to stray into therapeutic territory if you are using it in a coaching context.

When a Gestalt approach might not be appropriate

Peter Bluckert notes that the Gestalt method may be countercultural for some clients. He writes:

> Executives may be sceptical of it and impatient to see proof. If they don't see it quickly they can lose interest and commitment. Some managers and leaders operating in fast-paced, numbers-driven business environments may not be the natural client group for Gestalt coaching. Awareness-focused work may seem just too slow for them. (Bluckert, 2010)

Similarly, Julie Allan and Alison Whybrow write that:

> Gestalt approaches might not appeal to or be chosen by those people who would like a more gap-analysis based and/or cognitive-behavioural approach rather than an overtly holistic, systemic approach. (Allan and Whybrow, 2007)

EXERCISE 16.3

INTEGRATING IDEAS INTO YOUR COACHING PRACTICE

Look back on the ideas from solution-focused coaching, NLP and Gestalt described in this chapter.

- Which of these approaches would you like to investigate in much more detail?
- Which of these approaches do not appeal to you?
- Which ideas from any of the approaches might you use or modify to use within your own coaching practice?

17

SUPPORTING CONFIDENCE AND MOTIVATION

Introduction

One of the hardest challenges in coaching is to help a client for whom a lack of confidence or self-esteem prevents them from achieving their goals and aspirations.

Throughout this book we have summarised what you're trying to do as a coach in the equation:

Awareness + Responsibility = Performance

While this equation can take you a long way in coaching, it might be modified for situations when the client's lack of confidence stops them from taking action. There are times when a client is both aware of what they need to do and also keen to take responsibility to make things happen, but somehow fear or lack of confidence means that they don't act. On these occasions, when awareness and responsibility aren't enough, you could extend the equation to read:

Awareness + Responsibility + Confidence = Performance

In this chapter we look at a number of ways a coach may be able to help a client to overcome their lack of confidence and behave effectively. We begin by considering a client's motivation to be coached. We then look at how you might use some ideas from the approaches discussed in the previous two chapters to enable the client to think, feel and act differently and more successfully. We then discuss the notion that each of us is a community of selves, which you might use to help the client identify which self they wish to be in a challenging situation.

A related but different issue is working with a client who wishes to change but is held back by a lack of motivation or by some form of ambivalence. In the second part of the chapter we explore Motivational Interviewing, an approach which seeks to help someone ambivalent about changing their behaviour to find the motivation within themselves to change.

Issues of confidence, low self-esteem or lack of motivation often run very deep within a client. For some clients their lack of confidence is so profoundly ingrained that it may require referral to a therapist or counsellor to help them resolve this – and even this deeper level of intervention might not be effective in some cases. As a coach it is vital that you are clear about the level of intensity at which you can operate safely, ethically and effectively.

Motivation to be coached

A concern that many learner coaches, and some experienced coaches and mentors, sometimes have is that a client doesn't seem really to be fully engaged in or committed to coaching. Perhaps they turn up for a session without having any issues to work through, or maybe they agree some action steps but fail to carry these out before the next session. The coach or mentor may question themself and their ability.

In Chapter 14 we noted Tim Gallwey's observation that, 'If the learner doesn't want to learn, it doesn't make any difference if the coach is a great coach' (Gallwey, 2000). And in Chapter 12 we noted the view of Erik de Haan that the most important factor affecting the outcome of coaching is the client, including how committed the client is to being coached.

There may be occasions when the client is ambivalent about being coached. Geoff Pelham writes:

> there are many situations where coachees may not have freely chosen the coaching, perhaps because they think it is politic to 'go along' with the offer, or more subtly because coaching is part of a 'package', such as a leadership development programme, and has not been an explicit choice. The research would suggest that checking coachee motivation to ensure that there is real 'buy-in' is of paramount

importance at the beginning, and that there is a sense of active collaboration throughout the work. (Pelham, 2016)

Agreeing a clear contract – perhaps a three-way contract involving the sponsor from the organisation – may help here.

There may be other reasons or concerns that a client has which makes them unwilling to engage in coaching. And it could be that the coach is failing to create a sufficient amount of rapport and trust for the client to feel able to open up and explore issues or challenges.

Some ideas from different approaches

•   **Using the ABCDE model to dispute self-limiting thoughts and beliefs**

In Chapter 15 we summarised the ABCDE model where a cognitive behavioural coach disputes (D) the irrational or self-limiting beliefs (B) which are preventing a client from acting successfully:

A: Activating event

B: Beliefs and perceptions about this event

C: Consequences – cognitive, emotional, behavioural, physical or interpersonal

D: Disputing of self-limiting beliefs

E: Effective and new ways of thinking and behaving

As an illustration, let's suppose that you have a client who is afraid of flying and so unable to take a Mediterranean holiday even though they very much wish to. Exploring their thoughts and beliefs about flying might reveal that the client believes that air transport is inherently dangerous and it is likely that any plane in which they are travelling will crash. Moreover, they reckon that these days there is a significant risk of a terrorist attack on planes. They are worried too that if they went on a plane they would panic, lose control and create an embarrassing scene.

You might challenge their views on how dangerous it is to fly in a commercial aeroplane, which is in many ways safer than driving a car. You could share statistics which show that it's very unlikely to be in a plane crash and even less likely to be caught up in a terrorist incident. You might also assist them to master some relaxation techniques, and use imagery to help them envisage coping successfully with events such as boarding the plane, take off and the possibility of turbulence. These are some of the things – along with detailed technical information about flying and the opportunity to take an actual flight – that are covered in programmes offered by airlines to help people overcome a fear of flying.

In *Coaching Presence*, Maria Iliffe-Wood suggests that it is sometimes easier for the coach rather than the client to notice when assumptions or beliefs may be getting in the client's way. She recommends bringing this to the client's attention, encouraging them 'to consider what is stopping them from going forward and whether this still holds true for them now that they've considered it. Sometimes it's not enough to realize it logically – it needs to be felt too' (Iliffe-Wood, 2014).

This cognitive behavioural approach will help some clients to overcome their fear, particularly if you yourself believe in and have mastered the technique. However, if the client's fears are firmly entrenched it may be necessary for them to work at a deeper level with a therapist or counsellor.

- **Moving from a Child to an Adult ego state**

In the Chapter 15 we looked at the idea from Transactional Analysis of Parent, Adult and Child ego states. An example of when you might use this model is with a client who behaves passively when they would prefer to be assertive and whose passive behaviour arises from a lack of confidence. Explain the Parent–Adult–Child model to them, and help them to explore which ego state they are in at times when they are behaving passively. It is often the case that they are operating from an Adapted Child ego state. You can then ask them to consider how they might operate from their Adult ego state and thereby think, feel and act more confidently and effectively. You could also go on to invite them to rehearse speaking and behaving assertively in a simulation with you of the situation that they face.

- **Using the client's expertise to construct a solution**

Another possibility is to use a solution-focused approach, taking the view that the client knows what has worked for them in the past. You can invite the client to identify a time when they did well and felt confident – if possible when faced with a similar situation – and encourage them to focus on the things they did well. You can invite them to transfer behaviours they successfully deploy in one context to another. Not only might this help them to behave effectively, but translating their own ideas into successful actions might also build their confidence in a form of virtuous circle where a degree of confidence leads to achievement which in turn enhances confidence.

As an illustration, I recall working with a client whose lack of confidence was preventing them from contributing effectively in meetings. I asked them to think of a situation where they did feel confident and were able to perform well. They were in fact an accomplished singer who took the lead in fairly prestigious amateur musicals. I encouraged them to recall in detail the feelings and thoughts they had before a performance, and invited them to work out how they could get into that frame of mind as they sat down at team meetings.

EXERCISE 17.1

FOCUSING ON A SOLUTION

Think of a situation that you yourself encounter where a lack of confidence or inability to behave assertively prevents you from obtaining the outcome you want. On a scale of 1 to 10, how satisfied are you with your performance?

Now think of another situation where you behave confidently and effectively. On a scale of 1 to 10, how satisfied are you with your performance in that context?

- What is the difference that makes the difference?
- What ways of thinking and behaving can you translate from the successful situation to the problematic one?

Try this out when you are next in the problematic situation, notice what happens, and rate your performance on the same scale from 1 to 10.

EXERCISE 17.2

WHAT DRIVES YOU TO SUCCEED?

In *The Coach's Casebook,* Geoff Watts and Kim Morgan (2015) offer this powerful coaching question to tap into a client's self-knowledge:

- Think about times when you have been successful and have achieved what you wanted. In those situations, what was driving you?

As an exercise, write down some notes to answer this question for yourself.

- **Reframing**

Helping a client to see their situation differently may enable them to shift their thinking and their behaviour. In *The Coach's Coach*, Alison Hardingham writes that, 'Reframing is changing the meaning of something by putting it in a different context.' She offers as an illustration the example of a mother of a teenage son who argues with everything she says. She regards this as having no respect for her, and feels angry. A friend suggests that the boy may be trying to find some independence as he goes through adolescence, which helps her to feel compassion rather than anger. Hardingham writes that, 'Often when we are stuck, a reframe will help us to move forward.' She also makes the point that, 'Reframes that don't speak to people's underlying values, beliefs and motives won't work' (Hardingham, 2004).

- **Motivation 'away from' and motivation 'towards'**

There are times when your motivation is to avoid a situation, to move away from it. For example, you might have an unreasonable and unpleasant boss, and you decide to look for a new job to get away. At other times your motivation is to achieve an outcome or goal. For example, you might seek a promotion at work to obtain a more satisfying and better-paid role and move forward in your career.

Some people develop a pattern of motivation which is mainly 'away from'. They seek to avoid pain or discomfort. Their focus is often on what's going wrong. They look out for perceived threats or problems. They tend to avoid challenges or difficult situations. They can tell you what they don't want.

Others develop a pattern of motivation which is primarily 'towards'. They strive for success or pleasure. Their focus is on achieving goals, and they find this motivating. They are likely to know what they want, and can tell you this.

A motive to get away from a situation can be useful to get started. However, there are a number of problems with 'away from' motivation. It is undirected, it can be inconsistent, and it is often stressful. With 'towards' motivation that seeks to achieve a goal, you are aware of progress towards the goal and you can make adjustments if you go off track.

It may be clear from the language that a client uses that their motivation is primarily 'away from'. While recognising empathically their perspective, it can be useful to encourage them to focus on what it is that they would like to achieve.

- **Collapsing anchors**

In the previous chapter we mentioned the NLP notion of anchors. Recall that an anchor is simply a stimulus that generates a physiological response. For example, the sound of church bells ringing or the smell of burnt toast may have particular associations for you – you have a reaction that is anchored to this sound or smell.

A related NLP technique is the idea of **collapsing anchors**. The coach helps the client to create an anchor for a negative, problematic state they'd like to be rid of and another anchor for the positive state they want to experience instead. If a sufficiently strong positive anchor can be created, NLP practitioners consider that it's possible to use this to help the client break free of their negative thoughts and feelings. Having established in the client's mind and body two well-defined anchors, the coach asks the client to fire off both anchors simultaneously to enable them to shake off their unhelpful thoughts and feelings. It may be that a number of positive states has to be created and associated with the same anchor in order to create a powerful enough positive anchor to eliminate the negative anchor.

As an illustration of the technique, let's assume that you're working with a client whose key issue is a lack of confidence engaging with the senior executives in their organisation. You would help the client to create an anchor – for example, clenching their left hand – associated with feeling low on confidence. You then encourage them to imagine in detail an occasion – or perhaps a number of occasions – when they did feel confident. You help them to create an anchor for this positive state – for instance, clenching their right hand. To collapse anchors, you ask them to clench both hands simultaneously. If the technique is carried out successfully, this will enable the client to feel confident whenever they meet their directors.

This description simplifies the process, and it's essential to be very clear and competent before attempting to use a technique such as collapsing anchors. Please don't experiment with collapsing anchors unless you've been well trained in the technique.

Impostor syndrome

In *The Coach's Casebook*, Geoff Watts and Kim Morgan explore 12 traits which a coach is likely to encounter in their work with clients – traits such as performance anxiety or perfectionism. One of these is impostor syndrome, when a client tells themself that *Everyone else is better than me. I am not as good as people think I am and I am going to get found out.* I recall one executive coach telling me that she found this was often a topic brought to coaching by those who had risen to be chief executive at the very top of an organisation.

Watts and Morgan write that:

> Many people with Impostor Syndrome minimise their achievements and maximise their deficiencies. They often put their achievements down to factors outside their control. They might say, *'I was lucky'* or *'if only they knew the real me and what was going on'*. This is not through a sense of humility but simply because they struggle to internalise their achievements. (Watts and Morgan, 2015)

They go on to describe a number of tools and techniques that a coach might use to help 'clients acknowledge their qualities and achievements in order to begin giving themselves more credit'. One of these is to invite the client to imagine that they are being interviewed for a magazine article that wants to show them in the best possible light, and to write this interview in the third person. This might be set as an assignment between sessions, and the client might bring the article along with some photographs.

They also offer some powerful coaching questions that might be used to challenge the thinking of a client who is suffering from impostor syndrome:

- If you knew that everyone in the room had the same insecurity, how would that change your outlook?
- Which of your assumptions about yourself would your good friends challenge?
- How would you describe yourself if you were being as kind and generous to yourself as you are to your friends? (Watts and Morgan, 2015)

Impostor syndrome and the deference threshold

Geoff Pelham (2016) notes that a coach, perhaps one who is stepping up from being a participant on a coaching programme to working as an independent coach or a coach within an organisation, may well experience impostor syndrome – 'the sense of taking on an identity which you may not yet truly own'.

Peter Hawkins and Nick Smith (2006) discuss a phenomenon that has some similarities with the impostor syndrome and which they call the *deference threshold.* There are 'moments where it feels that the client or the situation have rendered us considerably less effective than we normally are'. In this situation the coach 'hands over their authority, presence and impact to the other person. We defer to the other person.' The coach becomes ineffective – they may lose the plot, go on the back foot, or feel the need for the approval of the client.

This can be triggered by all sorts of things. It may happen often for an inexperienced coach, but 'Even the most experienced coaches and supervisors can trigger this reaction in themselves.' It's important for a coach to know the things, situations or people that sometimes trigger their deference threshold.

Becoming aware in the moment during a coaching session of such an interference is the key to managing it. As with other interferences that may get in the way of you coaching fluently, simply notice that it's happening, and bring your attention and focus fully back on the client and their story. Reviewing it afterwards in supervision can be very useful to help you deepen your awareness of what triggered it, and how you will manage it when it arises again.

A community of selves

Robert Hobson describes the notion that each of us is a community of selves. A simple illustration of this is when we say, 'I am in two minds about … '. Hobson suggests that each of us has a number of unknown or dimly recognised subpersonalities or selves. He writes that this 'way of elaborating experience is often valuable in self-understanding and in therapy' (Hobson, 1985).

Hobson illustrates the idea with the example of a client who imagined his various selves as 'a troupe of actors (the Conversationalist, the Business man, the Country Bumpkin, the Adventurer, the Sentimental Lover, the Metropolitan Smooth Man and the Dreamer) with a vacillating and not very effective Producer'. Hobson emphasises that '"self as a community" is a metaphor within which some persons can express many aspects of experience in relation to themselves and others' (Hobson, 1985).

There is a hierarchy within the community of selves – 'all do not have the same power of willing and acting' .The Producer in the example has some kind of executive function, trying to coordinate the different actors or factions. Hobson adds that, 'These separate "identities" can be more or less related or they can be divorced. There is, however, a tendency towards an harmonious organization: a whole with an integrated activity of differentiated parts.'

Some clients will be able to work easily with this notion and express themselves through this kind of metaphor, and others won't. As an illustration, I was working with one client who behaved confidently and assertively in some situations but held himself back in others. I invited him to expand on how he thought, felt and acted in these contrasting situations. I then asked him to give these two versions of himself a name. When he was acting confidently and forcefully, he reckoned he was behaving like Alexander the Great. The name that occurred to him to capture how he felt when he was behaving hesitantly was Julian. We then explored how he might deliberately bring his confident Alexander self to the fore when he next found himself thinking and acting from his timid Julian self.

I had another client who found it very difficult to be assertive at work, which led to a situation where she felt overworked and undervalued. She lacked the confidence to ask for the resources she needed to carry out her role effectively. I asked her if she could make the statement *I have the right to ask for what I need*. She simply could not, even as a simulation in the coaching room.

I decided to trust a thought that came to me. Knowing that she was a linguist, I asked her if she could make this statement in another language. She was able to write down and vocalise a similar statement in French. This led to an intense and powerful 20 minutes' exploration of how she had felt very differently when she lived and worked for five years in Paris. She said she was a different person there and then, and that moving overseas had meant she didn't have to conform to other people's expectations of her. Her French 'self' was a far more confident and assertive person, and the challenge for her was how to access this self when she needed to in the present day.

The idea that each of us is a community of selves has many similarities to a psycho-therapeutic approach known as Psychosynthesis. Developed originally by an Italian associate of Freud's, Robert Assagioli, Psychosynthesis takes the view that each personality consists of a number of elements that need to be in harmony – to be synthesised – for healthy human growth and development. Each of us is a mixture of contrasting, changing elements, which in Psychosynthesis are termed subpersonalities.

These subpersonalities are like the instruments that make up an orchestra. Because we tend to identify with whichever subpersonality is dominant in a particular situation, the orchestra sounds like it's tuning up – a cacophony rather than a harmonious ensemble.

Psychosynthesis is a form of humanistic psychology which views individuals as having an inherent tendency towards synthesis and harmony. It also sees the individual as part of a bigger interconnected picture, part of a collective unconscious. To work with a client using the full range of ideas from Psychosynthesis is to work at a psychodynamic or psychoanalytic level, and requires an appropriate degree of training, experience and expertise.

Two selves

The theme of my coaching conversation with Lina was impostor syndrome. In this extract I invite Lina to explore two of her selves – in her words, *Cool and Collected Lina* and *Hot Mess Lina*. This led into Lina doing the reflective writing exercise that we looked at in Chapter 10.

In this clip when I reflect with Christian on my interview with Lina, I say more on the idea that we are different selves.

Link to Video 17.1
Two selves

Link to Video 17.2
Different selves

EXERCISE 17.3

DIFFERENT SELVES

Robert Hobson suggests that each of us is a community of different selves. Reflect upon how you yourself think, feel and act differently in different situations. Identify a number of different selves for yourself, and give each of these selves a name that is meaningful for you.

The person in Hobson's example had a somewhat ineffective Producer self who determined which self came to the fore. Which aspect of yourself determines which of your selves comes out in different contexts?

Motivational Interviewing

We turn now to an approach known as Motivational Interviewing. Many of the ideas in MI, as it's known, are very useful for someone coaching from a primarily non-directive stance. They are particularly relevant in situations where a client is feeling ambivalent about changing their behaviour, or is stuck and unable to choose between different courses of action. They also offer a potentially valuable way of helping clients for whom fear or a lack of confidence prevents them acting to achieve the goals that they desire.

Motivational Interviewing was developed originally by the American psychologist William Miller, based on his therapeutic work with problem drinkers. He explored the question *Why do people change?* He found that change often occurs naturally, and that the type of change that happens after counselling or therapy mirrors natural change. He also found that relatively brief interventions – too brief for the client to develop new behaviours or skills – could have a significant effect. When the counsellor or therapist demonstrated an empathic style, this facilitated change; when the counsellor or therapist was directive or confrontational, this created resistance to change. People who believed they could change – and who stated that they were committed to change – were more likely to change. Clients whose counsellor believed they could change were also more likely to do so.

Miller questioned whether approaches which used punishments of various sorts could motivate people to change. While rewards and punishments can be effective in some circumstances, people with alcoholism or drug addiction, for example, can be stuck in their pattern of behaviour even while suffering greatly. They are stuck because they feel ambivalent about change. They do see the downsides of their behaviour, but this isn't sufficient to motivate them to change. The way out of ambivalence involves the exploration of their experience and what truly matters to them. And this requires an empathic, accepting atmosphere that makes it safe for them to look at both the painful present and a future which satisfies their own desires and values.

Feeling ambivalent about change is normal, and working through ambivalence may be an essential part of change. However, it is being stuck in ambivalence that is problematic. William Miller and Stephen Rollnick (2002) write that, 'Ambivalence is a reasonable place to visit, but you wouldn't want to live there.' Exploring and resolving the client's ambivalence – *I want to change, but I don't want to change* – is the key challenge in facilitating change. It may even be that once the client has worked through their ambivalence satisfactorily then change occurs quickly – this is an important way in which a brief intervention which helps the client to resolve their ambivalence is effective.

On the other hand, when the counsellor or therapist seeks to force a resolution of a client's ambivalence – through punishment, persuasion or advice – this is likely to be ineffective and may even paradoxically increase the client's attachment to the very behaviour that was meant to be modified. When the coach appears to argue for one side of a possible change, the client is likely to respond with arguments for the other side. *Yes, but ... .*

The practice of MI is based on four guiding principles:

1. Express empathy

The ability of the coach to demonstrate to the client an empathic understanding and non-judgemental acceptance – that is, two of Carl Rogers' three core conditions – is of vital importance in MI. Listening respectfully to the client, without judging, criticising or blaming them, enables them to explore their ambivalence. Paradoxically, accepting people as they are seems to free them to change.

2. Develop discrepancy

This is where MI differs from a Rogerian person-centred approach. MI deliberately aims to help the client to resolve their ambivalence and move towards positive behavioural change. Thus MI intentionally seeks to help the client to amplify what they see as a discrepancy between their current state and where they want to be. The coach encourages the client to see the gap between where they are now and the goals or values that are important to them. It is vital, however, that it is the client not the coach who voices goals, concerns or reasons to change. The client is more likely to change when they themself realise and articulate that their behaviour is in conflict with their personal goals.

3. Roll with resistance

When the client is resisting change and presenting arguments against change, it is important that the coach does not oppose this, which is likely to be counterproductive. Rather, the coach works with the client's resistance, acknowledging that ambivalence is natural. The coach may offer a slight reframe, present information or invite a fresh perspective, but does not impose their views. The coach may turn a question or problem back to the client, with the assumption that the client is capable of solving their own problem. When the client is resistant, this is a signal for the coach, not the client, to do something different.

4. Support self-efficacy

In order to change, the client needs to believe in the possibility for change. This self-efficacy – the client's belief that they can succeed – is a good predictor of whether or not they will make the changes they desire. Moreover, the coach's belief in the client's ability to change can also have a powerful effect on what happens. The coach supports and encourages the client's belief in their ability to carry out their plans successfully, and seeks to enhance the client's confidence that they can make the changes they desire. Ultimately, of course, it is up to the client to change – the coach can only help them to do so.

In MI it is the client not the coach who must present the arguments for change. The coach's skill in eliciting change talk is the key strategy for developing discrepancy, resolving ambivalence and encouraging change. When the coach hears the client begin to talk of change, they invite the client to explore this further. Here are some illustrative open questions that the coach might ask to encourage the client to develop their thoughts on change.

- If the client talks of the disadvantages of the status quo: *What worries you about your current situation?*
- If the client talks of the advantages of change: *How would you like things to be different?*
- If the client expresses some optimism about change: *What strengths do you have that will help you to succeed?*
- If the client expresses some intention to change: *What do you think you might do?*

Eliciting change talk is intentionally directive, seeking to tip the balance in the direction of the change desired by the client. Note that this is not about manipulating the client or about the coach setting the direction for change.

In contrast to psychodynamic approaches which view a client's resistance as a defence mechanism, Motivational Interviewing regards resistance as something which arises in the interpersonal interaction between coach and client. Remember that resistance is a signal for the coach, not the client, to do something different.

How the coach responds to resistance is the hallmark of Motivational Interviewing which distinguishes it from other approaches. Faced with resistance, the coach or counsellor needs to double back to an earlier stage of the process rather than trying to attempt to drive on. Some of the ways in which the coach might respond to resistance are to:

- Reflect back to the client, acknowledging their perspective
- Reframe what the client offers, which acknowledges their view but offers a new light that may be more helpful to change
- Emphasise that the client has personal choice and control
- Come alongside the client to make the case against change – being careful, however, not to appear to be tricking the client

When MI is used with clients who have serious drug or alcohol problems or who are sex offenders there is a clearly desirable direction for change. However, MI can also be used when a client faces a choice where one outcome is not necessarily better than another. For example, the client may be considering whether to accept a new job or stay in their current role. One idea from MI that I find particularly useful in this type of situation is the notion of double sided reflection. Simply playing back to the client what they have said about both halves of their dilemma, taking care to give due weight to each side, often helps the client to clarify how they view things.

If you would like to find out more about MI and how you might use some of its ideas when working with clients who are ambivalent or lacking the motivation to achieve the goals they aspire to, then I recommend that you read Miller and Rollnick's classic book, *Motivational Interviewing: Preparing People for Change*. You might also visit the website of Guy Undrill, a psychiatrist who trains NHS staff to use MI techniques: www.guyundrill.com.

EXERCISE 17.4

FEELING AMBIVALENT

This is an exercise to try next time you are in conversation with someone who is feeling ambivalent about a change, or someone who is stuck in a way of behaving that they would like to change but haven't so far been able to.

When you are speaking with them, simply use the technique of double sided reflection to play back to them as accurately and empathically as you can what they are expressing. Make sure that you don't advocate any particular way forward. Then simply notice what happens.

18

COACHING AS A LINE MANAGER

Introduction

Myles Downey writes that:

> Coaching ... is the series of conversations that help a person perform closer to their potential, understand their role or task, help them learn what they need to learn in order to complete the role or task successfully, develop them for the next role, and on a good day help them achieve fulfilment at work and, maybe, a little joy. (Downey, 2003)

In this chapter we explore how you might use a coaching approach as the basis on which you line manage other people within an organisation. As the quote from Downey illustrates, you can use coaching to help people perform their role, develop their skills, obtain job satisfaction and prepare to move on to their next role. In other words, you can accomplish much of what you seek to do as a manager by coaching your people.

We begin by looking at a conventional **command and control** approach to management, consider a coaching approach, and describe some of the challenges of operating as a manager-coach. We next explore the idea of a coaching dance where you move gracefully between telling people what to do and asking them for their ideas, and discuss how this can be used to manage performance. We look at using a coaching style to conduct a development review conversation and then more generally at how coaching can provide a foundation for the long-term development of people. We discuss briefly the idea of coaching your boss. We end the chapter by looking at establishing a coaching culture in an organisation.

Command and control

A manager is someone who achieves results through other people rather than exclusively through their own efforts. So, how do you as a manager go about achieving results through others?

A conventional answer is that you set objectives for your people, communicate these clearly, and monitor their achievement. In effect, you tell your people what to do. This is often described – somewhat pejoratively but accurately – as a **command and control** approach to management.

Telling is about giving instructions, ensuring that these instructions are carried out and restricting the scope for discretion and judgement. It is directive. There are many situations in which this is appropriate. When I'm depositing a cheque at a bank, for instance, I want there to be well-defined procedures that the staff working in that organisation carry out consistently.

There are a number of advantages in a telling approach. Telling is quicker, certainly in the short run. Senior people often know more of the bigger picture and so can make more informed decisions about what is required. Sometimes it is obvious what needs to be done and it is entirely appropriate simply to say so. In an emergency or a crisis, a clear command is extremely useful.

Nonetheless, there are downsides in a management style which is exclusively telling. If you only ever tell your people what to do, then you don't tap into their experience, their knowledge of what is really going on, and their ideas about how to do things better. You run the risk of getting compliance but no real commitment or sense of ownership. When things go wrong, people will look to you for the answer rather than use their initiative. Continually telling can be very time consuming and, as you don't develop your people, you need to keep on spending your time telling them what to do.

A coaching approach

A coaching approach to managing people rests on the fundamental equation that we've considered at various points in the book:

Awareness + Responsibility = Performance

As a manager, you want your people to be fully aware of what they need to do and how to do it, and you want them to take responsibility for their actions. With awareness and responsibility, they will perform – that is, they will achieve objectives. This raises the question of whose objectives – yours as the manager or theirs? We'll consider this in a later section.

The fundamental skills you need to coach as a line manager are the same as those we looked at earlier in the book. First, you need to be able to listen with good attention and with empathy to understand how the world looks from the perspective of your team member. Second, you need to ask crisp, open questions that help them to think clearly. Third, you need to be able to play back what you've heard to check understanding and to help the individual to clarify or deepen their thinking.

You can also use a framework such as the GROW model to structure your coaching conversations with the people who work for you.

We have noted throughout the book that coaching is a relationship based on rapport and trust, and this relationship develops through a series of conversations. Similarly, as a manager, you have a relationship with each of the people who work for you, and this relationship evolves in part through the conversations you have with them. Establishing trust and rapport in these relationships creates a valuable foundation for managing your staff.

EXERCISE 18.1

METAPHORS OF MANAGER

In Chapter 10 we looked at how you can help a client use metaphor to explore their situation. We noted that all metaphors are partial, and that what matters are the insights yielded by a metaphor.

There are many metaphors you might use to think about the role of a manager. In this chapter we have spoken of the manager as commander or controller or coach. You could also, for example, think of a manager as a conductor or shepherd or parent or servant, and so on.

Here is an exercise to explore how you view the role of a manager.

- List some other possible metaphors for the role of a manager.
- Choose a couple of metaphors of manager that interest you. Which words or behaviours do these metaphors suggest?

- If you yourself are a line manager, which metaphors help to explain the attitudes and behaviours you demonstrate?
- If you work for a line manager, which metaphors help to explain the attitudes and behaviours that your manager demonstrates?

Challenges for a manager-coach

In some ways it is more difficult to coach if you are a line manager rather than an external or an internal but off-line coach. As a line manager, you have a direct interest in the results delivered by your staff. Your performance may be measured in part by their performance, and you may have strong views on how things should be done. It can be a real challenge to let go of control and use a coaching style to empower your people. On the other hand, while the external or off-line coach is keen for the client to succeed, they do not have the same responsibility for performance that a manager has.

It may also be that one of the issues facing the individual is their relationship with you, their boss, and they may be reluctant to explore this with you.

Another issue that poses a greater challenge for the manager-coach than for the external coach concerns confidentiality. Even if someone has a sound working relationship with their manager, they will probably and quite wisely put limits on how open and honest they will be. If they stay within the same organisation they may encounter their former manager years later in meetings or job interviews. Individuals will usually be more open and honest with a confidant who is from outside the organisation or is not perceived as part of the management hierarchy.

Jenny Rogers reflects these additional factors when she writes:

As a boss, it is entirely probable that you are part of whatever problems your coachee has and this can be difficult to see let alone acknowledge. Also, it is always more difficult to promise confidentiality, encourage or expect complete disclosure, set aside your own considerations or remain detached from the possible outcomes. As a boss you have a stake in the outcome, whereas when you are purely a coach you do not. (Rogers, 2008)

The coaching dance

Let us return to the issue that your objectives as a manager may differ from those of a member of your staff. A primarily non-directive approach to coaching implies that you can only coach someone – in the sense that we've been using the term – if you are on their agenda. And sometimes your agenda as a manager may not be the same as the agenda of one of your team.

I find the idea of the **coaching dance** a useful way of looking at this. I first heard about it from David Hemery, an Olympic 400 metres hurdles champion who has helped many managers learn how to coach. He suggests that there are times when you must **tell** people what to do and there are times when you need to **ask** them for their ideas. As a simple illustration, you might tell one of your team *I must have the report by Friday* and then ask them *What do you need to do to finish it by Friday?*

Hemery calls it a dance to indicate that the manager needs to move gracefully between telling and asking. The challenge to a manager-coach is to know which situations call for which approach, and to be able to move skilfully from one mode to another.

The coaching dance is summarised in Figure 18.1. It contrasts a *manager-centred* approach where the manager is *pushing* the performer for results and a *performer-centred* approach where the manager is seeking to *pull* results from the performer.

THE COACHING DANCE		
MANAGER-CENTRED		**PERFORMER-CENTRED**
(Pushing)		*(Pulling)*
(Telling)		*(Asking)*
• Set by the manager	**GOALS AND TARGETS**	• Discuss and agree with performer
• Reward and punish	**MOTIVATION**	• Ask what interests performer
• Encourage		• Performer challenges self
• Pass judgements	**FEEDBACK**	• Draw out performer's experience
• Praise and criticise		• Help performer to generate feedback
• Give feedback to performer		
• Tell what went well and what didn't	**LEARNING**	• From self-awareness
• Show how it could have been done better		• By reflection and discovery

Figure 18.1   The coaching dance

In a manager-centred approach the manager sets goals and targets. In a performer-centred approach goals and targets are discussed and agreed, and the performer might also set themselves some personal challenges.

In a manager-centred approach the manager uses a variety of carrots and sticks to motivate the performer. In a performer-centred approach the manager will find out from the performer what will motivate or interest them. If it's appropriate, they will try to build this into the task to be done.

We looked at feedback in some detail in Chapter 11. The manager-centred manager will give feedback, which is based on their judgement and which may contain a mix of criticism and praise based on this judgement. The performer-centred manager will seek to generate feedback in conversation with the performer, asking first how the performer viewed their performance before adding their own perspective – if this is necessary. People often know when they've made a mistake without having to be told.

Finally, as far as learning goes, the manager-centred manager will be in tell mode, stating how they think the task could have been done better. The performer-centred manager will be helping the performer to clarify and articulate what they think they have learnt.

Performance management

In some organisations performance management – often termed performance appraisal – is seen as an HR process that is accompanied by paperwork that needs to be completed once a year. The paperwork is often then filed away for 12 months until it's time for next year's appraisal.

An alternative – and much more useful – view is that performance management is a vital management process based on regular conversations between a manager and individuals who report to them. The conversations are the essence of the process – and this may be accompanied by user-friendly documentation that structures and supports these conversations.

In *Managing Performance*, Michael Armstrong and Angela Baron (2004) define performance management as a 'natural' management process which:

> contributes to the effective management of individuals and teams to achieve high levels of organisational performance.

In the factsheet *Performance Management: An Introduction*, the Chartered Institute of Personnel and Development (CIPD) state that:

> Performance management is key to enhancing organisational success. Employees need to understand their expected contribution to business objectives and be motivated and equipped with the skills, resources and support to achieve this. Various tools can be used but a good performance management process revolves around ongoing conversations on progress towards objectives. (https://www.cipd.co.uk/knowledge/fundamentals/people/performance/factsheet#6296)

Really effective performance management should:

- Be strategic – aligned with broad issues and the long-term goals of the organisation
- Be integrated – linking various aspects of the business and how people are managed
- Improve individual, team and organisational performance
- Develop people and teams
- Manage behaviour and foster healthy and productive working relationships

A coaching approach is an invaluable way of managing performance. Empathic listening, asking open questions and playing back to show understanding are great ways for a manager to set up constructive conversations and build cooperative relationships with the people who work for them. The coaching dance offers a practical template for a manager and a member of their team to agree goals, explore motivation, create feedback, and support learning. It does not take away the manager's right and responsibility to set objectives on behalf of the organisation, or to give feedback. But this can be done in a way that is much more collaborative and is more likely to gain commitment rather than compliance.

Managing underperformance

A specific situation that can arise in organisations is when an employee is underperforming. This is a situation which needs to be addressed rather than avoided.

Underperformance, or poor performance, can occur in a number of ways – failure to carry out duties to an acceptable standard, non-compliance with rules and procedures, or unacceptable or disruptive behaviour. It is less serious than misconduct in the form of, say, theft or assault, which may warrant instant dismissal.

There may be a number of reasons behind underperformance of an individual. It could be because the employee does not know what is expected of them, has not received any feedback on their performance or behaviour, or does not have the knowledge, skills, experience or resources to do what is being asked of them. It could be because of poor motivation, low morale in the team or a poor work environment. It might be because of interpersonal differences, bullying or cultural misunderstandings. Or, it might be because of personal issues outside the workplace that are affecting the person. It is worth checking out what are the reasons causing the underperformance.

Coaching is a powerful approach, but there are times when it's not appropriate. There are situations when it is vital to spell out – with specific examples – what is wrong in an individual's performance or behaviour. And there are times when more serious action, possibly termination of employment, is necessary.

Coaching and development reviews

In a previous role I helped run a programme to develop coaching skills in the middle managers working for our organisation. They attended a three-day workshop, practised their skills back at work, and then came on a two-day follow-up workshop. It was a significant investment, and had mixed results. Some managers really saw the benefits of a coaching approach to managing people, others picked up on things like the importance of listening or the use of the GROW model, and some participants seemed to be largely untouched once they'd returned to work.

Some of our managers found it difficult to deploy a coaching approach in the hurly burly of their everyday job. One situation, however, where they did find it possible to use their coaching skills was in the annual performance and development review meetings that they had with each of their staff. This kind of review is by its very nature set up to be a one-to-one conversation with a fair amount of time set aside to explore things.

If you are a line manager interested in using a coaching approach but not yet convinced as to whether it's possible or not, you might like to try it out in your annual review conversations with your staff. Although there may be lots of paperwork that seemingly needs to be completed, I'd encourage you to concentrate on having a meaningful conversation in which you listen attentively and ask crisp open questions. Having a fruitful conversation is far more important than the paperwork.

EXERCISE 18.2

QUESTIONS FOR A DEVELOPMENT REVIEW

Here are some questions that you might use or adapt to structure a conversation to help one of your people create their development plan. Note that the questions are worded to put the individual at the heart of the process. The questions are intended to open up a dialogue rather than to be followed mechanically.

- What are your strengths?
- What are your weaknesses?
- What are your aspirations for the future?
- What development goals do you want to set yourself?
- What experiences will help you achieve these development goals?
- How will you reflect upon and learn from these experiences?
- How can I best support you in carrying out this development plan?

You might like to answer the questions about yourself to create your own development plan to build your capability as a coach.

Developing people

One of the major benefits of a coaching style of management is that it is a great way of developing people.

In *The Fifth Discipline*, Peter Senge (1990) talks about 'real learning'. He writes, 'Through learning we become able to do something we never were able to do.' Real learning – that is, becoming able to do new things – requires real experience coupled with reflection to make sense of that experience. If this is indeed how people really learn, then as a manager seeking to build the capability of your people you need to do two things. First, offer them challenging experiences at the edge of their comfort zone. Second, use coaching and feedback to help them to review and learn from these experiences. This approach is not only more effective at developing people but also is far less expensive than traditional approaches based on attendance at courses and programmes.

If you adopt a coaching style, then your questions will prompt the individual to think more deeply or carefully about what they are doing, and will tap into their own ideas and skills. They become more aware of what's required and take more responsibility for delivering what the organisation needs. Since they are learning from their experience, their capability grows. Moreover, the individual's view of themself and what they can contribute grows too. They believe that they are a capable performer who is making a valuable contribution. They expect to bring their own ideas and strengths to the next task in hand. They begin to aim higher and so become a more capable performer who can take on bigger tasks and roles.

Manager offers a more challenging assignment,
and asks open questions of the individual.

Performer learns, develops confidence
and has greater self-belief.

With the support of the manager, the
performer thinks things through for themself.

Performer is more motivated, delivers
more and feels more satisfied.

Performer becomes more aware
and takes more responsibility.

Figure 18.2   Cycle of development

In other words, the organisation uses more of their potential, they make a greater contribution, they feel more satisfied, and their self-image expands. Coaching not only produces higher performance but also builds future capability and enhances the individual's self-image. You can picture this as a cycle of development, as shown in Figure 18.2.

Coaching your boss

A question that regularly arises when I run workshops to help managers to develop their coaching skills is *How do I coach my boss?* Invariably, when I ask the individual why they want to coach their boss, the answer is that they want to get their boss to agree to something. This isn't coaching! It may be influencing or persuading or manipulating, and it may be important, but it isn't coaching.

You can test this simply by asking *Whose agenda am I following?* or *What is my intention?* You can coach your boss – or anyone else – only if you are on their agenda.

Moreover, you can only genuinely coach someone who wants to be coached and is, therefore, willing to engage in the conversation. So, another question to check is *Is my boss willing to be coached by me?*

Creating a coaching culture

In *Building and Sustaining a Coaching Culture*, David Clutterbuck, David Megginson and Agnieszka Bajer note three ideas that writers on organisational culture generally agree upon:

* Culture is created over time through the interaction of people and their environment.
* Culture creates consistent patterns of meaning and behaviour that bind people together and make them unique as a group.
* Coaching is a combination of visible and invisible elements that exist on multiple levels. (Clutterbuck et al., 2016)

A coaching culture isn't one where everyone has an external coach, but rather one 'where people coach each other all the time as a natural part of meetings, reviews and one-to-one discussions of all kinds' (Hardingham, 2004).

A key reason why some of the managers who'd attended the coaching skills programme described earlier didn't translate what they'd explored in the workshops into their day-to-day practice at work was that the culture of the organisation was largely a more traditional command and control one. While I believe that it is possible to use a coaching style of management even when the surrounding culture of the organisation is indifferent to the notion of coaching, nevertheless it is much easier to do this when the prevailing organisational climate is one that supports the use of coaching.

To establish a coaching culture throughout an organisation – or indeed to change the culture in any way – requires the active commitment of the person at the top of the organisation. If the chief executive, or equivalent, hasn't experienced the benefit of being coached and doesn't adopt a coaching style of leadership themselves, then it's impossible to create a coaching culture. It may be possible to shift the culture within a part of the organisation whose leader is committed, but this will be an island of difference within the wider system.

Alison Hardingham describes how she faced up to this challenge when invited to coach the partners in a law firm. She writes:

> I insisted that the managing partner had coaching himself, to make it possible for his colleagues to take it up. He was puzzled; he genuinely wanted this help to be available to his partners, but felt no need of it himself.

> I knew that at that time, and in that highly competitive culture, having coaching would be seen as a sign of weakness unless the most powerful person in the firm led the way. (Hardingham, 2004)

She then illustrates the culture within the coaching firm Lane 4, set up by Olympic gold medal swimmer Adrian Moorhouse:

> The message 'coaching is a normal part of what successful people do around here' is communicated loud and clear. For anyone wanting to establish a coaching culture, that is the message that has to be got across. And it will be got across by actions, not words. (Hardingham, 2004)

She goes on to describe the values that 'are a solid foundation' for a coaching culture:

> Increasingly, organisations are looking for people who believe in teamwork rather than individualism, who are motivated by opportunity to build rapport with a wide range of colleagues and clients, who are committed to their own and other people's development. (Hardingham, 2004)

Clutterbuck et al. (2016) describe a set of core principles that underpin a coaching culture in an organisation:

- Attentiveness. When interacting with others, people give others their undivided attention.
- Collaboration. Achieving a goal requires collaboration with others.

- Curiosity. Asking good questions is as important as finding good answers.
- Ethicality. When faced with a dilemma, people engage in conversations on the ethical aspects of the situation.
- Growth. Each person has the potential to grow and develop and it is their responsibility to tap into that potential, both in themselves and others.
- Openness and honesty. People openly share what they think, how they feel and what their intentions are.
- Learning. True learning only takes place when people reflect on their experience.
- Respect. Respect is reflected by having positive feelings of esteem for others and valuing them irrespective of position, hierarchical power, or potential differences in opinions, interests or culture.

To create a genuine coaching culture across an organisation is likely to take several years. Peter Hawkins and Nick Smith (2006) describe seven steps that organisations may need to go through to evolve a coaching culture:

1. The organisation employs coaches for some of its executives.
2. The organisation develops its own coaching and mentoring capacity.
3. The organisation actively supports coaching endeavours.
4. Coaching becomes a norm for individuals, teams and the whole organisation.
5. Coaching becomes embedded in the HR and performance management processes of the organisation.
6. Coaching becomes the predominate style of managing throughout the organisation.
7. Coaching becomes 'how we do business' with all our stakeholders.

EXERCISE 18.3

THE COACHING CULTURE WITHIN YOUR ORGANISATION

In terms of Hawkins and Smith's seven steps to creating a coaching culture, what step is your own organisation currently at?

What needs to happen to take it to the next step?

19

COACHING A TEAM

Introduction

In this chapter we consider aspects of coaching a team of people rather than an individual person. We begin by offering a useful definition of what makes a number of people a team rather than a group, and then explore what team coaching is. We next look at the use of the GROW model when coaching a team, and consider the importance of ground rules. We then offer a model of how teams develop through several stages, consider working with teams, subteams and individuals, look at the difference between coaching and facilitation, and discuss how the ultimate goal of the team coach is for the team to be able to coach itself. We end by describing three exercises you might use when working with teams.

What is a team?

Bill Critchley and David Casey describe how they realised while running a team building event with the top management group of an organisation that:

> For most of their time this group of people had absolutely no need to work as a team; indeed the attempt to do so was causing more puzzlement and scepticism than motivation and commitment. (Critchley and Casey, 1984)

They point out that, for example, the Finance Director spent most of their time doing quite different things from the HR Director, and so on. Sometimes they had to speak to each other, and from time to time subgroups needed to come together, but most of the time this group simply didn't have to be a team. The main occasion when they did have to work as a team was when they were creating a strategy for the organisation, which is a shared task for which they were mutually accountable.

Similarly, I often find that groups of people who report to the same line manager spend – or rather waste – time and energy worrying about how to work as a team when they basically don't have to. They are a group of people who may have things to communicate to each other, but they essentially do different things and simply don't need to be a team.

Jon Katzenbach and Douglas Smith offer a definition of a team that explains why groups often struggle with this:

> A team is a small number of people with complementary skills committed to a common purpose, performance goals and ways of working together for which they hold themselves mutually accountable. (Katzenbach and Smith, 1994)

I think that the Katzenbach and Smith definition is extremely liberating. Many people sitting close to one another in an office don't have to be a team. And, as Critchley and Casey state, attempts to engage them in team development activities are likely to cause puzzlement and scepticism.

I also think that each phrase in the definition is precisely worded and worth careful consideration. For instance, each individual within a well functioning team will be committed to a common purpose and shared performance goals. They will have agreed ground rules – which we'll come back to later in the chapter – about how they will work together. And, interestingly, Katzenbach and Smith state that a team is a small number of people. They found that the majority of the effective teams they studied numbered fewer than 10 people.

For me, the key phrase in the definition is *mutually accountable*. In a healthy and successful team, each member feels mutually accountable to their colleagues.

What is team coaching?

Just as a team is more than the sum of the individuals within it, so too coaching a team is more than coaching the individuals in the team. However, the practice of coaching a team is not nearly as well developed as the coaching of individuals. Anne Scoular writes that:

> Team coaching is a huge subject, and is at the stage one-to-one coaching was 15 or 20 years ago, with very little direct research undertaken and not much yet published. (Scoular, 2011)

Myles Downey says that, 'Coaching teams has a very specific intent: to ensure that the team achieves its goals' (2003). He then gives an example of coaching a team which involved him engaging with them over a period of time:

> Some years ago I worked with a team that had been established to launch a new financial service. It involved the building of an entire organisation, from the people, to the systems, to the office buildings. This is team coaching at its most exciting, where it involves the delivery of tangible goals. (Downey, 2003)

These quotes from Downey suggest that the focus in team coaching is on helping the team to achieve its goals. David Clutterbuck extends this notion to include also helping the team to improve its processes – that is, how it works together. He offers this working definition of team coaching:

> Helping the team improve performance, and the processes by which performance is achieved, through reflection and dialogue. (Clutterbuck, 2007)

Peter Hawkins and Nick Smith explicitly include relationships with stakeholders outside the team as well as relationships among the members of the team. They define team coaching as:

> enabling a team to function at more than the sum of its parts, by clarifying its mission and improving its external and internal relationships. (Hawkins and Smith, 2006)

Because you are dealing with a number of people, coaching a team is inevitably more complicated than coaching an individual. There may be complex group dynamics going on within the team that affect how it operates and which might be difficult to fully understand. Myles Downey points out

> the obvious distinction between individual and team coaching: there are more people involved. At the surface level this means that more time is spent in the process of coaching. An individual can get to a level of clarity and make a decision relatively quickly. In a team that process takes much more time as each person needs to be heard, disagreement handled, consensus and commitment built. Now look beyond the surface, look to the interrelationships in the team, the dynamics and evolution of the team, and a whole new ball game emerges. (Downey, 2003)

Alison Hardingham recommends that two coaches work together when there are complicated group dynamics within a team. She writes:

And if the group dynamic in a team is very powerful and very destructive, it may be better for coaching to be done by a team of two coaches working together. It is much easier to resist the power of group dynamics when there is more than one of you. (Hardingham, 2004)

If we put together the various ideas just mentioned, we can say that team coaching is about helping the team to:

- Clarify and achieve their collective goals
- Communicate and interact with one another effectively
- Constructively explore and resolve differences within the team
- Make wise decisions
- Engage effectively with key stakeholders outside the team

Myles Downey (2003) defines coaching as 'the art of facilitating the performance, learning or development of another'. We might extend this to define team coaching as follows:

Team coaching is the art of enabling a group of people collectively to perform, learn and develop in order to achieve the goals for which they are mutually accountable.

Three stances a coach might occupy

David Clutterbuck (2007) develops the analogy of the coach of a sports team to describe three stances a coach might take. First, the coach might be on the field, participating in the match alongside the other players. Second, they could be on the touchline, observing the performance and able to provide feedback at intervals. Third, they might be in the grandstand, unable to influence the play directly but able subsequently to help the team take a wider perspective.

He goes on to suggest that the first role is similar to that played by a team leader, who needs to understand processes and be technically competent. 'In terms of managing perspective, the team leader coach has to focus primarily on achieving the short-term and medium-term goals.' The second role is similar to that played by a manager-coach – they 'engage with the task by providing direction, clarifying the link with organizational goals, aspirations and values, and providing both task-related and behavioural feedback'. The external team coach is one more stage removed – in the grandstand, as it were. They offer a wider perspective and 'have very little need to understand the technical processes, except insofar as they shape the nature and degree of interdependence between team members' (Clutterbuck, 2007).

Five disciplines of high-performing teams

In *Leadership Team Coaching in Practice*, Peter Hawkins (2014) describes five disciplines which are required for a team to be high-performing. These disciplines help the team to consider both task and process, and to focus internally within the team and on key stakeholders beyond the team. He offers key questions that a coach might use to help a team to focus on each of these disciplines.

- **Commissioning.** Who does your team serve and what is its commission? How does this align with the wider organisational objectives?
- **Clarifying.** What is the team's collective endeavour and core objectives? And is the team clear about its roles and working processes?
- **Co-creating.** How is your team working together, partnering internally and managing its team dynamics?
- **Connecting.** How is your team partnering with the various parts of the wider system and your key stakeholders?
- **Core learning.** How is your team learning from its experience and developing as a team? (Hawkins, 2014)

Hawkins emphasises the importance of viewing the team as a system which exists within a larger system (such as the whole organisation) and which serves the needs of an even wider system of stakeholders.

Using the GROW model with teams

Having noted that coaching a team is about far more than coaching the individual members, nevertheless many of the key ideas on coaching individuals that we've explored in earlier chapters apply also when coaching a team. The skills of listening to understand, asking open questions and playing back your understanding are vital in working with a team. It helps greatly if the team members – not just the coach – are able to deploy these skills when they are speaking together.

Moreover, the basic equation that we've been looking at throughout the book:

Awareness + Responsibility = Performance

applies also when working with a team. The two key challenges in coaching a team might be viewed as to raise awareness within the team and to encourage appropriate responsibility.

You can often very effectively use the GROW model with a team to structure their discussion. Let's look in more detail at this.

Goal: What do we want to achieve?

Establishing clear goals is vital in team coaching. Alison Hardingham (2004) high-lights a difference in coaching a sports team where the performance challenge – winning the contest – is evident to all of the team, and coaching a business team where goals may be more complex and less clearly understood by everyone. When they approach a new task, different members of a team within an organisation may have conflicting views on what the team's goal should be. There may be times when the team leader simply tells the team what the goal is, which may bring clarity but not necessarily win commitment. When commitment is crucial, it may be essential that the team spends a considerable amount of time exploring objectives, agreeing goals and building genuine buy in.

To put this another way, agreeing the goal is much more straightforward when coaching an individual than a team.

Reality: What is the current situation?

Similarly, clarifying the key aspects of the current reality is more complex when coaching a team since different people will have their individual perspectives on the situation and on what is important. A well functioning team will explore these varied perspectives. In terms of the levels of listening that we looked at in Chapter 3, this involves listening to understand what other people think and feel rather than listening to disagree. It is far more useful if people can appreciate the validity and value of multiple perspectives rather than arguing for one right way of seeing the world. Facilitating this exploration is one of the key challenges for the coach. Having a genuinely agreed ground rule about respecting everyone's contribution may be very important in generating a shared understanding of differing points of view.

Options: What could we do?

This is the one area of the GROW model where it may be easier to coach a team rather than an individual. Because there are multiple perspectives, the group will generate more options more quickly. They can brainstorm possibilities, and build on each other's ideas to create new and practical ways forward.

Will: What will we do?

Making a collective decision to which everyone is committed can be really difficult in a group. It may take considerable time to explore views and reach a consensus.

One option is for the leader to decide, taking into account to a greater or lesser extent the views of team members. Indeed this may be the only way of making a decision when the team cannot – or does not have the time to – reach consensus. This, of course, might get agreement rather than commitment.

On other occasions the coach might work very hard to enable the group to explore individual hopes and fears, to weigh up the pros and cons of different options, and to make a collective decision that everyone is genuinely committed to.

Ground rules

Alison Hardingham suggests that it is important to agree a set of ground rules with the team in order to focus the coaching. She summarises the set that she herself uses:

- Agree the purpose of conversations, and keep it in mind
- Share all relevant information
- Build shared meaning; clarify and give examples
- Balance advocacy and enquiry
- Discuss the 'undiscussable' (the 'elephant in the corner')
- Stay aware of feelings and use the information they provide. (Hardingham, 2004)

She makes it explicit to the team that she will be intervening to develop their 'capability to work together according to these ground rules'.

In my own experience of both facilitating and participating in away days and workshops, people find it much easier to apparently agree a set of ground rules than to genuinely commit to them. What each person understands the ground rules to mean is likely to become much clearer as the coach intervenes over time to highlight when they are not being kept.

EXERCISE 19.1

GROUND RULES

Imagine that you are in the early stages of working as a coach to a team. Draft a set of ground rules that you would recommend to the group to enable them to get the most from the time they spend working together and from the coaching that you will be doing with them.

Models of team development

Alison Hardingham writes:

> There are a number of models of team development to choose from … the important thing is for the coach to have and to communicate the one she is happy with. (Hardingham, 2004)

The model of team development that makes most sense to me is the one described by John Whitmore (2002). The three stages in this model that teams go through as they develop are:

- Inclusion
- Assertion
- Cooperation

In the *Inclusion* stage, people are gauging to what extent they are included in the group. They may be feeling insecure, and possibly asking themselves if they want to be in this group. Some people will deal with their anxiety about acceptance or rejection by being quiet or tentative, while others may compensate by being vocal or forceful.

In the *Assertion* stage, people who feel included begin to assert themselves in order to stake a claim for their territory within the group and their place in the pecking order. There may be power struggles and lots of competition within the group. This can make the group very productive. Many groups do not advance beyond this stage.

In the *Cooperation* stage, people who feel established begin to support each other and to trust one another. There is a lot of commitment to the team, patience and understanding of each other, and humour and enthusiasm. There is also a willingness to challenge ideas and debate issues constructively. The team is aligned well towards the achievement of its goals.

Note that it is entirely possible that a team will slip backwards at times to earlier stages of development. I like the way that the three stages are linked to the feelings and behaviours of individual members, which strikes me as a realistic basis for a model of group development. If someone new joins a team – even one that is cooperative – that person will still need to go through the inclusion and assertion stages, and this might affect how others behave. Moreover, someone who has been in the team for many years might revert back to asking themself if they feel included now that it's changed with the arrival of a new member or manager.

EXERCISE 19.2

TEAMS AND TEAM DEVELOPMENT

Take some time to reflect on your own experience of working in, leading or facilitating groups of people.

- Write down your own definition of what makes a group of people a team.
- Identify a model of how teams develop that makes sense to you and which you can use as the basis of work you do with teams.

Teams, subteams and individuals

When I worked in the gas pipeline business Transco I had the privilege of co-facilitating workshops to develop coaching skills in our managers with David Whitaker. An international hockey player himself, David coached the British men's hockey team which won the gold medal at the Seoul Olympics in 1988.

David used to describe how he worked with that team to raise their awareness of what they needed to do in different situations that might arise in a match. During a game, since he was on the sidelines, he had to rely on each player using their awareness to respond appropriately and very quickly to whatever emerged.

He also talked about how he worked with different subteams that make up a hockey squad at an international tournament. For instance, the defence and the attack face different challenges, and the midfield need to link up with both. Moreover, in a successful squad there are other teams, such as the support staff, the medical staff and indeed the team of coaches, that have to work effectively for the team on the pitch to succeed.

David and his coaching colleagues also worked with individual team members on whatever aspect of their game – technical, physical, psychological, etc. – each needed to improve to enable them to perform to the best of their ability at the peak event of their career. Alison Hardingham (2004) writes that, 'Although the focus of coaching is on team performance, the team is composed of individuals, and it will be the combined effect of many changes in individuals' behaviour that will lead to team development or team disintegration.'

Thus, when working with a team it may be necessary to spend time coaching the team, the subteams and the individuals within the team.

Coaching or facilitation

When I worked in a management development role, I facilitated two kinds of workshop. Some were learning and development events where a number of people from across the organisation came together to learn about a topic such as time management or handling conflict. And some were away days where a group of people in the same unit or department met to think strategically about the future or to develop as a more cohesive team.

I regard this as facilitation rather than coaching. There are similarities in the two activities. I use the key coaching skills of listening, questioning and playing back extensively when I am facilitating. Indeed, I often design a workshop simply around a set of open questions. I aim to create a safe and supportive environment to enable participants to explore issues that matter to them. I am looking to raise awareness and encourage responsibility, so that actions happen after the workshop to enable either individuals or the team to perform more successfully.

There are a number of differences between facilitation and coaching, however. One is that these workshops were generally one-off events. They are like a single coaching encounter. I believe that coaching a team requires an ongoing level of engagement over time. In the example noted earlier, Myles Downey worked with the executive team of a financial services organisation over an extensive period of time as they created and housed a brand new business.

Another difference concerns the extent to which the coach takes responsibility for managing the process. When I'm facilitating a workshop I do a lot of this. However, in coaching a team over time it is important that the team members take over much of the responsibility for things like managing the time, exploring different points of view, surfacing tensions within the group, and reaching decisions. If the coach is the only person managing these things, this creates an unhelpful dependency. The team has to be able to work these things out for themselves when the coach isn't there.

David Clutterbuck describes how the purpose of team facilitation differs from team coaching. He writes:

> The purpose of facilitation is to provide external dialogue management to help the team reach complex or difficult decisions. The purpose of coaching is to empower the team to manage its own dialogue, in order to enhance its capability and performance. (Clutterbuck, 2007)

The self-coaching team

David Clutterbuck (2007) notes that an effective team coach has to know 'when to back off and leave the team to its own devices. Failure to do so risks creating an unhealthy dependence.' The team needs to learn how to coach itself, and the coach needs to prepare them for this transition to being a self-coaching team. The members of the team take responsibility for coaching themselves and each other. Although they may bring in the coach occasionally if, for example, they are facing a new challenge, the self-coaching team:

- Finds the difficult questions, wherever they are
- Tracks down new knowledge
- Adapts and leads the coaching process
- Generates its own feedback, internally and from others
- Motivates itself to learn. (Clutterbuck, 2007)

He concludes that the ultimate goal of the team coach is self-sufficiency, when the team can 'apply coaching techniques with skill and insight into its own issues, in its own way and in its own time'.

Three exercises you might use with teams

I'd like to close this chapter by describing three exercises which you can use to help a team explore and improve how they work together.

1. Qualities of a high-performing team

This exercise offers a framework to enable a team to identify and build the qualities that will make it successful. It invites them, first, to articulate the qualities needed in an effective team and, second, to assess itself against its own template. All of the content comes from the members of the team based on their own experiences. Moreover, the exercise encourages everyone to contribute.

- Based on their own experiences of working in or leading teams – both at work and outside – each person writes down on Post-It notes the qualities they have observed in high-performing teams.
- These views are shared with the whole group, and the Post-It notes are placed in clusters on a flipchart. This enables a set of around half a dozen key qualities to be identified.
- Each individual then rates the team's performance on a scale from 1 to 10 on each of the key qualities. Capture these ratings on a flipchart.
- The group then explores these ratings, looking in particular at where individual ratings vary most and at the areas where they have scored poorly.

You can then help the group to identify actions to improve how they will work together. You can also ask each individual to note what they personally will do to bring more of the key qualities to the team.

2. Stages of team development

Here is an exercise you might use to help a team explore where its members are on the spectrum from Inclusion through Assertion to Cooperation.

- Each person takes a sheet of flipchart paper and draws three concentric circles, representing the spectrum from Inclusion through Assertion to Cooperation (see Figure 19.1).

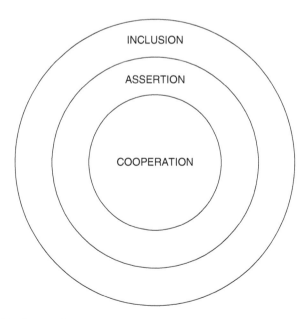

Figure 19.1 A model of team development

- They then write the names of each member – and themselves – at appropriate points on the chart to reflect where they see them on this spectrum and also their relative closeness to one another.
- Each individual presents their chart to the team, explaining why they have placed people where they did. This is likely to generate considerable discussion among the group.

You can then go on to explore with the group what actions or conversations need to happen to support individuals and to move the group forwards.

EXERCISE 19.4

STAGES OF DEVELOPMENT

- Refer back to the team which you identified in Exercise 19.3. List the names of each of the members of the team.
- Draw the three concentric circles, and write the names of each person at an appropriate point on your drawing to reflect where you see them on the Inclusion – Assertion – Cooperation spectrum.
- What might you do to help some of the people to move towards Assertion or Cooperation?

---

3. Group sculpture

This is an exercise to explore relationships among team members. First, clear a space in the room in which you are working. Invite a volunteer literally to position people in the room in a way which represents how they see their relationships with one another. With everyone remaining where they have been placed, you can then explore the thinking behind their positioning, and invite everyone to share how they feel about where they are situated.

This is sometimes described as a group sculpture since the person moves or guides their colleagues into position. You might go on to invite other members of the team to take their turn as sculpting the group. Some members might see the relationships among the group very differently from others.

It is potentially a very powerful exercise which can lead to a deep discussion of where people fit in the team and in relation to one another. This potency means also that you need to be very careful when and with whom you use it. It is an exercise which can engender very strong feelings in people. You need to be confident that you are experienced and skilled enough to facilitate the exercise, and the team members have to be resilient enough to handle their emotional reactions.

20

COACHING ACROSS CULTURES

Introduction

The type of coaching that we are exploring in this book is a Western, even British, notion. In this chapter we shall consider how coaching might be adapted for use in two very different cultures.

We begin by looking at the models of Geert Hofstede and of Erin Meyer who explored how people in various countries across the globe differ in a number of dimensions. We then consider how a British educator, Will Percy, adapted the idea of coaching in his work with young teachers in China. We'll then explore an approach to coaching in Islamic culture called Ershad.

We go on to discuss how cultural differences might be leveraged in coaching relationships. We end by considering individual differences between people – such as race or gender – that inevitably feature in coaching relationships.

Hofstede's dimensions of national culture

In the early 1970s Geert Hofstede, who founded and managed the Personnel Research Department in IBM International, analysed the results of surveys of 116,000 IBM employees working in 50 different countries. From the data he identified four patterns of similarity and difference – that is, four dimensions that could distinguish one national culture from another. He later added a fifth and subsequently a sixth dimension.

Hofstede defines culture as 'the collective programming of the mind that distinguishes the members of one group or category of people from others' (Hofstede et al., 2010).

Hofstede's original four cultural dimensions are:

- **Power distance:** This dimension explains the extent to which members who are less powerful in a society accept and also expect that the distribution of power takes place unequally.
- **Individualism vs collectivism:** The focus of this dimension is on the question regarding whether people have a preference for being left alone to look after themselves or want to remain in a closely knitted network.
- **Masculinity vs femininity:** Masculinity implies a society's preference for assertiveness, heroism, achievement and material reward for attaining success. On the contrary, femininity represents a preference for modesty, cooperation, quality of life and caring for the weak.
- **Uncertainty avoidance:** This dimension describes the extent to which people in society are not at ease with ambiguity and uncertainty.

He later added:

- **Long-term vs short-term orientation:** Long-term orientation describes the inclination of a society towards searching for virtue. Short-term orientation pertains to those societies that are strongly inclined towards the establishment of the absolute truth.
- **Indulgence vs restraint:** This revolves around the degree to which societies can exercise control over their impulses and desires.

www.cleverism.com/understanding-cultures-people-hofstede-dimensions/

You can compare the values for different countries on the six dimensions via this link to the Hofstede Insights website: www.hofstede-insights.com/product/compare-countries/

Table 20.1 presents the results on these dimensions (expressed on a 0 to 100 point scale) for the UK, China and Saudi Arabia.

Table 20.1 Hofstede's comparison of national cultural dimensions

	UK	**China**	**Saudi Arabia**
Power distance	35	80	95
Individualism	89	20	25

(Continued)

Table 20.1   (Continued)

	UK	China	Saudi Arabia
Masculinity	66	66	60
Uncertainty avoidance	35	30	80
Long-term orientation	51	87	36
Indulgence	69	24	52

The score for Power distance is much lower in the UK than in either China or Saudi Arabia, suggesting, for example, that management in the UK is likely to be more participative. The UK score for Individualism is much higher than in China or Saudi Arabia where there is more emphasis on harmony and hierarchy within groups. But there are differences between culture in China and Saudi Arabia, as the scores for Uncertainty avoidance and Long-term orientation suggest.

Meyer's culture map

In *The Culture Map*, Erin Meyer (2014), an American professor at INSEAD business school in France, sets out eight scales along which national cultures vary. These eight scales are shown in Table 20.2.

Table 20.2   Meyer's eight dimensions of national culture

Communicating	**Low-context**. Good communication is precise, simple and clear. Messages are expressed and understood at face value. Repetition is appreciated if it helps clarify the communication.	**High-context**. Good communication is sophisticated, nuanced and layered. Messages are both spoken and read between the lines. Messages are often implied but not plainly expressed.
Evaluating	**Direct negative feedback**. Negative feedback to a colleague is provided frankly, bluntly, honestly. Negative messages stand alone, not softened by positive ones. Absolute descriptors are often used (totally inappropriate, completely unprofessional) when criticising. Criticism may be given to an individual in front of a group.	**Indirect negative feedback**. Negative feedback to a colleague is provided softly, subtly, diplomatically. Positive messages are used to wrap negative ones. Qualifying descriptors are often used (sort of inappropriate, slightly unprofessional) when criticising. Criticism is given only in private.

Persuading	**Applications-first**. Individuals are trained to begin with a fact, statement, or opinion and later add concepts to back up or explain the conclusion as necessary. The preference is to begin a message or report with an executive summary or bullet points. Discussions are approached in a practical, concrete manner. Theoretical or philosophical discussions are avoided in a business environment.	**Principles-first**. Individuals have been trained to first develop the theory or complex concept before presenting a fact, statement, or opinion. The preference is to begin a message or report by building up a theoretical argument before moving on to a conclusion. The conceptual principles underlying each situation are valued.
Leading	**Egalitarian**. The ideal distance between a boss and a subordinate is low. The best boss is a facilitator among equals. Organisational structures are flat. Communication often skips hierarchical lines.	**Hierarchical**. The ideal distance between a boss and a subordinate is high. The best boss is a strong director who leads from the front. Status is important. Organisational structures are multilayered and fixed. Communication follows set hierarchical lines.
Deciding	**Consensual**. Decisions are made in groups through unanimous agreement.	**Top-down**. Decisions are made by individuals (usually the boss).
Trusting	**Task-based**. Trust is built through business-related activities. Work relationships are built and dropped easily, based on the practicality of the situation. *You do good work consistently, you are reliable. I enjoy working with you. I trust you.*	**Relationship-based**. Trust is built through sharing meals, evening drinks, and visits to the coffee machine. Work relationships build up slowly over the long term. *I've seen who you are at a deep level. I've shared personal time with you. I know others well who trust you. I trust you.*
Disagreeing	**Confrontational**. Disagreement and debate are positive for the team or organisation. Open confrontation is appropriate and will not negatively impact the relationship.	**Avoids confrontation**. Disagreement and debate are negative for the team or organisation. Open confrontation is inappropriate and will break group harmony or negatively impact the relationship.
Scheduling	**Linear-time**. Project steps are approached in a sequential fashion, completing one task before beginning the next. One thing at a time. No interruptions. The focus is on the deadline and sticking to the schedule. Emphasis is on promptness and good organisation over flexibility.	**Flexible-time**. Project steps are approached in a fluid manner, changing tasks as opportunities arise. Many things are dealt with at once and interruptions accepted. The focus is on adaptability, and flexibility is valued over organisation.

Meyer emphasises that 'cultural relativity is the key to understanding the impact of culture on human interactions'. She writes:

> when examining how people from different cultures relate to one another, what matters is not the absolute position of either culture on the scale but rather the relative position of the two cultures. It is this relative positioning that determines how people view one another. (Meyer, 2014)

As an illustration, consider the Communicating dimension. The United States is the lowest-context culture in the world, while Japan is the highest-context culture. Someone from the US may perceive someone from Japan as 'secretive, lacking transparency, or unable to communicate effectively'. Someone from Japan might perceive an American as 'inappropriately stating the obvious ... or even as condescending and patronizing'. Britain is low on this scale but not as low as the US. British irony, delivered with a deadpan face, is often lost on Americans.

Coaching in a Chinese context

Will Percy is a British educator who has lived and worked in China for over 15 years. He implemented a coaching programme with young Chinese teachers in an international school in China. He used the same definition of coaching that we have been exploring in this book.

Will notes that Confucianism is central to Chinese life and business. He lists five key aspects of Confucian values:

- Hierarchy and harmony
- Collectivism
- Guanxi (networks) and reciprocity in relations
- Mianzi (face) – showing respect for social status
- A long-term time orientation towards past, present and future. (Percy, 2017)

If you look back at Table 20.1 you'll see that the score for Power distance is 80 in China and 35 in the UK. Coaching is based on relationship, one which is ideally a partnership of equals rather than hierarchical. Percy notes that:

> The high power distance in Chinese culture ... may be a barrier to implementation. The hierarchical environment may cause the coachee to desire a more directive approach and a relationship that is not on an equal footing. ... [The coach] is expected to be someone who is more senior, more qualified and a source of wisdom.

China is a highly collective society – its score for Individualism is 20 compared to 89 for the UK. Individuals 'do not wish to risk standing out from the crowd by taking action and taking responsibility for their ideas'. Negative feedback and poor assessments of performance are generally avoided. Losing face for the Chinese 'is as bad as losing your mouth or nose'.

Factors such as these may create barriers to providing feedback, raising awareness and encouraging responsibility. This emphasises the need for skilful listening, questioning and play back.

These points are reinforced by a comparison of China and the UK using Meyer's culture map, shown in Figure 20.1. Percy notes that this

> further confirms the hierarchical nature of relationships in a Chinese business context; however, it also adds several other insights that should be considered when working with individuals in a coaching context. The more relationship based nature of trust in China may mean that it takes longer for the coach to develop a relationship with the client, while high context communication may mean that the coach needs to listen with greater intent, listening 'between the lines' for inferred meaning. In providing feedback and using the feedback of others to examine workplace reality it may be important to remember that in China negative feedback is given indirectly and that confrontation is often avoided. This may have implication for both playback and feedback, perhaps necessitating a need to peel back layers over time and in turn using a more high context communication method to provide this negative feedback and explore its implications. When providing information or seeking to persuade within the coaching relationship it may be beneficial to present facts first and underlying logic to follow, remembering the more mathematical approach to logic of the Chinese.

Percy conducted semi-structured interviews with the two experienced coaches who coached the Chinese teachers. They made the following points:

- Relationships took longer than usual to form, though they did become deep and often discussed personal issues.
- Listening was intensive and energy draining, given the need to listen for what was not being said.
- Follow-up activities were often not completed by the coachees, frequently because a superior or colleague had not played their part. The coachees in turn did not want to speak badly of their superior or colleague, or admit they hadn't carried out the action.
- Play back and feedback were initially difficult due to concerns about 'face', though this became less of an issue as relationships progressed and trust deepened.

Figure 20.1   Comparison of UK and China based on Meyer's culture map

Meyer does not include **Persuading** in this comparison.

Percy concludes that Power distance is a significant cultural factor that might suggest a preference for a directive style of coaching. He does not agree with this, however, and recommends that someone coaching in China needs to skilfully engage in the coaching dance – moving gracefully between the directive and non-directive ends of the spectrum – to support the development of the coachee. (See Chapter 18 for a description of the coaching dance.)

EXERCISE 20.1

COACHING DIRECTIVELY OR NON-DIRECTIVELY IN CHINA

In a Chinese context the coach may be expected to be someone who is more senior, more qualified and a source of wisdom. Will Percy suggests, however, that the coach moves fluently along the directive to non-directive spectrum.

Imagine that you were coaching in a Chinese context. How would you yourself manage the coaching relationship with a client who expected you to be directive?

Taking coaching to China

If you'd like to find out more about Will Percy's experiences in adapting coaching for use in a Chinese context, you might like to watch these videos where Will addresses these questions.

1. What were the main challenges in adapting the Western idea of primarily non-directive coaching to a Chinese context?
2. What are the key things that a coach working in China needs to bear in mind as they converse with a client?
3. In terms of managing a coaching relationship over time, what might a coach need to do differently in a Chinese context?
4. Thinking more broadly, how do you think coaching will develop in China over the next few years?

Link to Video 20.1
Challenges in adapting coaching to a Chinese context

Link to Video 20.2
Key things to bear in mind when coaching a client in China

Link to Video 20.3
Managing a coaching relationship in a Chinese context

Link to Video 20.4
Future development of coaching in China

Coaching in Islamic culture

In *Coaching in Islamic Culture: The Principles and Practice of Ershad*, Christian van Nieuwerburgh and Raja'a Allaho (2017) set out 'a culturally relevant coaching framework for use in Islamic contexts'. They chose the Arabic word *Ershad*, which has connotations of guidance, enlightenment and being on the right path, rather than the English word *Coaching*.

They view the Ershad framework as a process of self-guidance which allows a learner to set themselves on the right path according to their beliefs and values. This occurs through conversations with a facilitator who manages the process. 'The learner and facilitator work together to co-construct a safe, energising and reflective space in which the self-guidance can take place' (van Nieuwerburgh and Allaho, 2017).

They note that, 'The key purpose for which God has created the human race is to worship Him through building, constructing, and cultivating life on earth.' Thus the purpose of humankind is to worship God and to cultivate life on earth. The Arabic word *e'maar* captures the concept of building, constructing and cultivating life.

The Ershad framework incorporates:

- A respectful and trusting partnership between learner and facilitator
- A conversational process
- The concept of an alignment wheel which enables four key relationships to be explored – with beliefs, with self, with life and with people

The conversational process in Ershad incorporates four phases:

1. **Discovery** – understanding the current situation in relation to the topic for the conversation.
2. **Intention** – 'Intention has great stature in Islam. It is at the heart of how people will be judged by God and it underpins both worship and *e'maar*.' In this phase the learner seeks to identify their aspirations for the future and the true intentions behind these aspirations.

At this point in the conversation the learner should have a better understanding of their current situation and their intention for the future. The gap between these should be discussed before moving to the next phase.

3. **Pathways** – thinking broadly to identify a number of pathways or routes from the current position towards the intention. The alignment wheel can be used to check that the learner's pathways are aligned with their beliefs and environment.
4. **Effort** – the learner's determination to think and behave differently in order to move towards their intention. Both aspects – mindset and behaviour – are significant here. 'The learner should identify the new thinking (mindset) that will be needed in order to implement the adapted behaviour between coaching sessions.'

In the final chapter of their book, van Nieuwerburgh and Allaho share a number of case studies. In one of these, the coach (a British woman) was working with a young, female Gulf national. The coach drew these practical implications from the experience:

- Faith is personal and individual. Be mindful of making assumptions about what someone might think or how they might behave.
- Some people find it difficult to express their discomfort with a coach of the opposite sex. Be sensitive to this and facilitate the most positive coaching experience possible.
- Time is a cognitive construct and different cultures measure punctuality in different ways. Be open to these differences and challenge your own ways of thinking.

EXERCISE 20.2

HOW DISTINCTIVE IS ERSHAD?

Ershad is based on a respectful and trusting relationship. It allows a learner to set themself on the right path according to their beliefs and values. The four phases of the Ershad conversational process have similarities with the GROW – or rather the RGOW – model:

Discovery – Current Reality

Intention – Goal

Pathways – Options

Effort – Will

- In what ways do you think the Ershad framework is different from a non-directive approach to coaching using the RGOW framework?

Working with cultural differences in coaching relationships

In their chapter on intercultural coaching Philippe Rosinski and Geoffrey Abbott (2006) suggest that culture is 'an important influence in all coaching relationships'. They reckon that culture offers an opportunity that can be leveraged to enhance the impact of coaching, rather than being seen as irrelevant or as an obstacle to be overcome. They write that:

> Cultural influences are often subtle and operate beneath the surface, and people may have little awareness of the characteristics of various group cultures to which they are connected. They can therefore be oblivious to the influence culture may be having on their thoughts, behaviours and emotions. In organizations, often is it the outsider (such as the consultant, the coach, or the new employee) who can see patterns and forces of culture at work. (Rosinski and Abbott, 2006)

They suggest that, 'Intercultural coaching can bring to the surface issues and assumptions related to culture and harness them in unleashing coachee potential and facilitating positive change.'

Erin Meyer notes that:

> If your business success relies on your ability to work successfully with people from around the world, you need to have an appreciation for cultural differences as well as respect for individual differences. Both are essential. (Meyer, 2014)

Geoff Pelham agrees that knowledge of national differences in culture, as described earlier in the frameworks of Hofstede and of Meyer for example, is a useful starting point. But he goes on to add:

> Perhaps more fundamental, however, is a desire to reach out and 'meet' the other person, as underlying all the many differences there is a shared common humanity. In this sense working cross-culturally is not different to our usual practice, where the deepest challenge is always to connect with the other person. (Pelham, 2016)

In *The Reflecting Glass,* Lucy West and Mike Milan distinguish development coaching, which sits at the non-directive end of the spectrum, from skills coaching or training, which is at the directive end. They place performance coaching in the middle of the continuum. In their chapter entitled 'The Internationalisation of Coaching', they write:

> the more a coach works across cultures, the less directive he or she can afford to be as it is very likely that the coach's advice or guidance will not be appropriate for the different culture. Development coaching therefore seems particularly well positioned for working across cultures because of its non-directive, non-expert philosophy. The development coach's fundamental task is to enter his or her client's frame of reference, of which national culture is just another dimension. (West and Milan, 2001)

As West and Milan observe, a primarily non-directive approach is well-suited to coaching someone from a different cultural background to your own. A coach who works from the directive end of the spectrum needs to know in some detail the distinctive features of the culture of different nations, industries, professions and organisations if they want to offer advice or make suggestions that are culturally acceptable to their clients.

EXERCISE 20.3

HOW CULTURE MIGHT AFFECT YOUR COACHING PRACTICE

You may find it useful to consider the cultures that you are a member of – national or professional or religious, for instance. You might also like to reflect on how you view other cultures. How might your view of cultural differences influence how you operate as a coach?

Make some notes in response to the following prompt questions:

1. What cultures – national, regional, industry, profession, organisation, religious or spiritual, family, etc. – are important in shaping how you think and behave?
2. What are the implications of these cultural aspects for your own practice as a coach?
3. What are the distinctive cultural features of the people whom you coach?
4. Reflecting on your answers to these questions, as a coach what do you need to do differently?

Coaching and diversity

In this chapter we have focused on national culture. However, culture is also a feature of life in different industries, professions, companies and even families. And there may be sub-cultures in, for example, different departments of a company. Moreover, people bring their own individual personality, experience and values to their work and their interactions with others. Rosinski and Abbott (2006) comment that, 'Caution is required when making generalizations about culture. It is very easy to fall into unhelpful or negative stereotyping.'

Within any national or organisational culture there will be a diverse mix of people. Diversity refers to the differences between people – differences such as race, gender, sexual orientation, religion, age and class.

Helen Baron and Hannah Azizollah (2007) write that, 'Diversity is integral to coaching. To be a good coach it is necessary to work from a diversity perspective – even if the "d' word is not mentioned.'

They suggest that a coach tries to do two things in relation to diversity:

Help the individual value her or his difference and make effective use of it – this entails identifying and making use of positive diversity attributes.

Identify and work with negative diversity issues – in the client's mind and in the environment. This requires finding a balance between helping the person to operate within a flawed system ... and encouraging the client to challenge the status quo and change the environment. (Baron and Azizollah, 2007)

Geoff Pelham (2016) suggests that, while it is easy to claim that you treat everyone as equal, in reality differences in characteristics such as gender or race do make a difference. This may often be in a background way, but there may be times when it comes to the fore. This can produce feelings of anxiety when a coach is working with a client who is different from them in terms of race, gender or social class, for example. This might create one of three dynamics in the coaching relationship:

- **Difference and diversity invisible.** A dimension of difference (such as sexuality) is present but not apparent.
- **Difference and diversity avoided.** The difference is noticed but isn't spoken about, perhaps for fear of offending or, at a deeper level, because the coach feels in some sense 'guilty' of privilege or discrimination.
- **Difference and diversity compulsively addressed.** Difference is entangled with 'should' and 'must', and may be written in organisational policies and procedures.

To work appropriately, Pelham suggests that we have to:

> find a way of relating where difference and diversity is visible and spoken about, in a way and at a time that is not driven by rules, 'shoulds', 'musts' and 'oughts'. We are seeking a relationship where difference and diversity are part of the conversation because they have a natural place there and may be important for the coachee and their coaching agenda. (Pelham, 2016)

This is still likely to produce anxiety. He advocates an 'anxiety-lite' rather than an anxiety-free relationship. Moreover, the presence of the anxiety may be a signal that 'there is something important to address'.

EXERCISE 20.4

ASPECTS OF DIVERSITY

Geoff Pelham writes that he is 'white, British, male, able bodied, middle class and heterosexual'. He notes that he is on the 'right side of these power gradients, the side that in our culture is socially sanctioned as "good"'.

Make a list of the characteristics which reflect yourself in terms such as those used here by Pelham. You might add other dimensions, such as age or marital status or education or religion.

- Which of these dimensions of difference **in a coaching client** would you be comfortable to explore?
- Which of these dimensions may be invisible to you?

21
COACHING SUPERVISION

Introduction

In Chapter 9 we noted that the Global Code of Ethics for Coaches, Mentors and Supervisors emphasises the importance of supervision in maintaining and enhancing a high quality of practice. In this chapter we explore this key topic. We begin by presenting a number of definitions of supervision, and consider three functions of supervision – developmental, resourcing and qualitative. This raises the question of how supervision is different from simply coaching on coaching. We then discuss a primarily non-directive approach to supervision which parallels the definition of coaching we've been using throughout the book. We go on to introduce the seven-eyed model of supervision, a useful framework for structuring a supervision conversation.

Supervision offers a coach a safe place in which to reflect on their practice. We look again briefly at the cycle of learning from experience, and the ideas of reflection-on-action and reflection-in-action. This leads into the idea of an internal supervisor and of using a technique called Interpersonal Process Recall to review and learn from a recording of a coaching session.

We end by discussing some of the practicalities of finding and working effectively with a supervisor.

Definitions of supervision

Geoff Pelham describes supervision in very practical terms as follows:

> Coaching supervision is primarily about providing a safe reflective space where you can share your practice with someone who knows about coaching and is often more experienced in the field, with the intention of deepening your understanding of coaching and developing your capability to work more effectively. It is also a place to contain and work through the anxieties, uncertainties and confusions that arise in coaching. (Pelham, 2016)

In her definition Alison Hodge also describes well what happens in a supervision relationship. She defines coaching supervision as:

> A co-created learning relationship that supports the supervisee in his or her development, both personally and professionally, and seeks to support him or her in providing best practice to his or her client. Through the process of reflecting on his or her work in supervision, the supervisee can review and develop his or her practice and re-energize themselves. It offers a forum to attend to his or her emotional and professional wellbeing and growth. Through the relationship and dialog in this alliance, coaches can receive feedback, broaden their perspectives, generate new ideas and maintain standards of effective practice. (Quoted in Murdoch and Arnold, 2013)

Peter Bluckert offers this definition, noting two key purposes:

> Supervision sessions are a place for the coach to reflect on the work they are undertaking, with another more experienced coach. It has the dual purpose of supporting the continued learning and development of the coach, as well as giving a degree of protection to the person being coached. (Quoted in Hawkins and Smith, 2006)

In their own definition Peter Hawkins and Nick Smith emphasise two aspects – working systemically and the idea of transformational change:

> The process by which a coach/mentor/consultant with the help of a supervisor, who is not working directly with the client, can attend to understanding better both the client system and themselves as part of the client–coach/mentor system, and transform their work. (Hawkins and Smith, 2006)

Hawkins and Smith define three main functions of supervision – developmental, resourcing and qualitative – which are reflected in the above definitions.

- The developmental function is about developing the skills, understanding and capacities of the supervisee, through reflection on their practice.
- The resourcing function is about helping the supervisee to become aware of and deal with their reactions to the emotional intensity of their work with clients.
- The qualitative function provides quality control of the work of the supervisee, ensuring that the work is appropriate and ethical. (Hawkins and Smith, 2006)

EXERCISE 21.1

METAPHORS FOR SUPERVISION

In *Effective Supervision for the Helping Professions* Michael Carroll (2014) shares a number of metaphors which supervisees offered to complete the sentence *'For me supervision is …'*. Here are three of the metaphors he quotes:

- A torch – which illuminates my work.
- A container – where I feel safe and held.
- A playpen – where we play with ideas, feelings, intuitions, hunches, theories.

As an exercise, write down some metaphors with which you would complete the sentence *'For me supervision is …'*.

What ideas or behaviours do your metaphors evoke?

Coaching on coaching

Hawkins and Smith (2006) quote Mary Beth O'Neill on the importance of a coach receiving coaching on their practice. She writes that, 'One of the best ways that coaches can stay effective in their role is to receive coaching themselves.' After 20 years of experience as an executive coach continuing to have a coach herself, she reckons that *using a coach is a smart investment*.

This raises the question: To what extent – if any – is coaching supervision different from coaching on coaching?

A common answer to this question would make two points. First, in supervision there is always a third party – the coach's client or clients – in the room (as it were) during a supervision conversation. There might be other parties, such as the client's organisation, in the room too. In their definition Hawkins and Smith emphasise the importance of a systems perspective. Second, the qualitative function of supervision suggests that the supervisor has a quality assurance responsibility to see that the coach is working ethically. This extends to the notion that the supervisor has a responsibility to the coaching profession, ensuring good practice within the profession.

A non-directive approach to supervision

Throughout the book we've been basing our discussion on a definition of coaching that is primarily non-directive. Here is a parallel definition of supervision:

> Coaching supervision is a relationship of rapport and trust in which the supervisor assists the coach to reflect upon their practice in order, on the one hand, to develop their capability and enhance their effectiveness as a coach, and, on the other, to process their emotional responses to their work with clients.

This definition views supervision as being first and foremost a relationship. It also states two purposes of supervision: first, to develop capability and enhance effectiveness, and, second, to work through the emotional impact of the role on the coach. These mirror Hawkins and Smith's developmental and resourcing functions.

In *Freedom to Practise: Person-centred Approaches to Supervision,* Keith Tudor and Mike Worrall (2004) write that

> a supervisee's experience of being empathically understood and unconditionally accepted is perhaps the single most important factor in effective supervision, and we retain in our thinking about supervision the idea that a supervisee will benefit to the degree that he feels fully received. (Tudor and Worrall, 2004)

They note that the belief which a person-centred supervisor has in the self-actualising tendency within people

> helps free supervisors to hold a high level of trust in the work that their supervisees are doing, and in the capacity of their supervisees' clients to make the most of and take the best from that work. It follows from this that supervisors do not normally need to assess, monitor or police the work of their supervisees, and can instead devote their attention to helping supervisees explore their own thoughts and feelings about their work. (Tudor and Worrall, 2004)

The third, qualitative function is not explicit in my definition. I think that the qualitative function sits awkwardly with a non-directive approach to supervision. If the supervisor takes on a responsibility to ensure the quality of the coach's work and to monitor the coach's compliance with a relevant code of practice, then I think their acceptance may become conditional. The coach knows that the supervisor is making judgements about their competence and their practice. This is likely to limit the degree of rapport and trust that is established in the relationship.

Let me stress that I agree that there is a legitimate place for judgement of competence and for the confronting or reporting of unethical practice. However, this creates a different relationship and a different way of working in a supervision session. The supervisor who is also the line manager of a team of counsellors, the senior social worker who is judging whether a novice social worker is fit to qualify or practise, or the teacher who is deciding whether a student on a coaching programme is to be accredited do indeed have a qualitative function within their remit. They inevitably have to balance their quality assurance role with the importance of creating an effective supervisory relationship. This is likely to hinder them in working non-directively. There is nothing wrong with that, but it is useful to be clear about it.

EXERCISE 21.2

DEFINING SUPERVISION

Look back at your own metaphors for supervision and the various definitions offered above.

- Write down your own definition of supervision.
- To what extent, if any, does your definition differ from *coaching on coaching*?

The seven-eyed model of supervision

In *Supervision in the Helping Professions* Peter Hawkins and Robin Shohet (2006) set out their model of the supervision process, which they call the seven-eyed model. The supervision process involves two interlocking systems:

- The client/coach system
- The coach/supervisor system

The model describes seven modes which a supervisor might focus on through, for example, the questions they ask or the concerns explored. Although the modes are numbered, this does not indicate an order in which they are used in a supervision conversation. Rather, the supervisor might move in and out of a mode as seems appropriate. And not all modes are likely to be covered within a single session.

The seven modes, perspectives or eyes are:

- **Mode 1: Focus on the client and how they present**

This mode aims to help the coach to 'pay attention to the client, the choices the client is making and the connections between the various aspects of the client's life'.

- **Mode 2: Exploration of the strategies and interventions used by the coach with the client**

The aim here is to increase the coach's 'choices and skills in intervention'. This mode is often used near the end of a supervision session by inviting the coach to consider how they will work with the client in their next session together.

- **Mode 3: Exploration of the relationship between the client and the coach**

This mode explores 'what was happening consciously and unconsciously in the relationship' between the coach and their client, enabling them to 'develop a greater insight and understanding of the working relationship with a particular client'.

- **Mode 4: Focus on the coach**

This mode focuses on the coach's development and how they resource themself. It aims to increase the capacity of the coach 'to engage with their clients and more effectively to use their responses to the clients'.

- **Mode 5: Focus on the relationship between the coach and the supervisor**

This mode looks at what is going on within the supervision session. There are two aspects of this. First, it gives attention to the quality of the working relationship between the supervisor and the coach. Second, it explores how this relationship might be unconsciously paralleling the dynamics of the coach's work with clients. This **parallel process** occurs when 'a process which happens in one situation or relationship is repeated in another'. As an illustration, a coach might be talking somewhat hesitantly to their supervisor when discussing a client who is often hesitant in their coaching sessions.

- Mode 6: The supervisor focusing on their own process – what is going for them, here and now

The supervisor pays attention to the feelings, thoughts and images that are emerging for them in the session. This might reflect how they are working with the coach, or it may be in response to the material the coach is sharing about their work.

- Mode 7: Focus on the wider context in which the coaching happens

The client–coach–supervisor threesome does not exist in isolation but rather sits within a wider context. Professional codes, organisational realities and culture, other stakeholders and aspects of the business environment are examples of factors that may need to be taken into consideration.

(Hawkins and Shohet, 2006)

The seven-eyed model is represented diagrammatically in Figure 21.1. The model is usually presented with the supervisor at the top, the coach in the middle, and the client at the bottom. I have reversed these to suggest that the supervisor is supporting the coach who, in turn, is supporting the client.

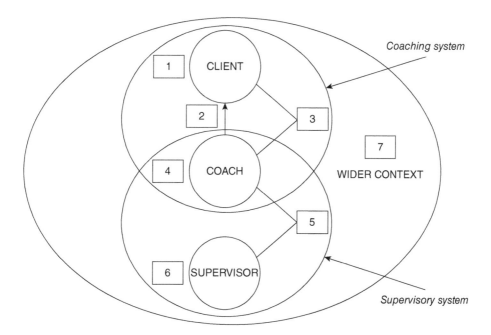

Figure 21.1 The seven-eyed model of supervision

Peter Hawkins and Nick Smith write:

It would be very unusual to find a supervisor who remained entirely in one of these seven modes of supervision and we would hold that good supervision must inevitably involve a movement between modes. However, distinguishing between the modes in their pure form is very fruitful. It allows supervisors to clarify their own style, its strengths and weaknesses – and which possible modes of supervision they might be avoiding out of habit or lack of familiarity and practice.

Not only does our model provide a way of increasing the options for the supervisor, it can also be used by the supervisee as a map within which to negotiate changes in supervision style and is a suitable tool in a regular two-way review and appraisal of the supervision. (Hawkins and Smith, 2006)

EXERCISE 21.3

REINFORCING YOUR UNDERSTANDING OF THE SEVEN-EYED MODEL

Think back to a coaching conversation you had which was particularly challenging. Imagine that you have brought this to a supervision session. The supervisor might be your own supervisor, or an imaginary supervisor if you don't have one.

1. Write down seven questions, one for each of the modes of the seven-eyed model, which the supervisor might ask you, the coach.

   o Mode 1: A question about the client
   o Mode 2: A question about an intervention you made with the client
   o Mode 3: A question about the relationship between you and the client
   o Mode 4: A question about yourself that is relevant here
   o Mode 5: A question about how you might be relating to the supervisor as you discuss this
   o Mode 6: A question that the supervisor might ask themselves as they discuss this with you
   o Mode 7: A question about the wider context

2. When you have written down the seven questions, write down the answers to these questions.
3. What would you do differently if you had another session with this client? (This is a Mode 2 question.)

Developing your internal supervisor

In Chapter 6 we discussed the idea of the experiential learning cycle, and noted the importance of experience, coupled with reflection upon that experience, to develop coaching skills and confidence. The definitions of supervision from Pelham, Hodge and Bluckert quoted earlier, and my own definition, all contain the word *reflecting* or *reflective* or *reflect*. Supervision is a place for reflecting on – and learning from – experience.

Peter Hawkins also emphasises the importance of learning by reflecting on your experience and practice:

> In workshops you can learn models and develop competencies, but these do not by themselves produce an excellent coach. Supervision provides the reflective container for the trainee to turn his or her competencies into capabilities and to develop his or her personal and coaching capacities. (Hawkins, 2006)

In *The Reflective Practitioner* Donald Schon distinguishes two types of reflection that are both important in how professionals learn. Reflection-on-action takes place after an experience as we look back on what happened. Keeping a journal might be one way of doing this. A supervision session is another.

Reflection-in-action takes place during the experience itself as we reflect on what is happening here and now. We reflect on our actions as we are doing them, perhaps noticing our feelings or considering what theory we are trying to employ. As we engage in our practice, we may build some new understanding while a situation unfolds.

A powerful example of reflection-in-action is the idea of the *internal supervisor*, which Patrick Casement describes in his book *On Learning from the Patient* (1985). Casement was originally a social worker who then became a psychoanalyst. In the book he reflects deeply and honestly on his practice, particularly on the mistakes he made in his work. By listening closely and without preconception to what his patients were communicating to him at many diverse levels, he was able to learn what they needed from him and how, in turn, he needed to respond. Although he draws mainly on examples from psychoanalysis, he invites readers from other caring professions to relate the ideas to their own spheres of work.

He points out that support from a supervisor can offer *hindsight* on earlier sessions and *foresight* in relation to future sessions. However, therapists – and coaches and supervisors – also need *insight* within a session. He writes, 'As a counterbalance to the many pressures upon a therapist in a session, I have found it useful to think in terms of an internal supervisor.'

An important aspect of the internal supervisor is what Casement calls *trial identification*. He writes that, 'This can also be thought of as related to empathy in seeking to understand a patient.' He uses trial identification in a number of ways:

- Thinking or feeling into the experience being described by the patient
- Putting himself in the shoes of someone being referred to by the patient
- Imagining how a patient might hear a possible comment from the analyst
- Reflecting on how the patient has in fact responded to a comment from the analyst

The internal supervisor enables the analyst to 'be in two places at once, in the patient's shoes and in one's own simultaneously'.

Interpersonal Process Recall

One method for reflecting on your practice that can contribute to the development of your internal supervisor is a technique known as Interpersonal Process Recall. IPR is a technique to help a coach or other professional to look back – through the use of video or audio tape – at a session with a client in order to recall what was going on for them at various points in the conversation. Through recall, the coach can become more aware of what they were thinking and feeling during the session, and can recognise things that they might have but didn't say or do. They may also become aware of some of the unconscious factors or interpersonal dynamics that influenced their behaviour in the session.

The technique was developed by Norman Kagan and his colleagues at Michigan State University in the 1960s. Coming from a client-centred perspective, Kagan reckoned that, 'The individual knows best about the meaning of their own experience' (Kagan, 1980). In IPR, the coach rather than the supervisor is the authority on what was going on for the coach during the taped coaching session. The job of the supervisor within an IPR session is to offer a safe, supportive relationship that leaves the coach free to reflect and thereby to become less fearful and more skilled in their practice.

Here is one way in which an IPR session might be run:

1. Prior to the session, a coaching conversation between the coach and a client is taped with the client's permission, using video or audio tape.
2. This is played back between the coach and another, who is often called an inquirer in IPR.
3. The coach, not the inquirer, pauses the tape when they recall something that was going on for them *at that point* in the coaching conversation.
4. The coach speaks about the thoughts or feelings they had at that time.
5. The inquirer asks open questions to facilitate the coach's discovery process.

Note that the role of the inquirer is not to teach, offer opinions or pass judgements. Rather, the role of the inquirer is first and foremost to provide a safe place where the coach can deepen their understanding and acceptance of themselves, and thereby enhance their ability to coach others well.

It is generally the case that there is far more contained within a coaching session than can be processed, so the coach may wish to focus on particular sections of the tape or aspects of their coaching practice.

The use of Interpersonal Process Recall can be very helpful in developing your internal supervisor. Penny Allen writes that:

> my experience of the IPR method can be a helpful guide in processing a session for myself. I have the experience of knowing how to access stuff going on in me. Often that is all that is needed. (Allen, 2004)

While IPR can play a useful part in supervision, complementing other supervision sessions, it is not by itself a substitute for appropriate supervision.

Finding a supervisor

In many walks of life, personal recommendation by word of mouth is a very effective way of finding someone to provide a service that you need. The plumber who has taken care of our central heating, showers and leaks for the last 20 years was first mentioned to us by a friend who works as an electrician and knew the local trades people well.

Personal recommendation is one way of finding a supervisor. Another way is more serendipitous – perhaps someone that you meet at a conference or through your training as a coach. However, it is likely that many people will search for a supervisor through one or more of the main coaching professional bodies.

As an illustration, the website of the European Mentoring and Coaching Council (www.emccouncil.org/) contains helpful information if you are seeking a supervisor.

The EMCC offers a European Supervision Individual Accreditation. This 'demonstrates that an individual practising as a professional mentor/coach supervisor has the appropriate level of knowledge and the ability to apply it effectively in his/her practice'. The website lists the names and countries of supervisors who have this accreditation.

They recommend the following criteria in selecting a supervisor, though they acknowledge that this may be difficult in some countries:

- They have experience as a coach/mentor.
- They have experience of being supervised and are themselves currently supervised.
- They have had training in supervision and are qualified as a supervisor.
- They can explain a theoretical framework for their own coaching/mentoring practice.
- They can explain a theoretical framework relating to supervision.
- They show commitment to continuing professional development for themselves and their supervisees.
- They agree to abide by the Global Code of Ethics for Coaches, Mentors and Supervisors.

They also suggest some useful questions you might ask of a prospective supervisor. These emerged from a webinar they ran on *How to Choose your Supervisor*:

- What is your coaching and/or supervision model that informs you in your practice?
- How many supervisees do you work with and thus what is your availability?
- What would a normal session look like: how structured, how conversational?
- How do I feel when in the conversation with this person (be that face to face or virtually)?
- Willingness to work flexibly in terms of geography, time of day, methods

Geoff Pelham offers a number of important considerations to bear in mind in choosing a supervisor:

- Be choice-full. Identify a number of possible supervisors and check out their backgrounds.
- Have an initial 'chemistry' meeting with a number of people before you settle on someone who feels right for you.
- Spend some time on agreeing the contract: confidentiality, fee, time, place, frequency, missed sessions and so on. (Pelham, 2016)

Working with a supervisor

Jenny Rogers offers the following practical tips to help you get the most from a supervision session:

- Choose your supervisor carefully. Liking and mutual respect are important.
- Prepare for a supervision session carefully, constructing your agenda in just the way you expect your clients to do.
- Notice your own reactions to the sessions. It is highly probable that you will be feeling apprehension combined with excitement, pleasurable anticipation and interest.
- Build the relationship on candour and trust, just as you would expect from one of your own clients. If you are not getting value from the sessions, stop.
- Expect to get non-judgemental comment.
- Concentrate on you and your coaching style, not on yet another intellectual analysis of your clients' issues. (Rogers, 2008)

Geoff Pelham echoes many of these points. He suggests that you:

- Prepare for a supervision session. Identify the coachees you'd like to discuss, have the coachees fresh in your mind and be clear about why you are bringing each coachee.

- Check in as to whether there is something you'd like to get from a session.
- Review the session with your supervisor. How are you getting on with each other? What's going well, not so well? What would enhance your work together?
- Be courageous in being honest about things that have happened that you are embarrassed about because you seem to have done badly in the session. Having the courage to 'own up' to 'mistakes' can open the door to the deepest understanding, and the possibility of transforming the coaching. (Pelham, 2016)

Other forms of supervision

While one-to-one supervision is in many ways the ideal, practical considerations of time, money and the availability of a suitable supervisor may mean that you have to make other arrangements for supervision. Group supervision, where a group of coaches meet with a supervisor, offers the benefit of sharing experiences with one another. On the other hand, individual attention may be less than in one-to-one supervision. You can obviously combine different modes of supervision – for instance, you might have a personal supervisor and engage in group supervision too.

Another possibility, which might be a more realistic option for someone learning to coach, is to set up a co-supervision arrangement with one or two other coaches so that you supervise each other, working as a pair or as a trio. Apart from being an affordable option, this also brings the benefit of experiencing the roles of being supervisor, supervisee and, in a trio, observer of a supervision session. If you are a participant on a coaching skills development programme, you may be able to work with one or two colleagues on the programme to supervise each other on your work with practice or other clients.

EXERCISE 21.4

YOUR OWN SUPERVISION

- If you do not currently have supervision, what might you do to set this up?
- If you do currently have supervision, consider these questions:
  1. On a scale from 1 to 10, how satisfied are you with your current supervision arrangements?
  2. What might you do to raise your level of satisfaction one or two points higher?
  3. What will you do?

22

CONTINUING YOUR DEVELOPMENT JOURNEY

Introduction

In this final chapter we consider how you can continue your journey of development as a coach. We begin by considering the requirements for formal accreditation as a coach by three of the leading coaching bodies. We then discuss what you might look for if you intend to take a coaching qualification or sign up for one of the many commercially available training programmes.

Developing your skills and confidence as a coach requires ongoing experience, coupled with reflection on that experience. We look briefly at five generic possibilities of working as a coach to obtain this experience. We end by discussing continuing professional development activities that can keep your practice fresh and informed.

Accreditation as a coach

In this section we look at the accreditation requirements of three of the leading coaching bodies – the Association for Coaching (AC), the European Mentoring and Coaching Council (EMCC) and the UK branch of the International Coach Federation (ICF).

I've chosen to focus on a few bodies rather than attempt to be comprehensive. If you are interested in becoming accredited, I recommend that you check the latest position by visiting their respective websites (and perhaps also the websites of other professional bodies):

- www.associationforcoaching.com/page/AccreditationPage
- www.emccouncil.org/accreditation/
- www.coachfederation.org.uk/credentialing/

The ICF website summarises well the benefits of accreditation, stating that it:

- Enhances your credibility
- Reassures potential clients that you are an experienced and professional coach
- Demonstrates that you:
  - have high professional standards
  - stand by a strong code of ethics
  - have a high knowledge and skill level
  - take ongoing professional development seriously

- Reinforces the integrity of the coaching profession nationally and internationally

Each of the bodies has different levels of accreditation:

- AC: Foundation Coach, Coach, Professional Coach and Master Coach
- EMCC: Foundation, Practitioner, Senior Practitioner and Master Practitioner
- ICF: Associate Certified Coach, Professional Certified Coach and Master Certified Coach

The AC has two options – the Executive Coach Scheme for coaches working primarily in an organisational context, and the Coach Scheme for all other coaches (such as, for example, life coaches). To become accredited by the AC requires you to meet a number of criteria. The two options have similar levels, and the requirements are:

- Being a member of the AC
- Hours of training (e.g. at least 60 hours for Professional Coach or Professional Executive Coach)
- Hours of coaching (e.g. at least 750 hours for Professional Coach or Professional Executive Coach)
- Supervision (e.g. minimum of nine months' supervision for Professional Coach or Professional Executive Coach)
- Continuing professional development (e.g. 36 hours per year for three years for Professional Coach or Professional Executive Coach)

- Client references and reference from supervisor
- Holding professional indemnity insurance, if appropriate
- Meeting a number of coaching competences

You can download a 35-page Applicant Guide for the AC's Coach Accreditation Scheme and Executive Coach Accreditation Scheme via this link:

> https://cdn.ymaws.com/www.associationforcoaching.com/resource/resmgr/
> accreditation/coach_accreditation/supporting_documentation/ca_applicant_
> guide.pdf

The other professional bodies also offer support to assist you in making an application to them. The EMCC publish deadlines for submission throughout the year. You can work flexibly and fit the work of completing your application for their European Individual Accreditation around your other commitments. Their website says that:

> Once applications go forward for assessment, the process is likely to take three months until a final decision is made. Depending on their circumstances, applicants may find that completing the application can take anywhere between 150 and 400 hours.

It's worth noting that putting your application together is likely to be time consuming. Another factor to bear in mind is the cost of obtaining the accreditation.

Is coaching accreditation for you?

1. What would be the advantages for you in gaining accreditation as a coach?
2. How much time, energy and cost are you prepared to invest in achieving this?
3. Balancing these two aspects, do you want to seek accreditation in the near future?
4. If you answered *Yes* to the previous question, what are the next steps you'll take?

Coaching qualifications and programmes

Opportunities to learn how to coach have expanded considerably over recent years. These range from one-day or two-day courses up to Master's-level degrees and doctorates. I won't even begin to list the options, a list which would probably be out of date by the time this book is published. Rather, I will summarise the key features of the Certificate and Diploma in Coaching which I set up some years ago at the University of Warwick's Centre for Lifelong Learning. These offer a useful checklist to bear in mind if you yourself are choosing a coaching development programme in which to invest your time, emotion and money.

The Certificate is suitable for someone new to coaching, and offers a foundation of relevant models and practical skills. It involves attendance at nine one-day workshops spread over six months. It is assessed through two written assignments and observation of a coaching session with a fellow participant. It requires you to work over a number of sessions with a practice client, whom you need to find. You also work in trios with fellow participants during the workshops in which you have the experience of coaching, of being coached, and of observing a coaching session.

The Diploma builds upon this and is suitable for someone who has taken the Certificate or an equivalent qualification, or who has experience of coaching or other forms of one-to-one work. It aims to deepen your knowledge of the theory and practice of coaching, and to help you to clarify your coaching presence and your unique coaching approach. It involves attendance at nine one-day workshops – or alternatively four two-day workshops – spread over six months. It also is assessed through two written assignments and observation of a coaching session with a fellow participant. It requires you to work with three practice clients. The programme is designed to develop a community of learning, so that all students learn together and from each other.

On the final morning of both the Certificate and Diploma, students are assessed against these five competencies:

- Listening empathically to understand the client's perspective
- Asking crisp, open questions
- Paraphrasing, summarising and reflecting back
- Managing and focusing the conversation
- Making clear and appropriate choices about where to intervene on the directive to non-directive spectrum

The following key elements of the Certificate and Diploma offer a checklist that may help you evaluate other programmes or qualifications.

- They contain a significant amount of coaching practice – both with fellow participants and with practice clients. If you want to develop your coaching skills, there is no substitute for experience.
- They encourage reflection on experience through classroom discussion, feedback from others, and the requirement to capture your views in writing.
- Written assignments also invite you to read some of the coaching literature and to weave together what you take from theory with what you put into practice.

Expressing in writing what you think is a great way to clarify for yourself what you do.

- There is one-to-one support and conversations.
- There is a sense of a learning community, with participants learning from one another as well as from faculty.

Bearing these points in mind, here are some questions to consider if you are choosing whether or not to sign up for a coaching programme:

- Who are the people who will be running the programme? How much experience do they have of coaching or supervising others? Do they favour one approach to coaching?
- What is the background of other participants? How much experience of coaching, mentoring or other forms of one-to-one work do they have?
- How much coaching of others (fellow participants or practice clients) does the course require?
- How much face-to-face contact is there? What other means of sharing ideas and experiences are used?
- How practical are the logistical arrangements for you? In particular, where are workshops held?
- How is the programme assessed?
- Who, if anyone, accredits the programme? To what extent will completion of the programme contribute to your meeting the requirements of coaching bodies for individual accreditation as a coach?
- What are the fees? How much value for money does the programme offer (which is balancing cost with the quality and quantity of what is being offered)?

A coaching programme for you?

Here are some further questions to consider whether or not you wish to take a coaching programme or qualification in the near future.

1. How do you like to learn?
2. If you were to sign up for a programme, what are the important practical factors that you need to take into account?
3. On a scale of 1 to 10, how interested are you in taking a programme or qualification at this point in your coaching journey?

If you do wish to take a programme now, here is one further question to consider.

4. What will you do to find out which options are feasible for you?

Ways of working as a coach

In this section we shall consider a number of possible ways in which you might operate professionally as a coach.

1. Internal coach

One way of becoming a coach is to find or shape a role within an organisation which involves one-to-one coaching as a key part of the job. If you currently work within a medium to large sized organisation, you might explore if such jobs exist there and then work out how you could secure one of them. Alternatively, if you are already in a position where you are using your coaching skills extensively, you may be able to move to another organisation in a coaching-type role. To make both changes at the same time – to start coaching others in a different organisation – is likely to be very difficult if you don't already have relevant coaching experience.

2. Coaching firm

There are a number of companies and consultancies who provide one-to-one coaching as their main service or as one of their key offerings. This is often described as executive coaching or leadership coaching. It may also be some form of career coaching, often in situations of redundancy. There are also consultancies offering a range of management development activities – including coaching – where you might be employed as a coach or more generally as a facilitator who does coaching as one of their roles within the firm.

3. Independent coach

Setting yourself up as an independent coach is, in principle, straightforward, and you don't need to convince someone to give you a job. You do, however, need to convince – and go on convincing – people to pay for your services as a coach. And this requires skills in marketing, in selling, and in organising yourself – as well as the ability to coach well and manage coaching relationships over time. Many people who can coach well are less good at selling their services as a coach – these are different skill sets.

4. Associate

One way of reducing the need to market and sell your coaching services is to work as an associate for one or more other coaches or companies. For example, you might establish a relationship with a coaching firm which employs your services to work with their clients. This means that you will receive a fraction – perhaps one half – of what they charge their clients for the work.

Another advantage of being an associate is that you will be interacting with others, which helps to offset the isolation you can feel as an independent.

As you build your coaching business over time, you may find that sometimes you win a contract where you need to employ associates while at the same time you are working as an associate for others. Being linked as an associate to a number of firms or individuals spreads the effort required for marketing, and balances the risks of winning and losing tenders for new work.

5. Mixed portfolio

A final possibility is to combine coaching with other paid or unpaid activities. For example, you might move from a full-time job to working three or four days a week for an employer, using the rest of the time to build your coaching practice. Or you might make part of your living working as a trainer or musician or accountant – whatever fits with your skills and interests – while also working as an independent coach or as an associate. One advantage of coaching part-time is that this offers variety and a chance to recharge your batteries doing something different from the satisfying but intense and demanding role of coaching people.

Winning business as a coach

In the previous chapter we mentioned that recommendation by word of mouth is an ideal way to find a supervisor. It is also a good way to win business as a coach. For many coaches, however, finding new clients and bidding for work is essential. If you have to tender for new work, then you may be asked about your qualifications or accreditation. In thinking about whether you yourself want to take a coaching qualification or seek accreditation, a key point to bear in mind is the extent to which this may help you to win business as a coach.

Maria Iliffe-Wood (2014) summarises the position as follows:

> Some clients are not interested in qualifications, all they want to know is – can you help me? It can depend on the size of business you want to engage with. The bigger the business the more likely you are to be asked for qualifications.

> The same companies that might ask for qualifications might also require coaches they employ to be accredited by one of the professional bodies.

In *Developing a Coaching Business* – a book which I'd thoroughly recommend that you read if you're thinking of establishing yourself as an independent coach – Jenny

Rogers offers practical help on how to find your niche as a coach, how to promote your business, how to sell your services, and how to manage your brand. Coaches often struggle with the necessity to sell to clients. She describes an approach that she calls selling with integrity which has many similarities to non-directive coaching. She reframes the role of the seller as being to facilitate the client's decision to buy, helping them to decide what they want. She writes:

> When you are selling coaching your role is to work with the client to facilitate the decision to buy. It's not about pushing your product (the selling equivalent of giving advice). So, exactly as in coaching, it's about asking questions, rather than giving answers. (Rogers, 2006)

She goes on to add that:

> Selling works best when it is based on an entirely non-manipulative approach and is a partnership of equals, based on mutual respect. The decision to buy emerges out of this partnership. (Rogers, 2006)

Continuing professional development

Continuing professional development enables you to maintain and enhance your knowledge and skills, helping you to refine your practice and support your clients even more effectively. Throughout the book we have emphasised the importance of reflecting on your experiences in order to continue to learn and develop. In the previous chapter we looked at how supervision offers a safe space in which to do this.

There are a variety of other activities which you might engage in. Taking a formal qualification, such as those discussed earlier in the chapter, is one way. The process of putting together your portfolio for accreditation by one of the professional coaching bodies will also require you to reflect systematically and deeply on your practice. Other possibilities include attending workshops or seminars; taking part in an online course; or reading blogs, articles and books on coaching and related subjects. Keeping a journal may appeal to some people as a way to reflect regularly on their experiences.

Some of the topics discussed in earlier chapters might suggest areas in which you would like to learn more and perhaps assimilate into your own approach to coaching. You might, to give just three illustrations, wish to find out more about clean language, or Gestalt, or psychometrics. And there are other areas, such as neuroscience or mindfulness, that we haven't explored but which may be of interest to you.

We talked earlier about seeking accreditation by one of the professional coaching bodies. Another possibility is to become a member of one of them, which is a much simpler process. The website of the AC (and of the other bodies) offers a rich variety of opportunities to continue your development as a coach. Many of these are available to non-members too, though AC members receive a discount to all AC events. Opportunities listed on the AC website include:

- International and national conferences
- Skills development workshops; masterclasses with thought leaders; and coaching exchange workshops that provide the opportunity to network with others as well as listening to a guest speaker
- Online webinars on a broad range of topics
- Local co-coaching forums which offer the opportunity to try new ways of coaching in a safe environment where you can receive constructive feedback
- Group supervision experience calls – these offer members a taste of what supervision is like. There is a maximum of five participants on a call, supported by an experienced AC coach or supervisor.

www.associationforcoaching.com/page/EventsOverview

Your continuing professional development

Take some time to work through these questions, based on the GROW model, to explore what you wish to do to further your development as a coach.

- Where do you want to be as a coach in two years' time?
- What are the current challenges facing you in developing your coaching practice?
- What might you do to address these challenges?
- To continue your development as a coach what specifically will you do, and by when?
- How will you review your progress?

I wish you well on your coaching journey!

BIBLIOGRAPHY

Allan, J. and Whybrow, A. (2007) 'Gestalt coaching', in S. Palmer and A. Whybrow (eds) *Handbook of Coaching Psychology*. London: Routledge. pp. 133–159.

Allen, P. (2004) 'The use of Interpersonal Process Recall (IPR) in person-centred supervision', in K. Tudor and M. Worrall (eds) *Freedom to Practise*. Ross-on-Wye: PCCS Books. pp. 153–169.

Allworth, E. and Passmore, J. (2008) 'Using psychometrics and psychological tools in coaching', in J. Passmore (ed.) *Psychometrics in Coaching*. London: Kogan Page. pp. 7–25.

Antiss, T. and Blonna, R. (2014) 'Acceptance and commitment coaching', in J. Passmore (ed.) *Mastery in Coaching*. London: Kogan Page. pp. 253–281.

Armstrong, M. and Baron, A. (2004) *Managing Performance: Performance Management in Action*. London: Chartered Institute of Personnel and Development.

Bachkirova, T., Jackson, P. and Clutterbuck, D. (eds) (2011) *Coaching and Mentoring Supervision*. Maidenhead: McGraw Hill.

Baron, H. and Azizollah, H. (2007) 'Coaching and diversity', in S. Palmer and A. Whybrow (eds) *Handbook of Coaching Psychology*. London: Routledge. pp. 367–384.

Bisson, M. (2017) *Coach Yourself First*. Kibworth Beauchamp: Matador.

Blakey, J. and Day, I. (2012) *Challenging Coaching*. London: Nicholas Brealey.

Bluckert, P. (2004) *The Four Dimensions to a Coaching Session*. Littleport: Fenman. Available at: www.fenman.co.uk/cat/product_info/CTC%20issue%201%20sample.pdf (accessed 5 May 2013).

Bluckert, P. (2010) 'The Gestalt approach to coaching', in E. Cox, T. Bachkirova and D. Clutterbuck (eds) *The Complete Handbook of Coaching*. London: Sage. pp. 80–93.

Bonhoeffer, D. (1954) *Life Together*. New York: Harper & Row.

Bourne, A. (2007) 'Using psychometrics in coaching', in S. Palmer and A. Whybrow (eds) *Handbook of Coaching Psychology*. London: Routledge. pp. 385–403.

Brooks, B. (2001) 'Ethics and standards in coaching', in L. West and M. Milan (eds) *The Reflecting Glass*. Basingstoke: Palgrave. pp. 95–101.

Carroll, M. (2014) *Effective Supervision for the Helping Professions*. London: Sage.

Casement, P. (1985) *On Learning from the Patient*. London: Tavistock.

Cavanagh, M. and Grant, A. (2010) 'The solution-focused approach to coaching', in E. Cox, T. Bachkirova and D. Clutterbuck (eds) *The Complete Handbook of Coaching*. London: Sage. pp. 54–67.

CIPD Factsheet (2017) *Performance Management: An Introduction*. London: Chartered Institute of Personnel and Development. Available at: www.cipd.co.uk/knowledge/fundamentals/people/performance/factsheet#6296

Clarkson, P. (1989) *Gestalt Counselling in Action*. London: Sage.

Clutterbuck, D. (2007) *Coaching the Team at Work*. London: Nicholas Brealey.

Clutterbuck, D., Megginson, D. and Bajer, A. (2016) *Building and Sustaining a Coaching Culture*. London: Chartered Institute of Personnel and Development.

Cooper, M. (2008) *Essential Research Findings in Counselling and Psychotherapy: The Facts are Friendly*. London: Sage.

Covey, S. (1989) *The 7 Habits of Highly Effective People*. London: Simon & Schuster.

Cox, E., Bachkirova, T. and Clutterbuck, D. (eds) (2010) *The Complete Handbook of Coaching*. London: Sage.

Critchley, W. and Casey, D. (1984) 'Second thoughts on team building', *Management Education and Development*, 15 (2): 163–175.

de Haan, E. (2008) *Relational Coaching*. Chichester: John Wiley.

de Jong, A. (2006) 'Coaching ethics: Integrity in the moment of choice', in J. Passmore (ed.) *Excellence in Coaching*. London: Kogan Page. pp. 191–202.

Downey, M. (2003) *Effective Coaching*. London: Texere.

Egan, G. (2007) *The Skilled Helper*. Belmont, MA: Thomson.

Frisch, M. (2008) *Use of Self in Executive Coaching*. New York: i-Coach Coaching Monograph Series 2008 No. 1. Available at: http://icoachnewyork.com/wp-content/uploads/2015/09/Monograph.pdf (accessed 10 June 2019).

Gallwey, T. (1975) *The Inner Game of Tennis*. London. Jonathan Cape.

Gallwey, T. (2000) *The Inner Game of Work*. New York: Random House.

Gillie, M. (2011) 'The Gestalt supervision model', in J. Passmore (ed.) *Supervision in Coaching*. London: Kogan Page. pp. 45–63.

Grimley, B. (2007) 'NLP coaching', in S. Palmer and A. Whybrow (eds) *Handbook of Coaching Psychology*. London: Routledge. pp. 193–210.

Hardingham, A. (2004) *The Coach's Coach*. London: Chartered Institute of Personnel and Development.

Hawkins, P. (2006) 'Coaching supervision', in J. Passmore (ed.) *Excellence in Coaching*. London: Kogan Page. pp. 203–216.

Hawkins, P. (ed.) (2014) *Leadership Team Coaching in Practice*. London: Kogan Page.

Hawkins, P. and Shohet, R. (2006) *Supervision in the Helping Professions*. Maidenhead: Open University Press.

Hawkins, P. and Smith, N. (2006) *Coaching, Mentoring and Organizational Consultancy*. Maidenhead: Open University Press.

Hobson, R. (1985) *Forms of Feeling: The Heart of Psychotherapy*. London: Tavistock.

Hofstede, G., Hofstede, G.J. and Minkov, M. (2010) *Cultures and Organizations*. New York: McGraw Hill.

Iliffe-Wood, M. (2014) *Coaching Presence: Building Consciousness and Awareness in Coaching Interventions*. London: Kogan Page.

Iordanou, I., Hawley, R. and Iordanou, C. (2017) *Values and Ethics in Coaching*. London: Sage.

Isaacs, W. (1999) *Dialogue and the Art of Thinking Together*. New York: Currency Doubleday.

Kagan, N. (1980) 'Influencing human interaction: Eighteen years with IPR', in A. Hess (ed.) *Psychotherapy Supervision: Theory, Research and Practice*. New York: Wiley. pp. 262–283.

Katzenbach, J. and Smith, D. (1994) *The Wisdom of Teams*. New York: Harper.

Kirschenbaum, H. and Henderson, V. (eds) (1989) *The Carl Rogers Reader*. Boston: Houghton Mifflin.

Kline, N. (1999) *Time to Think*. London: Ward Lock.

Kolb, D. (1984) *Experiential Learning*. Englewood Cliffs, NJ: Prentice-Hall.

Long, K. (2011) 'The self in supervision', in T. Bachkirova, P. Jackson and D. Clutterbuck (eds) *Coaching and Mentoring Supervision*. Maidenhead: McGraw Hill. pp. 78–90.

McCall Smith, A. (2003) *The Full Cupboard of Life*. Edinburgh: Polygon.

McDermott, I. (2006) 'NLP coaching', in J. Passmore (ed.) *Excellence in Coaching*. London: Kogan Page. pp. 106–118.

McMahon, G. (2010) 'Coping imagery', in G. McMahon and A. Archer (eds) *101 Coaching Strategies and Techniques*. London: Routledge. pp. 16–18.

Meyer, E. (2014) *The Culture Map*. New York: PublicAffairs.

Miller, W. and Rollnick, S. (2002) *Motivational Interviewing: Preparing People for Change*. New York: Guilford Press.

Mitton, M. (2004) *A Heart to Listen*. Abingdon: Bible Reading Fellowship.

Morgan, G. (1996) *Images of Organization*. Thousand Oaks, CA: Sage.

Murdoch, E. and Arnold, J. (2013) *Full Spectrum Supervision*. St Albans: Panoma.

Neenan, M. (2006) 'Cognitive behavioural coaching', in J. Passmore (ed.) *Excellence in Coaching*. London: Kogan Page. pp. 91–105.

Neenan, M. (2009) 'Using Socratic questioning in coaching', *Journal of Rational-Emotive & Cognitive-Behavior Therapy*, 27 (4): 249–264.

O'Connell, B. and Palmer, S. (2007) 'Solution-focused coaching', in S. Palmer and A. Whybrow (eds) *Handbook of Coaching Psychology*. London: Routledge. pp. 278–292.

Palmer, S. and Whybrow, A. (eds) (2007) *Handbook of Coaching Psychology*. London: Routledge.

Passmore, J. (ed.) (2006) *Excellence in Coaching*. London: Kogan Page.

Passmore, J. (ed.) (2008) *Psychometrics in Coaching*. London: Kogan Page.

Passmore, J. (ed.) (2011) *Supervision in Coaching*. London: Kogan Page.

Passmore, J. (ed.) (2014) *Mastery in Coaching*. London: Kogan Page.

Pelham, G. (2016) *The Coaching Relationship in Practice*. London: Sage.

Peltier, B. (2010) *The Psychology of Executive Coaching*. New York: Routledge.

Percy, W. (2017) *Implementing a Professional Coaching Program in Elite K-12*. Dissertation submitted for MBA degree at the University of Warwick.

Prochaska, J. and DiClemente, C. (1983) 'Stages and processes of self-change of smoking: Toward an integrative model of change', *Journal of Consulting and Clinical Psychology*, 51 (3): 390–395.

Rogers, C. (1961) *On Becoming a Person*. Boston: Houghton Mifflin.

Rogers, J. (2006) *Developing a Coaching Business*. Maidenhead: McGraw Hill.

Rogers, J. (2008) *Coaching Skills: A Handbook*. Maidenhead: McGraw Hill.

Rosinski, P. and Abbott, G. (2006) 'Intercultural coaching', in J. Passmore (ed.) *Excellence in Coaching*. London: Kogan Page.

Schon, D. (2016) *The Reflective Practioner*. Abingdon: Routledge.

Schwenk, G. (2007) 'Bath Consultancy Group develop four key areas of an effective coaching strategy', *The HR Director*, June 2007.

Scott, S. (2002) *Fierce Conversations*. London: Piatkus.

Scoular, A. (2011) *The Financial Times Guide to Business Coaching*. Harlow: Pearson.

Senge, P. (1990) *The Fifth Discipline*. New York: Currency Doubleday.

Shackleton, M. and Gillie, M. (2010) *The Use of Self and Self Disclosure in Coaching*. AoEC Conference 2010. Available at: www.thegilliepartnership.co.uk/Use-of-self-and-self-disclosure-in-coaching.pdf (accessed 5 May 2013).

Shaw, P. and Linnecar, R. (2007) *Business Coaching*. Chichester: Capstone.

Starr, J. (2011) *The Coaching Manual*. Harlow: Pearson.

Starr, J. (2014) *The Mentoring Manual*. Harlow: Pearson.

Sullivan, W. and Rees, J. (2008) *Clean Language: Revealing Metaphors and Opening Minds*. Carmarthen: Crown House Publishing.

Thomson, B. (2009) *Don't Just Do Something, Sit There*. Oxford: Chandos Publishing.

Thomson, B. (2013) *Non-directive Coaching*. Northwich: Critical Publishing.

Tudor, K. and Worrall, M. (eds) (2004) *Freedom to Practise: Person-centred Approaches to Supervision*. Ross-on-Wye: PCCS Books.

van Nieuwerburgh, C. (2017) *An Introduction to Coaching Skills*. London: Sage.

van Nieuwerburgh, C. and Allaho, R. (2017) *Coaching in Islamic Culture: The Principles and Practice of Ershad*. London: Karnac.

van Nieuwerburgh, C. and Love, D. (2019) *Advanced Coaching Practice*. London: Sage.

Watts, G. and Morgan, K. (2015) *The Coach's Casebook*. Cheltenham: Inspect & Adapt.

West, L. and Milan, M. (2001) *The Reflecting Glass*. Basingstoke: Palgrave.

Wheatley, M. (2002) *Turning to One Another*. San Francisco: Berrett-Koehler.

Whitmore, J. (2002) *Coaching for Performance*, 3rd edition. London: Nicholas Brealey.

Whitney, G. (2001) 'Evaluating development coaching', in L. West and M. Milan (eds) *The Reflecting Glass*. Basingstoke: Palgrave. pp. 85–94.

Whitten, H. (2014) 'Cognitive behavioural coaching', in J. Passmore (ed.) *Mastery in Coaching*. London: Kogan Page. pp. 151–189.

Williams, H., Edgerton, N. and Palmer, S. (2010) 'Cognitive behavioural coaching', in E. Cox, T. Bachkirova and D. Clutterbuck (eds) *The Complete Handbook of Coaching*. London: Sage. pp. 37–53.

Williams, M. and Penman, D. (2011) *Mindfulness: An Eight-week Plan for Finding Peace in a Frantic World*. New York: Rodale.

Wright, J. and Bolton, G. (2012) *Reflective Writing in Counselling and Psychotherapy*. London: Sage.

INDEX